To David & Martin.

Bon voyages, always.

Christopher Rynd
Commodore

Queen Victoria.
1 May 2015

The triumph of a great tradition

The story of

CUNARD'S
~175~
YEARS

Eric Flounders · Michael Gallagher

Published by: Ferry Publications, PO Box 33, Ramsey, Isle of Man IM99 4LP

Tel: +44 (0) 1624 898445   Fax: +44 (0) 1624 898449   E-mail: ferrypubs@manx.net   Website: www.ferrypubs.co.uk

Contents

*The **Queen Mary 2** under construction in Saint-Nazaire, France. (Chantiers de l' Atlantique)*

Acknowledgements

No book is the work solely of the author. All of them depend to varying degrees on the effort of others. Those others deserve to be thanked.

Our thanks go firstly to a variety of authors - the authors of shelves of files in the Cunard archives at Liverpool University, and also some still retained by Cunard, and the authors of many books either about various aspects of Cunard or touching on the subject. Principal among those are the late Professor Francis Hyde, whose dense factual tome 'Cunard and the North Atlantic 1840 - 1973' is virtually a précis of the University archive and an invaluable source of commercial information; Peter Newall and the late Duncan Haws, whose meticulous and detailed analyses of every ship in the fleet in 'Cunard Line: a Fleet History' and 'Merchant Fleets: Cunard Line' respectively have saved others a lifetime of poring over ship registries.

Thanks are also due to Brian Williams who has patiently and painstakingly re-typed drafts in a blizzard of re-edits. Our thanks also goes to Sian Wilks at the University of Liverpool for all her help with many of the historical views from the Cunard collection.

And finally we thank our publisher, Miles Cowsill, without whom we would not be here.

Eric Flounders and Michael Gallagher

October 2014

This book is dedicated to

Frank Gallagher
Michael Gallagher's grandfather without whose tales of life at sea told on rainy Saturday afternoons Michael would not have his passion for Cunard.

and **Hur Flounders**
Eric Flounders' father whose vivid recollections of being in a crowd of thousands watching the **Mauretania** *pass Scarborough on her final journey on 2nd July 1935 awakened Eric's interest in ships.*

Foreword

by HRH The Duke of Edinburgh

As the British Isles are stuck out in the Atlantic off the west coast of Europe, it would seem only natural for some of the inhabitants to be sea-farers. When the Europeans discovered the existence of the Americas, it must have inspired many to find out more for themselves what this new land was like. Exploration led to settlement, and settlement led to regular communication, although the North Atlantic posed some serious problems for the early navigators. It was not long before trade and passengers demanded regular communication by sea, which, in turn, stimulated bigger and better ships.

This story begins with the Novia Scotian, Samuel Cunard, and it covers the development and apogee of the trans-Atlantic passenger trade. The Cunard Company was probably the most enterprising and successful in that specialist trade, and its whole story deserves to be recorded. It covers a very special period in

*HM The Queen and HRH The Duke of Edinburgh on board the Royal Yacht **Britannia**, 27th July 1990, reviewing the Cunard fleet. (Cunard)*

Britain's maritime story, and this book pays appropriate tribute to the managers, ship designers, maritime engineers and shipbuilders, who together achieved quite remarkable technical advances in the design and management of the great trans-Atlantic ocean liners. It is a story of which the people of the British Islands can be justly proud.

Philip

HRH The Duke of Edinburgh

*The **QE2** in the Engish Channel. (FotoFlite))*

Introduction

*Pamela Conover, second from the left, at the naming of **Queen Mary 2** on 8th January*

At 4.00pm on the afternoon of 8th January 2004, Pamela Conover – then President of Cunard Line – walked, probably nervously, to a podium facing a thousand invited guests. Among them were The Queen and The Duke of Edinburgh, members of Parliament, peers of the realm, eminent businessmen, and journalists from around the world. Her purpose was to deliver a speech which would lead to the royal naming of the *Queen Mary 2*, the world's first transatlantic liner for 37 years, and the largest passenger ship ever built.

In that speech she captured, with moving simplicity, why the name Cunard means so much to so many.

"Transatlantic liners are the thread that runs through Cunard history," she said. "We were the first company to offer regular scheduled transatlantic crossings and, though many others have come and gone, we are now the last.

"Every year since 1840, without fail, in peace and in war, Cunard liners have crossed and recrossed the wide Atlantic, weaving together like a gigantic loom the United Kingdom, the United States and Canada.

"And that thread also runs through the fabric of British history.

"They were Cunard ships that in the nineteenth century carried millions of the dispossessed from the Old World to a new life in the New.

"It was a Cunard ship, the little *Carpathia*, which sped through ice fields in the dark to rescue all the survivors of the Titanic.

"They were Cunard ships that carried to Crimea all the horses that charged with The Light Brigade.

"They were Cunard ships, the *Queen Mary* and *Queen Elizabeth*, which indubitably shortened the last war by carrying American GIs - 15,000 at a time - across the Atlantic to Europe. And afterwards took them home.

"And it was Cunard's *QE2* that, with others, dashed to the South Atlantic when her services were needed in The Falklands War.

"The heartbeat of Cunard, for 165 years, has been as one with the heartbeat of the nation".

She could have gone on. She could have reminded her audience how Cunard faithfully championed Scottish shipbuilding in the face of fierce competition from the Thames, and how "the hammer's ding-dong" became not just the song of the Clyde, but often the song of a new Cunarder under construction.

She could have reminded them also how Liverpool flourished anew once Cunard made the port both its home and the hub of a huge global operation. How, just 30 years after the company's inception over 8,500 Liverpudlians were employed at sea by Cunard, with a further 3,000 onshore repairing and refitting, loading and unloading; and how, at the same time, over 15% of tonnage dues paid to the port of Liverpool were paid by Cunard. Liverpool, for over 120 years, was a city where everybody knew somebody who worked for Cunard.

For the Americans, she could have pointed to the incalculable boost given to the economy of the eastern seaboard of the USA once Cunard's relentlessly reliable connection to Britain made the distant so much nearer. It helped to increase the prosperity of Boston, whose population soared by 39,000 between 1840 and 1845, and whose trade doubled.

It is a fact: the lives and livelihoods, the aims and

eeen Mary 2

2004, with Micky Arison, Commodore Warwick and HM The Queen. (Cunard)

aspirations, of millions of people across the globe have owed much over the years to Cunard. That is why it is a magical name, a revered name, which means so much to so many.

Of course, the cynic might say, surely everything that can be said about Cunard has been said. That is true, but mainly what has been said has been said in part and in a vast array of books covering a range of topics.

There cannot be a book on Atlantic shipping, on steam pioneers, on a litany of wars from Crimea onwards, on the history of New York, on Boston, on Halifax or Liverpool, which does not contain a chunk about Cunard. There have been books by the score on a number of the company's ships – on the *Mauretania, Lusitania, Queen Mary, Queen Elizabeth, Laconia, Lancastria* and *QE2*; several have merited more than one book. And, of course, there is print by the acre dealing with Cunard's glory years, the days when royalty, moguls and movie stars shuttled to and fro in some style on the Atlantic ferry.

Many of the Line's Captains and Commodores have themselves become celebrated enough to produce autobiographies.

So it has to be admitted that Cunard history is there by

the bookload for those with the persistence and patience to sift through it. But there are relatively few books which give an overview of the company's history in its entirety. Why? Because it is a huge subject – not only long in years, but complex and massively eventful. The company has done so much for so long a mere volume cannot encompass everything. And nor does this book attempt to do that; its purpose is to set out the story of Cunard passenger shipping comprehensively, but succinctly, drawing together many of the strands to be found elsewhere. Much of Cunard's commercial history is complex, with a web of agreements, ownerships, inter relationships, takeovers, amalgamations and contracts which may be of interest to Cunard aficionados for whom every esoteric morsel is a joy, but for the general reader such details present an impenetrable jungle. As this book is aimed at that general reader, such complex detail is omitted or simplified without, it is hoped, affecting the integrity of the story but rather directing the focus to the main events.

Also, the book concentrates on Cunard's passenger ships; early ships, and indeed some until the 1960s, carried cargo as well as passengers, and they are here, but vessels of the company's dedicated cargo and tanker fleets are omitted from the main text though they are recorded in the fleet list.

There is also much Cunard archive material missing. For a company of such historical significance and such international repute, Cunard has had a peculiarly cavalier attitude to its own heritage. As, in recent years, offices have been downsized, much material has been destroyed. Similarly, artefacts – and especially models and paintings – have relentlessly been given away over the years so that, of a potentially very rich heritage, little is left. By necessity there is still much missing in this book and much which would benefit from more detail were space to allow, but it can be hoped that despite the shortcomings it will give the reader a flavour of the rather rollercoaster excitement that is the history of one of the greatest names in international commerce.

This book also contains some hitherto unpublished material from the mid-1970s onwards, and brings the Cunard story up to date.

Chapter One

Great oaks from little acorns

It is difficult now, in an age of instant communication and rapid travel, to appreciate not only what a significant event the establishment of the first transatlantic steamship service proved to be, but just how technologically advanced it was.

Small steamships providing canal and coastal services had been in operation for almost two decades or so in 1840, when Samuel Cunard's transatlantic service began, but the first genuinely successful steamship crossing of the Atlantic took place only in 1838 – a mere two years earlier.

Two steamships made that initial critical advance virtually simultaneously, arriving in New York almost within sight of each other. One was the tiny *Sirius*, a coastal steamship chartered for the express purpose of making the first historic transatlantic crossing, albeit a ship quite unsuited for the purpose. The other was Brunel's magnificent *Great Western*,

*The **Britannia** in Liverpool in 1840; a specially-commissioned portrait by Robert Lloyd presented by Cunard to the City of Liverpool on the occasion of **Queen Mary 2**'s first visit to Liverpool on 20th October 2009. (Cunard)*

the first steamship specifically built to cross the Atlantic.

The *Sirius* left Cork in Southern Ireland on 4th April 1838, while the *Great Western* set off from Bristol - one day's steaming further from the destination, New York - four days afterwards. The *Sirius*, her coal reserves almost spent, arrived in New York on 23rd April, with the *Great Western* a mere twelve hours behind, despite having left later and from a more distant port. The *Sirius* may have arrived first and could claim

The story of
CUNARD'S
175
YEARS

to be the first ship to have successfully crossed the Atlantic entirely under steam, but by any measure the *Great Western* was the winner.

The success of Brunel's ship and her subsequent crossings in 1838 and 1839 undoubtedly placed the Great Western Steamship Company as the favoured candidate to establish a timetabled service, and that it failed to do so provides an almost comic twist to the story of the Atlantic ferry.

For how odd it is that it should fall to Samuel Cunard, a cautious, conservative, prudent and long established businessman of some standing, to take the almost incalculable risk of setting up such a service - a venture regarded by many as so foolhardy, hazardous and potentially ruinous financially that he was unable to persuade any of his fellow Nova Scotians to invest in it. We can easily imagine the maverick genius Brunel forging ahead with such a scheme regardless of financial risk or technological challenge, if only to extend his spectacular new railway from London beyond Bristol to New York – something he had mused over as early as 1835. But the quiet, orthodox, settled Samuel Cunard? Surely not!

By the time he first proposed his transatlantic service in 1839, Samuel Cunard, a resident of Halifax, was a substantial figure in Nova Scotia and beyond. His father, Abraham, had been born in the United States of America of German stock, and was 'deported' in 1783 for having had the temerity to back the British Crown in the War of Independence. He arrived in Halifax with nothing, save for the woman who was

Samuel Cunard. (Cunard)

to become his wife and whom he met on the ship carrying him to exile.

Samuel, the second of nine children, was born in Halifax to Abraham and Margaret on 21st November 1787. America's loss was Canada's gain.

Industrious Abraham began his business, A. Cunard and Sons, in 1812, dealing in timber and the West India trade. In 1813 the company purchased the *White Oak*, its first ship, and by 1815 had six ships involved in, among other things, the carrying of mail to and from New York, and the London mail

*The **Britannia** leaves Halifax for Boston on 17th July 1840. In the background is the **Unicorn** - the ship whose place in history has been eclipsed by the **Britannia**. The Admiralty Contract awarded to Samuel Cunard called for a feeder service from Halifax to Pictou and Quebec so the **Unicorn** was chartered by Cunard for six years to undertake this feeder service. The **Unicorn** left Liverpool on 16th May 1840 and so made the first Cunard crossing. This 2014 painting by Robert Lloyd was commissioned by John Langley, Chairman of the Cunard Steamship Historical Society.*

Isambard Kingdom Brunel's **Great Western**, *the first steamship specifically designed to cross the Atlantic.*

bound for Halifax which was picked up in Bermuda on return trips from the West Indies.

On Abraham's retirement in 1819 the firm became S. Cunard and Company as Samuel took over and, already prosperous, it had increased its fleet under his careful stewardship to over seventy sailing ships by 1833. Samuel was not only industrious, he was principled and capable. Burdened by an alcoholic mother, he took it upon himself to arrange and oversee the education of his brothers. Such family loyalty resurfaced throughout his life.

But Cunard's ambition did not rest with coastal trading. Apart from shipping, Samuel's interests now extended to shipbuilding, canals, banking, whaling, tea importing, railways, timber, mining and land ownership. He was a founder of the Halifax Steamboat Company, a small ferry, and he took shares in the Quebec and Halifax Steam Navigation Company which operated the *Royal William* from Quebec. The *Royal William* was a financial failure and, ironically, as a result of being sold became in 1833 the first steamship to cross the Atlantic though under sail for most of the voyage. These were his only serious contacts with steam before embarking on his big transatlantic adventure.

So there he was: prosperous, rich even; settled, with his large house and his eight children around him; thriving businesses to keep him busy; and a great deal of influence and political clout in his native Nova Scotia. Even more significantly, in the light of the precarious course he was to follow, in 1839 Samuel Cunard was already 52 years old - an age by which most people at the time were already dead.

He was also probably lonely; his wife, Susan, had died in 1827 bearing the couple's ninth child. But that we cannot know, other than to guess it was a motivation for his brainstorm.

For despite his success, his wide interests, his family, despite his age, and despite his cautious and prudent approach to business affairs, Samuel Cunard was prepared to risk everything, absolutely everything - including uprooting himself from Nova Scotia and starting a new life 3,000 miles away. All this on a project which to most observers was an impractical folly likely to be ruinous: the establishment of a steamship service across the Atlantic only two years after the first successful crossings and reliant on engineering which was at the very edge of current competence.

It was, surely, a brainstorm.

The catalyst was an advertisement placed in *The Times* by the British Admiralty on 7th November 1838, and which was reprinted two months later on 10th January 1839 in the *Novascotian*, where Samuel saw it. (What better argument for a steamship service than it took *The Times* two months under sail to reach Nova Scotia?). The advert invited interested parties to bid to provide a timetabled steamship service across the Atlantic, principally for the carrying of the Royal Mail (for which the Admiralty was at that time responsible). The deadline for bids was December, by which time Samuel had not even seen the advertisement, but his reaction on doing so was immediate; he took the first packet sailing to Falmouth, and was in London by February 1839. He had no steamships, little knowledge of steam, no backers and was two months late - but he was ready to make a bid.

The Admiralty found its responsibility for carrying mail overseas was becoming an embarrassment. It was dependent largely on its own fleet of sailing brigs which were at best slow, being reliant on the vagaries of the wind, and at worst profoundly unsafe as so many of them - one in six - failed to arrive at all. For those which did cross safely, there was no way of knowing exactly when they would arrive, and generally a transatlantic crossing would take at least six weeks - some taking longer. In 1836, just three years earlier, 17 passengers on board sailing ship the *Diamond* died of starvation on a journey from Liverpool to New York which took 100 days.

The Admiralty had been made very aware of the failings of its own sailing ships by the rapid development of railways on land. Mail which had previously taken days to reach provincial cities by mail coach from London was now being delivered in hours. But the overseas mail juddered to a halt in port, and then slowly proceeded overseas at a pre-steam pace.

Isambard Kingdom Brunel.

Robert Napier.

It wasn't good enough, and the Admiralty finally decided that steam power needed to be applied to the sea.

This is not to say the Admiralty was forward thinking. It was not. The *Great Western* had been shuttling back and forth on the Atlantic for some months by this stage. Their reluctance to innovate was demonstrated again later by their refusal to countenance iron ships which, bizarrely, they thought would be more vulnerable in war time, and by their refusal to allow Cunard to swap from paddlewheels to screw propellers until 1862. And so it came to place its advertisement in November, with bids to be submitted in December, and for the successful applicant to commence the service in April 1839. So tight a timetable, of course, effectively restricted contenders to those with suitable ships already - which narrowed things down to the Great Western Steamship Company whose *Great Western* had completed five crossings during 1838, and the St George Steam Packet Company, owners of the *Sirius*.

So why did the company which possessed the only proven transatlantic steamship not scoop the contract? Why did it go to a late starting colonial who possessed no steamships at all?

The truth seems to be that the Board of the Great Western Steamship Company was so smug in its assumption that they were the only viable option available to the Admiralty, that they ignored the Admiralty's express wishes and substituted their own preferred contractual details. They maintained that the *Great Western* was not sufficient for the task, and that they would need two years in which to build new, more powerful ships to provide a monthly service in each direction for the sum of £45,000. No senior civil servant likes

to be treated in this haughty fashion and, no doubt leaving Brunel in despair at the idiocies of his Board, the Admiralty rejected the bid on 10th January 1839. They also rejected a bid from the St George Steam Packet Company.

Cunard submitted his bid a month later, offering not a monthly service as the Great Western Steamship Company had, but a weekly one. The Admiralty felt twice monthly was sufficient, and that Cunard's proposed fee of £55,000 a year was better value than Great Western's. There were potentially ruinous clauses in the contract, however - £15,000 penalty for a missed sailing, and £500 penalty for a 12-hour delay in departure - and, in a move to be repeated throughout Cunard history, the Admiralty reserved the right to make use of the vessels during times of war.

You do not need to be a mathematical genius, of course, to work out that just four missed sailings – statistically likely with untried technology on the Atlantic – would obliterate the entire annual subsidy. Such concerns were at the front of the minds of some of Cunard's eventual investors, especially David MacIver, and almost finished the venture before it started.

Of course, Cunard still had no ships. He travelled north to the Clyde, and on 18th March 1839, agreed terms with the eminent engineer Robert Napier and shipbuilder John Wood for the construction of three 960-ton ships of 375 hp at a cost of £32,000 each and to be delivered within twelve months. So far, apparently, so good. Except that Cunard had a problem in that he was acting alone and the entire financial burden fell upon him alone. Despite his wide commercial interests, he was at that time financially stretched as a result

11

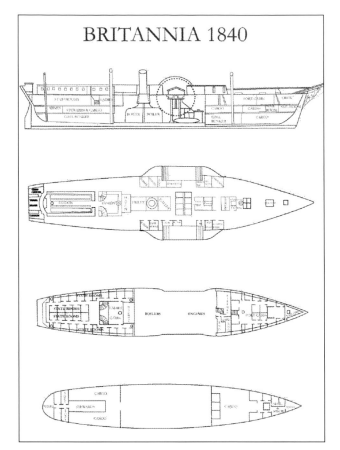

BRITANNIA 1840

*Deckplan and cross-section of the **Britannia**. (Cunard)*

of a significant land deal back in Nova Scotia. When Napier visited his bank to redeem Cunard's first payment of £5,000 there was a disquieting delay in the process. The delay certainly disquieted Napier, and Cunard was forced to act by finding investors.

On 4th May Cunard signed his first contract with the Admiralty – a contract which was revised many times before the service commenced.

On 14th May, guided by Napier, who became an investor himself, Cunard settled on Glaswegian George Burns and the Liverpool-based brothers, David and Charles MacIver, as partners in the venture. Both parties had owned and operated coastal steamship services between Glasgow and Liverpool since 1823 and 1831 respectively; rivals became united under the Cunard banner and their companies subsumed for operational purposes within the new British and North American Royal Mail Steam Packet Company, known from the start as Cunard Line. These men were invaluable additions to the future functioning of Cunard's embryonic line.

Cunard's agreement with Burns and MacIver gave them the right to bring others into their share of the company. This

they did and eventually on 28th May 1840 what was known as 'the Glasgow Proprietary' was first signed with additional local shareholders. The final agreement, with 33 shareholders, was signed on 23rd July; Cunard, Burns and MacIver held only 28% of the shares.

In June a new contract was signed with the Admiralty specifying four ships, rather than the three already ordered, for delivery in May 1840 to provide a fortnightly service at a sum of £60,000 a year. The potentially ruinous clauses remained, as did the requirement to place the ships in the service of the government if required. The new ships were also to be considerably larger than those originally specified, on the advice of Robert Napier – and thus more costly. On 4th July 1839 the Admiralty signed an amended contract to take account of the increased size.

In order to have the four ships ready as rapidly as possible, construction was divided between four Clyde yards: Robert Duncan was to build the *Britannia*, brothers John and Robert Wood were to build the *Acadia* and *Caledonia* respectively, and Robert Steele was to work on the *Columbia*.

While this quartet were to form the first timetabled steamship fleet to tackle the Atlantic, none of them, perversely, was the first steamship to cross the Atlantic under Cunard colours. That honour belonged to the tiny *Unicorn*, previously owned by Burns' coastal steamship company and transferred to the new company to provide a 'feeder' service for the mails from Halifax to Quebec. She left Liverpool on 16th May 1840 for Halifax with Samuel Cunard's son, Edward, and 23 passengers on board and she arrived on 1st June. Though not part of the embryonic timetabled service, she was in reality the first of the line.

The *Britannia* was the first of the four to enter the waters of the Clyde, launched on 5th February 1840 by Isabella, daughter of Robert Napier. The chosen names of the four ships were, of course, the names of Roman provinces – a theme continued more or less throughout Cunard history; hence the preponderance of 'ia' endings.

Her construction, like the others, was traditional and was of the conservatism that was a Cunard hallmark for most of its history. The company did not experiment, and did not readily adopt innovations; rather it let others try out new ideas and waited to see which were successful before adopting them itself. This had good effect and bad; in later years the company was constantly perceived to be old-fashioned because it refused to adopt each new passing fad, but on the other hand taking on only that which had been thoroughly tested by others helped develop a culture of steadfast reliability which served the company well.

But Samuel Cunard had travelled several times on the *Great Western*, and had observed deficiencies which he addressed in the construction of the new fleet in two ways. Firstly, he ensured the furnaces and boilers were well insulated to obviate the problem of excess heat suffered by passengers on the *Great Western*; and secondly the coal bunkers were incorporated into the hulls so coal could be shovelled out of hatches adjacent to the furnaces, rather than having to be hauled in baskets from holds at the bow as on the *Great Western*.

The *Britannia* was not a pretty ship, but traditionally sturdy with a clipper bow and three fully rigged masts. Two huge paddle boxes adorned each side, linked by a 'bridge' - from which the current term derives. She was just 207 feet long and 1,455 tons and could have fitted inside one of the public rooms of many modern liners. Despite her four boilers and two paddle wheels, she retained masts and sails – just in case. And although Cunard's primary interest was the mail, she had space for 115 passengers. She also carried a cow, slung in a hammock on deck, to provide fresh milk and a flock of chickens to supply eggs. Three cats were on hand to deter vermin. The *Britannia* was registered in Glasgow, as were all Cunard ships until 1878.

It may be helpful at this stage to clarify 'tonnage', or more accurately gross tonnage as applied to ships, and used throughout this book. It is not a weight, but a volume of all the internal space in cubic feet, divided by 100. This originates from the word 'tun', or barrel, which was generally of 100 cubic feet. So, if a ship had space for 1,000 tuns, it had a 'tunnage' of 1,000. Precise definitions have changed over the years, but the important fact is that tonnage is an expression of volume. So pouring lead into a ship would not increase the ship's gross tonnage, but building cabins on the deck space would.

The *Britannia* arrived in Liverpool from Greenock on 11th June 1840, and berthed at the Coburg Dock until the day of departure – which was originally intended to be 2nd July. On 3rd July she moved from Coburg Dock to the middle of the Mersey, and the following day at noon the 63 passengers – including Samuel Cunard and his daughter, Ann, embarked by tender from the Egremont Ferry Slip. Under the command of Captain Henry Woodruff, and with a crew of 93, she weighed anchor at 2pm. She thus started a timetabled service which has never stopped, and is generally regarded as the first of the line.

Despite her status, the *Britannia* was not a lucky ship and

Charles MacIver.

was involved in a series of groundings, breakdowns and collisions. Cunard finally divested itself of the *Britannia* in 1849 when the ship was sold to the Prussian navy. Finally, in 1880, she suffered the indignity of being sunk when used for target practice.

Cunard has traditionally measured its existence from the date of the sailing of its first transatlantic steamship on 4th July 1840. The company was actually incorporated over a year earlier but the view has always been that a shipping company only exists in reality when its first ship enters service. Preparations were well advanced to celebrate the century in July 1940, though Hitler put paid to that party; the 150th anniversary was marked in 1990 when The Queen and the Duke of Edinburgh visited the then flagship, the *Queen Elizabeth 2*; and now 2015 celebrates the 175th. Of course, if Cunard were to include the steamship companies already owned by two of the ruling triumvirate, Burns and the MacIvers, and now incorporated operationally, though not by register, within the British and North American Royal Mail Steam Packet Company, the company would be considerably older. But they weren't transatlantic steamers. And, as Pamela Conover reminded us, it is transatlantic liners that form the thread that runs through Cunard history.

Chapter Two

Triumph
and
disaster

While Samuel Cunard, the biggest shareholder in the British and North American Royal Mail Steam Packet Company, stepped aboard the *Britannia* on 4th July 1840 in readiness for the maiden voyage, his two colleagues in the triumvirate which was to run the company stayed behind.

George Burns remained in Glasgow where it was his job, along with his brother James, to oversee the construction of the *Britannia's* sisters, and that of vessels to follow. He was a busy man. In the 35 years after the company began operations, he oversaw construction of many steamers. Not all were transatlantic steamships, of course; the number included two tenders, the *Satellite* and *Jackal* (the former holding the record for the longest serving Cunard vessel at 54 years) which ferried passengers out from the Pier Head to liners anchored in the Mersey and it included a whole new Mediterranean fleet which took to the water after the repeal of the Navigation Acts in 1849.

But whatever the vessels were, they were built to the meticulous standards for which Cunard became known - not standards of grace or comfort necessarily, but of robustness and capacity to do the job required. It was Burns' task, as one of the most experienced shipowners on the Clyde, to ensure that the ships were delivered on time and that the maxim "Clyde built is well built" had meaning. The impact of the steady flow of orders from Samuel Cunard and his colleagues was pivotal in establishing the Clyde as the principal shipbuilding river in Britain; it is difficult to believe now, but its supremacy at the time was challenged by the Thames.

David MacIver, meanwhile, along with his brother Charles, established himself in Liverpool where he oversaw the operational conduct of the company's hub, the centre of a rapidly expanding network.

As might be expected, there remained some nervousness among potential passengers about the safety of these new fangled steamships. Many convinced themselves that it was inevitable that a boiler would blow up taking the entire ship, and everything therein, with it; others thought it folly for a wooden ship to have at its heart a voracious furnace fed 24 hours a day from great stockpiles of highly combustible coal, while a tall and gaudy funnel rained sparks onto the wooden deck. Cunard funnels, incidentally, have been an iridescent red with black bands from the outset, apart from a brief period when the *QE2*, *Cunard Adventurer*, *Cunard Ambassador* and *Cunard Countess* were not so blessed and had funnels painted white in the name of modernity; they have long been a welcome sight to weary travellers in foreign ports. The black bands were for the practical purpose of disguising the leakage of soot and tar through the joints in the funnel; an image consultant would be paid a fortune now to dream that up. The iridescent red was achieved by a mixture of red ochre and whey, which baked onto the hot metal funnel, whereas paint just blistered and peeled.

The respected maritime historian, Duncan Haws, noted that Robert Napier built a steam yacht, the *Menai*, in 1830 and delivered her with a striking red funnel rather than the customary black. It may be that, but for the *Menai*, Cunard might now have plain black funnels instead of the heartwarming red.

The fears of those nervous about explosion and fire were merely confirmed in 1848, when White Diamond Line's the *Ocean Monarch* caught fire just after leaving Liverpool, resulting

Of course there were accidents and there were deaths. But, for example, the five passengers washed overboard from the *Campania* by a freak wave in 1905 were taken by an act of God and not by carelessness on the part of the company. Many have gone overboard from ships over the years, usually by accident but sometimes by design. One crewmember on the *Russia* dived overboard in an attempt to save the life of a colleague who had plunged into the sea. The ship, travelling at 14 knots, turned back and rescued him - though unfortunately not the man he had been trying to save - and the passengers were so impressed by his valour they collected 100 sovereigns for him by way of reward. He went on to become famous as a swimmer, notable as the first man to swim the English Channel. That Cunard crewmember was Captain Matthew Webb.

Cunard's funnel colours remain unchanged since 1840 with the **Queen Mary** *(left) and the* **Queen Elizabeth 2** *(right). (Miles Cowsill)*

in the unpleasant deaths of 400 passengers and crew.

But as the years ticked on, Cunard's reputation for safety steadily grew until it was commonplace for travellers to wait in port for the next Cunarder, rather than entrust themselves to anyone else. The line's almost obsessive concern with safety came into its own in later years, as we shall see, when rivals such as Collins Line and White Star found their cavalier attitude to safety led not only to the loss of thousands of lives but eventually to the deaths of the companies themselves. To this day, Cunard's record on the Atlantic is unsurpassed, never having been responsible for the loss of a single life or a single mailbag.

This impeccable safety record can be traced back partly to Samuel Cunard himself, whose instruction to Captain Woodruff, the first master of the *Britannia*, was simply this "Your ship is loaded, take her. Speed is nothing. Follow your own road; deliver her safe and bring her back safe; safety is all that is required". But it also owes a vast amount to David MacIver, who today would probably be classed as being in the grip of obsessive compulsive disorder. He, or his brother Charles (who took on the entire responsibility in 1845, when David died prematurely) personally inspected, with the Captain and Marine Superintendent, every ship from poop to prow, from boat deck to bilges, once it was ready to sail and before passengers had embarked. This was no rapid skimming; no languid ticking of boxes.

The entire crew, of every position, was lined up on deck for inspection. Each had an allocated lifeboat - and contrary to modern myth there was a place in a lifeboat for every soul on board - and each had allocated tasks to perform in any emergency. A drill was carried out to ensure each man knew his role, and that evacuation could be carried out swiftly and without fuss, that there was no confusion, no duplication - just quiet and rapid efficiency. Then each boat was swung out to ensure full competence in the task. The same procedure followed with fire drill, with each man required to rehearse his allotted task, and then with manning the pumps. There was no doubt, no excuse for anything other than the calm execution of what was necessary in any emergency.

The storerooms were inspected, the watertight doors tested and the general condition of the ship assessed. If the smallest defect was discovered by MacIver, came the order "out with it". The reign of order on Cunard ships was as absolute and complete as on a naval man o' war.

Some of Cunard's safety precautions caused passenger annoyance, and the company itself extra expense, but it was not swayed by such considerations.

One source of passenger irritation was the company's insistence on sailing from the Mersey in the morning; afternoons were avoided in case any unforeseen delay resulted in departure in darkness - which was regarded as an unnecessary risk. But the demands of the tide sometimes meant very early departures, and passengers complained loudly about the pre-dawn hour they had to vacate their lodgings ashore in order to get on board. But the company suffered too, albeit financially rather than physically; a ship could only depart after clearance from an official of the Board of Trade, and the Board of Trade would not countenance such a task being

*The wrecking of **Slavonia** exemplified Cunard's diligent attention to safety. (Cunard)*

carried out by its officers outside normal office hours without a substantial supplementary payment. Needless to say, the officials themselves did not benefit from the extra levy; all that went straight into the coffers of the Board of Trade.

Despite the company's efforts, though, accidents did happen and there were numerous groundings in those first few years. But the first serious incident, and the first total loss, came in July 1843 when the *Columbia*, en route from Boston to Halifax, went aground in dense fog just off Seal Island. All the passengers - and all the mail bags - were saved, transferred to another Cunard ship and arrived in Liverpool only a week later than scheduled. By the standards of the time - a time when ships constantly foundered or were lost without trace - this was a minor incident, but it was one which Cunard would have preferred not to have.

Altogether in its 175-year history, Cunard has lost 15 ships other than through enemy action, almost all of them in the first fifty years. Only two, the *Sidon* in 1885 and the *Demerara* in 1887, both on the Mediterranean routes, resulted in passenger deaths – four in the former and two in the latter. That is a strikingly impressive record.

That MacIver's emphasis on calm and orderly behaviour in emergency endured, as can be determined from the evidence of a passenger on board the *Slavonia*, which was impaled on rocks at Flores in the Azores almost 70 years later in 1909 – an incident which prompted the first ever use of the SOS signal. Writing home to Canada following her rescue (and that of all the other passengers) Agnes Lucas wrote:

"We soon got orders to dress, and after doing so we went on deck where officers and stewards were assisting people in putting on… the life preserver'.

The ship was wedged between rocks 'towering away above the masts' – and was in no immediate danger, so the passengers were invited to pack and have breakfast - 'though we did not have the usual variety' - before taking to lifeboats.

'We were in the fifth boat. The men were left till last, though there were any number of boats to accommodate many more than the number of passengers aboard. (The crew) were splendid, and spared no effort to help us in every way. Our bedroom steward was most kind".

The company continued, to devise ways of improving safety even further. Rigorous eye tests were introduced for look-outs, masthead and port and starboard lights were introduced in 1847 long before they became mandatory, and in 1850 different eastbound and westbound routes were established in order to minimise the risk of mid-Atlantic collision. Charles MacIver, David's successor, spent much effort trying to get this system generally adopted by all shipping companies, but it was many years before this was achieved.

Within 35 years of its inception, Cunard was carrying 60,000 passengers a year across the Atlantic - all of them safely.

But while they were being carried safely they were not being carried comfortably. Samuel Cunard, as we have noted, was an austere man accustomed to the rigours of Canadian winters, and his notion of comfort did not accord with that of urban softies. "I want a plain boat' he had said on ordering the *Britannia*, 'with no unnecessary expense for show". He never moved from that position, and in it found an ally in David MacIver who put utilitarian practicality way before swags and curtains.

The cabins were, at best, spartan with just two small bunks, a small sofa, a washstand and pegs for clothes. Light came from a lamp fixed at the top of the bulkhead, where passengers could not fiddle with it and so risk fire and which, economically, illuminated two adjacent cabins and the companionway. Charles Dickens, travelling on the *Britannia* in July 1842, was scathing, complaining that his bunk had "a thin mattress spread like a surgical plaster on a most inaccessible shelf". His pillow, he said, resembled "a muffin beaten flat" and the cabin as a whole was "a profoundly preposterous box" into which he had 'as much chance of getting his wife's luggage as persuading a giraffe into a flower pot". Which it was. Yet the company insisted on referring to what were little more than horse boxes as 'staterooms', a grandiose euphemism that would make even a modern marketing man blush.

The saloon, Dickens moaned in another sideswipe, was like an elongated hearse with windows, and continuing the funereal theme he complained of his bunk that "nothing smaller for sleeping was ever made except coffins".

It is to be hoped Cunard was not expecting eminent third party endorsement from the great man, though he was so impressed by the seamanship of Captain Hewitt that he acted as treasurer of a passenger committee which raised $300 to present the Captain with a silver plate in gratitude for their safe passage across the Atlantic. The plate was presented by Dickens himself at the Tremont Theatre in Boston; it was Dickens' first public appearance in the US.

Dickens was unfortunate in that he endured a particularly rough crossing - which he milked for all it was worth with tabloid hyperbole in *American Notes* - but such a small ship battling against a head wind was bound to pitch and roll. It was not unusual for the cabins to be ankle deep in water, and an

Charles Dickens' cabin, ostentatiously called a 'stateroom', on the **Britannia**. *(Cunard)*

apocryphal story relates how one terrified passenger wailed "Officer, officer - there's water coming down the stairs"; "We only worry, madam," he calmly replied," when it's coming up the stairs".

It wasn't just the crew that operated like clockwork; so did the passengers in accordance with MacIver's strict 'rules and regulations'. Meals were frequent, albeit to our modern stomachs at rather odd hours. Breakfast was on the table at 8.30am, with lunch at 12 noon. So far so good, but dinner was at 4 pm and tea at 7.30 pm. Supper, if required, was to be taken before 10pm.

Order extended to other things too. The saloon lights were extinguished at 11.30 pm, and those serving the cabins and companionways at midnight. Too bad if anyone had thoughts of reading - the latest Dickens perhaps - in bed.

Food was plentiful. David MacIver, as part of his meticulous concern with safety, made certain that all the ships were over provisioned. In summer they carried 30 days' supply for a 10 day voyage and in winter 40 days' supply. The staple, however, was salted meat and fish together with dry or dried goods; fresh meat ran out after the third day at sea, though fresh milk was plentiful courtesy of the unfortunate cow slung in its hammock on the deck.

But although gathering and gossiping in the dining saloon helped to pass the long hours, it is doubtful if many relished the wholesome but staid and repetitive menus. Many passengers were, in any event, preoccupied with not being sick - so common an occurrence that one of the first jobs of the stewards on leaving port was to remove the rugs in the saloon.

There were compensations, though, to help passengers through the wearisome day; the bar opened at 6am, and remained so until 11 pm. And whisky and brandy, perfect for the nauseous stomach, were available for just 2s6d -12.5 pence - a pint!

But most Victorian passengers were thankful to Cunard for two things: firstly that the company's steamships got the agony of a transatlantic crossing over with relatively quickly - 10 days as opposed to six weeks or more under sail - and secondly, that they actually got you there.

In 1861 the Secretary to the Treasury, Mr F. Peel, was asked in the House of Commons how many breaches of contract and how many penalties had been incurred by all the companies

originally to have been ready to depart Liverpool on 4th June. In the event she did not reach Liverpool until 11th June, and a new maiden voyage date was set at 2nd July. That deadline, too, was missed and so "by happy coincidence" 4th July it was.

After a genuinely historic and rough but nonetheless uneventful first crossing, largely unremarked by newspapers in the UK, the *Britannia* arrived in Halifax late on 17th July - a crossing of 11 days and four hours. Despite the significance of the occasion and the welcoming gun salute, the *Britannia* did not tarry and was onward bound for Boston in just eight hours. She arrived there at 10pm on 18th July to a cannon salute, and despite the lateness of the hour, cheering crowds.

The *Britannia's* departure from Liverpool may not have been headline news, but her arrival in both Halifax and Boston

From left to right: President James Polk, Charles Dickens and Edward Knight Collins.

transporting the mail overseas. In the case of Cunard, Mr Peel replied, "The Cunard Company has been in existence since 1840….. and there has been no breach of contract. They have incurred no penalties. They have carried the mails with undeviating regularity during the 21 years the contracts have been in force".

The ship that Samuel Cunard boarded in Liverpool on 4th July, accompanied by his daughter and 61 other passengers, was, according to *The Times* of 17th November 1875, "Like a hand stretched out from England to invite America to assume its proper place in the comity of nations". But contrary to the common assumption that 4th July was deliberately selected to woo the Americans, it was in fact "by happy coincidence which was unpremeditated". In fact, the *Britannia* had been subject to delays and, following her launch on 5th February 1840, she was

certainly was.

The citizens of Boston were more than aware of the commercial impetus the new steamship service would give the city, and Samuel Cunard was feted not only at a vast public dinner at the Maverick House Hotel on 21st July - complete with bands, speeches, toasts and a new rendition of 'Rule Britannia' - but he also received over 1,500 individual invitations to private dinners. Cunard himself was to have spoken at the public dinner, but as we have noted, he was a shy and diffident man. He rose and, barely audible, thanked the crowd but said that as he was unaccustomed to public speaking, he wouldn't. And he sat down. The townsfolk also collected subscriptions in order to commission a silver cup, two and a half feet high, from the leading silversmith of the day, Obadiah Rich, to present to Cunard in recognition of his achievement.

This ornate confection is currently carried on board the line's present flagship, the *Queen Mary 2*, and can be seen in the Grand lobby.

Even more telling than this extravagant and expensive gift came four years later when the *Britannia* was stuck in 7 feet of ice in Boston harbour, and the gratitude of the citizens extended to digging a channel seven miles long and over 100 feet wide to the open sea in order to allow her to resume her journey. When Cunard offered to meet the £1,500 cost of the labour he was refused, and the merchants of the city met the cost themselves.

But the merchants were both shrewd and correct; in the first year of the *Britannia's* operation the city's trade doubled in both volume and value and its population had increased by 39,000 by 1845. By 1841, even though there were 150 sailing ships crossing the Atlantic for every one steamship, steamships were carrying 20% of all cargo. In the years 1840-1850 Cunard alone paid $10 million in duty to the United States customs. But despite business being brisk, Cunard's accumulated losses by the end of 1842 were £63,954 – a gloomy situation that soon changed for the better.

For the next decade, save for the loss of the *Columbia*, Cunard's steamship company prospered and grew with only minor setbacks and a total absence of any serious steamship competitors.

But for Samuel personally it was a difficult time and his own prosperity was seriously compromised by an unfortunate concourse of circumstance.

Stretched as he was by the cost of establishing the British and North American Royal Mail Steam Packet Company, he was further burdened by litigation over a significant land deal in Prince Edward Island into which he had entered some years earlier. His personal debt in that year totalled £130,000 - in excess of £10 million in today's prices - and he was being pursued by creditors. At one point, having hidden in a back room in the premises of his solicitors in London to avoid being served with a writ, he fled up to Liverpool to be ferried out to one of his ships already outward bound from the Mersey in order to make his escape to Halifax. By 1851 he had repaid all his personal debt.

His problems were compounded by the misfortunes of his brother Joe who owned sawmills and shipbuilding yards in the town of Chatham in New Brunswick. His businesses began to founder as early as 1842, and collapsed entirely in 1849. Burdened as he was by his own difficulties, Samuel did not abandon his brother but personally guaranteed to pay all the debts in full himself. It took years and wasn't fully achieved until

*The **Britannia** in the ice at Boston in 1844. (Cunard)*

1871, six years after Samuel's death. Samuel Cunard had always taken responsibility for his siblings, including educating them, and he didn't fail his brother at his time of need.

These episodes were ignominy for a proud and prudent man like Cunard, not least because he was forced to borrow money from his partners, but despite recording losses in the first two years the line continued to thrive in a virtual monopoly. By 1846, it was so confident of its dominance that it increased its transatlantic fares to £46 - equivalent to £4,000 today.

Such unchallenged supremacy of the Atlantic by a British company was badly received in the United States, not least by the country's singularly undistinguished President, James Polk, who intemperately raged in 1845 "when the Treasury of some other nation is poured into the lap of one chosen individual for the purpose of destroying America, I say we must act and act now!".

The consequence of this feeling, which took no account of the hugely beneficial effect Cunard was having on the Eastern Seaboard, was that Congress voted to provide a subsidy of $385,000 - far more than Cunard was receiving - for the carrying of American Mail to Europe by steamship. The contract went first to the Ocean Steam Navigation Company, a modest outfit whose ships turned out to be significantly slower than Cunard's; and so Cunard remained masters of the Atlantic. Until along came Edward Knight Collins.

Collins had a long history of running sailing packets, but in 1846 he made the transition to steam, setting up the New York and Liverpool United States Mail Steamship Company. And just as sensible people ignored the Cunard Company's official moniker, so they did with this one - and it was known from the outset simply as Collins Line. Collins Line was Cunard's first serious challenger.

The American mail contract was awarded to Collins on the understanding that his ships would be faster than Cunard's, and

*The Charge of the Light Brigade – all the horses that took part were carried by the **Arabia**.*

*The **Arabia** not only carried horses to Crimea but also Cunard's first Royal passenger.*

the first two of his five planned vessels came into service in 1849. These challenged Cunard head on. Not only did they prove to be faster, but they were considerably more comfortable with such novel luxuries as steam heating and barber shops, and fine woods and brocade in the public rooms. They even mocked Cunard by using the same funnel colours in reverse - black with a red top - which may have been an early sign of their

*The Boston Cup currently resides on the **Queen Mary 2** designating flagship of the fleet status.*

propensity for style over substance as the red topping had to be repainted after every voyage as the soot turned it black. But there is no doubt these ships were grand hotels, and Cunard's mere boarding houses.

To try to match the rise of the American steamers Cunard swapped its US terminus from Boston to New York in 1847, and also ordered two new ships, the *Arabia* and *Africa*. These, though, turned out to be slower than their American rivals and considerably less plush. The public opted in increasing numbers for the novelty of speed and luxury rather than dependability and safety. In 1852 Cunard carried 3,000 passengers across the Atlantic while Collins took over 4,000. The only lining to Cunard's cloud was that it was at least making a profit; Collins, extravagant, flamboyant and a prodigious user of expensive coal, was running at a loss.

Suddenly, in 1853, the situation worsened for Cunard with the outbreak of the war in Crimea (1853-56). It had been written into Cunard's early Admiralty contracts - against Samuel's commercial instinct though his commercial judgement told him acquiescence was necessary if he were to gain the contract - that the fleet should be available to the Admiralty in times of war for military transport. Indeed, the Admiralty had a hand in drawing up the specifications of some of the newer ships in order to ensure suitability for this purpose, and they continued so to do for the next sixty years.

Almost at once most of Cunard's transatlantic fleet was 'taken up from trade'. The *Andes* and *Alps* were consigned to take the dead and the dying from Balaclava to Florence Nightingale's hospital at Scutari; on 13th February 1854, the *Niagara* docked in Liverpool from New York and within ten days had been converted to carry troops and horses. Likewise, sister ship the *Cambria* arrived on 14th February and was converted with similar speed.

The *Jura*, *Europa*, *Arabia* and *Etna* were requisitioned, the

Captain Matthew Webb.

Arabia specifically to transport horses, 203 at a time – 7,500 of them in total through the war, and she took to Crimea all the horses that charged with The Light Brigade.

The conversions may have been rapid but the journey was slow, with the ships sailing in convoy, each towing two barges, at a speed of 4 knots. Not quite the Atlantic greyhounds they were meant to be. All told, by September 1854 14 Cunard vessels had been requisitioned, making multiple journeys carrying 100,000 troops, horses and tons of equipment.

It is easy to skim over the words; but it is sobering for us now to think how unpleasant conditions must have been for hundreds of soldiers crammed with hundreds of horses onto ships, devoid of stabilisers, refrigeration and air conditioning. They had to endure the rigours of the Bay of Biscay, men vomiting and distressed horses unable to, followed by the long, dreary six-week journey to Crimea becoming progressively hotter as they moved east.

But while Cunard was serving the country, albeit not entirely voluntarily, Collins Line was scooping up the passenger trade on an Atlantic from which Cunard was forcibly absent. Crimea earned Samuel Cunard a baronetcy, in 1859, but it almost earned the company bankruptcy.

But perversely it was a disaster which saved Cunard from obliteration.

On 27th September 1854 Collins Line's the *Arctic* left Liverpool bound for New York and in heavy fog off Cape Race was rammed by a French steamer, the *Vesta*. As the water in the *Arctic* rose it extinguished the boilers, and all power was lost; any prospect of reaching land was gone and the ship doomed. The Captain gave the order to abandon ship and take to the lifeboats (which could accommodate only 40% of those on board) and the crew did exactly that. They commandeered the lifeboats at gunpoint, physically throwing passengers out, and rowed away leaving the ship to sink and passengers to their own

British and North American Royal Mail Steam Ships,
Appointed by the Admiralty to sail between New York and Liverpool direct—and between Boston and Liverpool, the Boston ships only calling at Halifax to land and receive passengers and Her Majesty's Mails.

The Ships Composing this Line are the following:

...a, Capt. Judkins.		Africa, Capt. Harrison
" Lott.		Europa, " Shannon.
...ara, " Leitch.		America, " Lang.
...a, " Ryrie.		Cambria, " Douglas.
...da, " Stone.		

Proposed Dates of Sailing.

Between Boston and Liverpool.		Between New York and Liverpool.	
FROM LIVERPOOL.	FROM BOSTON.	FROM LIVERPOOL.	FROM NEW YORK.
September 2d,	September 13th,	September 9th,	September 20th,
September 16th,	September 27th,	September 23d,	October 4th,
September 30th,	October 11th,	October 7th,	October 18th,
October 14th,	October 25th,	October 21st,	November 1st,
October 28th,	November 8th,	November 4th,	November 15th'
November 11th,	November 22d,	November 18th,	November 29th,
November 25th,	December 6th,	December 2d,	December 13th,
December 9th,	December 20th,	December 16th,	December 27th,
December 23d,	1855	December 30th,	1855
1855	January 3d,	1855	January 10th,
January 6th,	January 17th,	January 13th,	January 24th,
January 20th,	January 31st,	January 27th,	February 7th,
February 3d,	February 14th,	February 10th,	February 21st,
February 17th,	February 28th,	February 24th,	March 7th,
March 3d,	March 14th,	March 10th,	March 21st,
March 17th,	March 28th,	March 24th,	April 4th,
March 31st,	April 11th,	April 7th,	April 18th,
April 14th,	April 25th,	April 21st,	May 2d,
April 28th,	May 9th,	May 5th,	May 16th,
May 12th,	May 23d,	May 19th,	May 30th,
May 26th,	June 6th,	June 2d,	June 13th,
June 9th,	June 20th,	June 16th,	June 27th,
June 23d,	July 4th,.	June 30th,	July 11th,
July 7th,	July 18th,	July 14th,	July 25th,
July 21st,	August 1st,	July 28th,	August 8th,
August 4th,	August 15th,	August 11th,	August 22d,
August 18th,	August 29th,	August 25th,	September 5th,
September 1st,		September 8th,	

Price of Passage, 1st Cabin, Boston to Liverpool, $110.
" " " 2d " " " $ 60.
" " " 1st " " Halifax, $ 20.
" " " 2d " " " $ 15.
" " " 1st " New York to Liverpool, $130.
" " " 2d " " " $ 75.

Apply in Boston to S. S. Lewis ; in New York to E. Cunard ; in Halifax to S. Cunard ; in Havre and Paris to Donald Currie ; in Liverpool to D. & C. Mac Iver ; in London to J. B. Ford ; in Glasgow to G. & J. Burns.

An early Cunard advertisement. (Cunard)

devices. Of 281 passengers, only 32 survived; of 109 women and children, none survived; of 153 crew, 61 survived – including four of the top five officers. All told, 350 died. How this compared with the quiet and ordered efficiency displayed during emergencies on Cunard ships.

But Collins' misfortunes did not end there, and just 16 months later their steamship the *Pacific* disappeared without trace off Ireland. Having lost 536 lives in less than two years the line's reputation was in tatters. Once Cunard ships were back on the Atlantic in January 1856 after war service was over, passengers flocked back to a company which may not have got you there as quickly or as comfortably as its competitors, but which at least got you there. By 1858 Collins Line, Cunard's first major competitor was gone.

Chapter Three

Expansion, retrenchment & reform

With its ships back on an Atlantic from which Collins had conveniently exempted itself, Cunard experienced a period of alternating expansion and consolidation, and an onslaught not just by a single serious competitor but by a phalanx of seriously ferocious ones. By the end of the century, having for years clung to the Samuel Cunard mantra of 'slow and steady', eschewing both luxury and innovation, the company was forced by its opposition on the Atlantic to move eventually to the era of grand hotels for which it is best known.

The expansion and consolidation partly involved the further development of trade to the Mediterranean, which had begun in a modest way in the previous decade and which was able to grow following the repeal in 1849 of the Navigation Acts, a move which enabled goods from Europe to be trans shipped through Britain to both the USA and the Mediterranean. This culminated in the same principal investors in the British and North American Royal Mail Steam Packet Company - Cunard, MacIver, Burns and their families - establishing the British and Foreign Steam Navigation Company which initially operated eight ships to the Mediterranean.

The transatlantic fleet continued to shuttle back and forth with commendable regularity and an exemplary safety record between Britain and North America. New York had become the company's principal US terminus with the maiden call of the *Hibernia* in 1847, and after Crimea, Cunard provided a weekly service from Liverpool for eight months of the year and a fortnightly one in winter. The Admiralty contract had risen to £155,000 as a consequence - a comfortable financial cushion for the operation.

Initially Cunard continued with its policy of considered conservatism, reluctant to innovate on matters of technology or passenger comfort. They were supported in this by the Admiralty, whose contract specified both wooden ships and paddle wheels. But change did happen slowly, and the *Arabia*, which entered service in 1853, had the distinction of being the last of the company's wooden hulled ships; it went on to further distinction by carrying to Crimea all the horses that charged with the Light Brigade, and of being the first Cunard ship to carry a member of the Royal family when, in 1861, it brought Queen Victoria's second son, Prince Alfred, home from Canada.

Wood, of course, restricted the size of ships and a new commercial opportunity was developing which required bigger vessels and greater passenger capacity - emigration. And so, in 1856, Cunard introduced its first iron-hulled

The story of
CUNARD'S
~175~
YEARS

Brunel's **Great Britain**.

transatlantic steamer, the *Persia*, which was both the largest ship in the world and, it soon proved, the fastest.

While the Board had agonised over the change to iron, and had then had to carry a reluctant Admiralty with it, an even greater source of dispute was the transition from paddle wheels to screw-driven ships - a dispute which led to a serious rift between Samuel Cunard and George Burns from which their relationship never recovered.

Burns was of the opinion, backed by significant and growing evidence, that propellers were more efficient than paddle wheels, providing greater speed for lower fuel consumption. In addition, they released a great deal of space amidships for passenger accommodation - the paddle wheels and attendant machinery having occupied much prime space, while screws allowed the mechanics of the ship to be moved down and aft. Samuel Cunard, however, saw no point in such expensive investment when the current paddle-driven fleet was performing its allotted task by conforming well to the requirements of the mail contract. The Admiralty agreed with him.

Notwithstanding Samuel's objections, the eventual move to propellers had been inevitable ever since Brunel had introduced the screw-driven *Great Britain* as far back as 1843. Perversely, some of Cunard's Mediterranean fleet - admittedly smaller than the Atlantic liners - had been both screw driven and of iron construction since the *Alps* and *Andes* of 1852. But the last Cunard transatlantic liner to be built with paddle wheels was the *Scotia*, as late as 1861 - almost 20 years after Brunel had revolutionised propulsion with the *Great Britain*, and three years after Burns, the great advocate of propellers, had retired.

The change to screws was accelerated by the growing success of the new Inman Line (properly called the Liverpool, New York and Philadelphia Steamship Company) set up in 1850 with two iron-hulled, screw-driven liners - the *City of Glasgow* and *City of Manchester*. Inman pitched itself directly at the emigrant trade; the ships had accommodation for just 52 First Class passengers and 85 second - but had space for 400 emigrants in steerage.

So it was in October 1861 that Cunard introduced its first iron-hulled screw-driven transatlantic liner, the *China*, just four months after launching the paddle-driven *Scotia*. The *China* was also revolutionary for Cunard in being the first of its ships to have significant accommodation specifically for emigrants - a full ten years after Inman had recognised the potential.

However, in the 1850s, as more and more shipping lines began to envy Inman's cash cow, competition had become ferocious. Moreover, in the 1860s business fluctuated wildly as a result of the American Civil War and the resulting economic downturn dampened the enthusiasm of Europeans to travel to the New World. Steerage fares hovered at around £5 or £6 for many years, falling in the early 1870s to an all-time low of just £2. Cunard, in effect, entered the trade at the worst possible time. Nonetheless, between 1860 and 1900, 11 million emigrants crossed the Atlantic of which over a third passed through Cunard's home port of Liverpool. Early in the process, before Inman instituted the habit of calling at Queenstown, Irish emigrants first had to take a ferry to Liverpool in order to join the westbound flood. Continental migrants mainly made their way to the North Sea ports, and from there ferries would carry them to Hull – more widely associated with fish than emigrants – whence they travelled by train to Liverpool. A massively complex operation built up, in Cunard's case based at its Head Office at 8, Water Street, whereby it was possible to book in central European cities all the necessary components of the journey – rail, ferry, hotel, transatlantic crossing and, should it be required, rail transport across the United States and Canada. All organised by means of the telegraph and scores of clerks, and fuelled not just by the push factor of poverty at home but also by the pull factor of alluring tales of a California Gold Rush and the offer of free land on the Canadian Prairies.

Inman Line was the undisputed leader of the pack in the

Queenstown, now Cobh, to embark Irish emigrants. Like Inman and Collins before it, Guion also suffered a number of losses which, while impacting badly on both image and finance, did not incur great loss of life. After barely two years in operation Guion's the *Chicago* sank in 1868, the *Colorado* in 1873, the *Dakota* in 1877 and the *Montana* in 1880 - the cumulative effect of which was company bankruptcy in 1896. Apart from the attrition of losses, the catalyst for collapse was Guion's construction of the *Oregon*, designed to be - and succeeding in being - the most glamorous of the time. But it was also a financial disaster. Ironically, the *Oregon* was bought by Cunard and gained the company the Blue Riband for the first time in 20 years.

But although Cunard still plugged bravely away in the 30

From left to right: An early print of the **China** *at sea and William Inman. (Cunard)*

business of emigration, but again - as with Collins Line - Cunard's near perfect safety record helped the company eventually to see off an innovative and competent competitor. For, while Cunard continued to plod back and forth across the Atlantic in old-fashioned ships of dubious comfort, it did so without loss of life. Inman, meanwhile, experienced casualties even greater than Collins; the *City of Glasgow* was lost in 1854; the *City of Philadelphia* the same year; the *City of New York* in 1864, and the *City of Boston* went missing without trace in 1870; the *City of Washington* was wrecked in 1873, while the *City of Limerick* disappeared in 1881 and the *City of Brussels* was sunk in a collision in 1883. At that point the firm's owner, William Inman, gave in and sold up; Cunard sailed on.

Other competition in the 1860s flowed primarily from Guion Line, established in 1866 with the intention of securing a slice of the emigrant trade. It operated between Liverpool and New York, but with an outbound call at

or so years between entering the emigrant trade and the final demise of it main competitors, that period of stiff competition from rivals with better ships, of fluctuating trade and of high capital expenditure in new tonnage in an attempt to catch up, was a difficult one for the company. But it was able to keep going not just because of its reputation for reliability and safety above all, but more practically because a major advantage it held over its rivals was the safety net of the Admiralty contract. Even that, though, was snatched away in part in 1867 as a result of the escalation of a row between the Admiralty and the Post Office. The former valued above all the security of Cunard's proven record and the potential availability of a powerful fleet in times of conflict; the Post Office, however, simply wanted mail to be delivered as cheaply as possible. Ultimately responsibility for the mail was transferred to the Post Office alone in 1880, but in 1876 a compromise had to be reached where rather than affording

Cunard a fixed price contract, payment was to be determined by the type and amount of mail carried. At a stroke, Cunard's subsidy was almost halved.

Nonetheless, the mail contract continued to give the company a degree of financial stability denied to others - which is why competitors railed against what they perceived to be an unfair advantage to Cunard. A degree of financial stability was also provided by Cunard's Mediterranean business to which ships could be transferred when Atlantic business was slack and from which they could be 'borrowed' when business was brisk. And a further aid to stability for Cunard was that it still retained a high proportion of non-emigrant passengers, whose fares remained considerably higher and less prone to fluctuation than the emigrant fares on which competitors relied so heavily.

But until the 1880s Cunard continued to be hamstrung by its perception as old fashioned and uncomfortable. Even among emigrants, whose expectations were not high, Cunard gained a reputation for inferior steerage accommodation. Inman Line really set the standard, providing not only individual berths, clean linen and three meals a day for just £6 for the Liverpool to Philadelphia crossing, but also such refinements as iced water and information leaflets in three languages. This was a standard of living generally superior to that which the emigrants had enjoyed at home, and vastly superior to the standards suffered by emigrants on sailing packets who were required to take with them sufficient food for the entire crossing.

By the time Cunard entered the emigrant fray in the 1860s, government intervention had already set rules for the transport of steerage passengers to which all shipowners had to conform, but nonetheless the company continued to be trumped on both comfort and speed, though not, of course, on safety.

Speed and comfort are easy messages to convey to potential passengers, as any marketing man can confirm, and Inman and Guion did this most effectively. Questionable safety, however, is a slow realisation drummed in only by a succession of losses over a number of years. Consequently, in 1870 Inman carried 44,100 passengers across the Atlantic and was the biggest carrier; Guion took almost 29,000; and Cunard, which just 20 years earlier had dominated the Atlantic passenger trade, carried fewer than 25,000.

This situation changed after 1873 when a four-year depression in the United States caused the number of emigrants to plummet, and Cunard's mail contract and its non-steerage passengers carried the company through. But even so, the period up to 1880 was largely one of retrenchment and more of the same. New tonnage was traditional, apart from a move to compound engines, and included the *Parthia*, the first Cunard ship to have baths – one on each side. She, like others built in the decade, had space for over 1,000 emigrants – the *Batavia*, *Bothnia* and *Gallia* all followed suit – and this increased Cunard's exposure to fluctuation.

Cunard's problems were exacerbated in this period by the emergence in 1871 of the most serious challenger of them all, White Star Line. Whereas Collins Line had challenged Cunard for a mere eight years, soaring and crashing in under a decade, and both Inman and Guion were challengers for 30 years, White Star was to be an arch enemy for the next sixty years.

White Star had existed since 1845 as an American sailing packet company which crashed with massive debts in 1867. It

*The **Parthia** at sea.*

Cunard's Liverpool Office, 8 Water Street. (Cunard)

*Above: The **Servia**. (Cunard)*

Left Sir Samuel Cunard shortly before his death in his London home at the age of 78 in 1865. (Cunard)

was bought by a Liverpudlian, Thomas Ismay, in 1868 and renamed the Oceanic Steam Navigation Company - a clear indication of the company's intended direction. But as with all these things, the ponderous official name was ignored and the company continued under its name from days of sail, White Star.

Under Ismay, White Star began an aggressive programme of shipbuilding and ordered four liners from Belfast shipbuilder Harland & Wolff - the yard which went on to produce all White Star's vessels. Ismay decided that the future lay not just in speed, but in luxury and modernity. In came low clean lines, the straight bow and jaunty raked funnels together with interior refinements as yet undreamt of by Cunard - hot and cold running water in cabins, steam central heating throughout, steam-powered shoe brushes, bells with which to summon the steward and impressive dining rooms the full width of the ships with menus to match. By 1872 all

four ships were in service - the *Oceanic, Atlantic, Baltic* and *Republic* - and White Star, apart from the occasional blip, became the line from which Cunard had most to fear.

At the same time as the splendid new White Star ships came on stream, Cunard was doing little. As we have seen it had invested heavily in new though not spectacular ships in the 1860s and early 70s in its quest for a share of the emigrant trade, and now that the trade was in the doldrums the 1870s saw a slowdown in Cunard investment. To an extent, and to use an appropriate phrase, Cunard Line had been left rather rudderless by the death of Sir (as he had been since 1859 on the recommendation of Lord Palmerston) Samuel Cunard on 28th April 1865; conservative he may have been, but Cunard had drive, and a keen business brain, and the company missed him.

Indeed, throughout the 1870s after White Star ships took to the water, competition in speed, service and refinement was largely between White Star and Inman, with plodding Cunard looking distinctly dowdy. The Blue Riband for the fastest crossing of the Atlantic passed from Inman to White Star and back again with Cunard failing to make any impact at all.

But yet again, as with Collins, Inman and Guion, the spectre of safety haunted White Star throughout its existence. In March 1893 the line's *Atlantic* hit the coast of Nova Scotia at full speed, with the loss of 585 lives. It was damaging to White Star not only because it was the biggest loss of life at sea in the nineteenth century, but because of carelessness implicit in the loss; the ship had been on diversion to Halifax because it was running out of coal, something unthinkable at ever cautious Cunard. It was also the first of a toll of White Star losses, which culminated almost 30 years later with the *Titanic*.

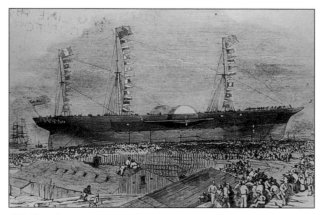

*The **Persia**.*

Left: Bruce Ismay, son of White Star founder, Thomas Ismay.

Centre: Cunard Chairman John Burns, the first Lord Inverclyde. (University of Liverpool Cunard archive)

Right: Inventor Guglielmo Marconi.

In 1878, partly to regularise the situation between the British and North American Steam Packet Company (Cunard had dropped 'Royal Mail' from the name in 1868) and the British and Foreign Steam Navigation Company, which tended to operate as one, and more importantly to raise cash for much needed investment, a limited company was formed incorporating the two former companies; the new company almost immediately went public with great success. And so two companies with grandiose titles simply became The Cunard Steamship Company Limited, sailing under its new house flag - a golden lion on a red background holding a globe - the same house flag that is in use today.

John Burns, son of one of the original triumvirate, George Burns, became Chairman of the new company in 1880 and major changes began to happen. Burns seems to have been a confident character with a plan, and he steamrollered the Board into accepting a major programme of investment in new ships. The austere, no-frills approach of Samuel Cunard and the MacIver brothers still lingered in the upper reaches of the company, though they themselves were long gone, and

A postcard showing White Star's second **Oceanic**.

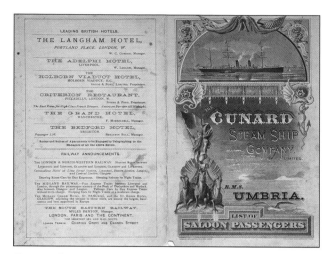

*Passenger list for the **Umbria**. (Cunard)*

*The **Servia**. (Cunard)*

there was resistance to Burns' plans. But he could see that, regardless of the company's enviable record over forty years, Cunard could not regain its place as the premier line on the Atlantic simply by trading on its past. It had to match and surpass White Star, Inman and Guion in the race to turn ships into grand hotels. Frills mattered, even for emigrants.

Burns' plans began with the introduction of the *Servia* in 1881, the first Cunard ship to be built of steel and the first to be lit by electricity. She was destined for the New York run, but Burns also enhanced the Boston route with the launch in 1881 of the *Catalonia*, followed in 1882 by the *Cephalonia* and *Pavonia*. The *Aurania*, principally for cabin class passengers,

followed in 1883. In 1884 Cunard purchased Guion Line's superb *Oregon*, capable of 20 knots, which Guion was unable to sustain because of the 268 tons a day coal consumption. As a result Cunard regained the Blue Riband after two decades. Sadly, the *Oregon* also became one of Cunard's few peacetime losses, sinking in 1886 after being rammed by another vessel.

But the ship so impressed Cunard that even before purchase the company decided to replicate it, and in 1884 they took delivery from the yard of John Elder – the *Oregon's* builder –

*The **Campania** under construction. (Cunard)*

*The grand First Class Dining Saloon of the **Campania** and **Lucania**. (Cunard)*

*The **Lucania**. (Cunard)*

the *Umbria* and *Etruria*. This pair were the first Cunard ships to truly resemble twentieth century liners and the last to carry sails. Their speed was remarkable – in excess of 19 knots in all weathers – and the *Etruria* captured the *Oregon's* Atlantic record. They were the peak of Cunard's achievement in that decade.

It is worth noting, in this Cunard's 175th year, that the company's fiftieth anniversary was celebrated with a grand dinner on board the *Etruria*, anchored in the Mersey. The top rank of north-west society was there, along with others from more distant parts, including the Mayors of Bootle and Birkenhead (Liverpool could not attend), the American and Japanese Consuls, the chairmen of virtually every other shipping line, local MPs, representations of every major insurance company and those of every railway company. The only notable absence was that of John Burns, kept away by the recent death of his father, Sir George Burns, one of the company's founders, who had been made a baronet just the year before.

During the 1890s, still under the dynamic leadership of John Burns, Cunard stepped up its fight back against its competitors by investing in bigger, faster and more modern ships. The most notable were the *Campania* and *Lucania*, the first twin-screw Cunarders and, at almost 13,000 tons, the company's biggest yet. They were also the fastest, notching up speeds in excess of 21 knots – and they remained without challenge on the Atlantic from their introduction in 1893 until the debut of the *Kaiser Wilhelm der Grosse*, the world's first four-funnelled liner, in 1897.

These ships looked even more modern than the *Etruria* and *Umbria* of the previous decade; both pleased passengers with public rooms that would have blended into a land-based hotel, and the clumsy paraphernalia of rigging disappeared. These were proper steamships that reduced the transatlantic crossing to just over 5 days – faster than is achieved now. And they were the first hint of Cunard's future fame as a company of elegance, fine food and service – which was to develop early in the twentieth century. Oddly, the dining rooms remained like something from a public school – with passengers seated at long, communal tables, albeit now with fine linen and porcelain. The transition to a country house at sea had not quite arrived. The Cunard Board may have been critical of John Burns' determination to build bigger ships, faster ships and more comfortable ships, but he lived long enough – until 1901 – to see that he had been right. And he earned acknowledgement by being created the first Lord Inverclyde.

October 1901 was significant in that the *Campania* and the

*The **Umbria**. (Cunard)*

Lucania communicated with each other in mid-Atlantic courtesy of Signor Marconi's new wireless telegraphy. The ships were in contact for over five hours, until they were 170 miles apart and in that time 75 messages were exchanged; it is hard to imagine now that before this time contact between ships, and between ship and shore, had been entirely visual. This was a major advance for Cunard – and, of course, for the world.

Now that the Cunard Board, thanks primarily to John Burns, Lord Inverclyde, was at ease with speed and luxury, they entered the twentieth century fully receptive to grand ideas and modernity. Not a moment too soon, in fact, as White Star Line – which had never gone away, unlike Cunard's other nineteenth century British competitors – was about to be reborn as part of a voracious American conglomerate, the International Mercantile Marine Company.

*The **Campania**. (Cunard)*

Chapter Four

From great things to greater

In 1902, J. Pierpoint Morgan, an American financier, began to buy up steamship companies which he forged into the International Mercantile Marine Company with the undoubted aim of dominating the North Atlantic - something the United States had not achieved since the days of the clippers. He could afford to: in 1896 the multi-millionaire had been able to lend the US government $62 million! Dominion Line and Leyland were gobbled up, as were National Line, the Atlantic Transport Line, Shaw Savill and Albion, together with control of Red Star and a 25% holding of Holland America. And finally, White Star was bought for £10 million. The government was aghast. The prospect of anyone other than Britannia ruling the waves, and the North Atlantic in particular, did not appeal. Something had to be done.

And it wasn't just the government that was aghast: so was the public at large. In the days before aeroplanes, shipping companies mattered and big shipping companies mattered a lot. In homes across the land, with no maritime connection greater than an annual fortnight in Bridlington, the rise of American and German sea power and the clear decline of British sea power mattered. Security was at stake, and they knew it just as the government knew it.

Cunard was accustomed to dealing with governments - and, as we know, even the earliest mail contracts required the company to make vessels available for trooping and transport duties, something which it did throughout the nineteenth century. Cunard served not only in major conflicts like Crimea (1853-56) and the Boer War (1899-1902), but in lesser known incidents in Egypt, Canada, Ireland and Russia.

This relationship took on a more regular turn in 1883 when Cunard was paid an annual retaining fee of £20,000 per ship for constructing and maintaining gun placements beneath the teak decks of the *Etruria*, *Umbria* and *Aurania*, for ensuring that half its crews were RNR ratings, and for guaranteeing that the ships could be fitted out as armed auxiliary cruisers in less than a week should the need arise.

The Admiralty didn't hesitate to requisition eight Cunard vessels for the Boer War – two of which were given the lowly task of conveying not men but mules from New Orleans to South Africa.

And so, in 1903, the government signed a 20 year agreement with Cunard intended to protect British interests on the Atlantic - but not before the company had been required to amend its Articles of Association to ensure that it could not fall under foreign control. Shares in the company could henceforth only be owned by British subjects, and no foreigner could be a director or 'principal officer' – which included captains and officers on board any of the company's ships. Three quarters of the crew had to be British. Today such requirements would be called racist; then they were called prudent security.

The agreement provided for the construction of two large, fast four-funnelled liners to be built in accordance with Admiralty requirements - including the fitting of gun placements beneath the decks. These, though never used, were much later to become of profound importance to the fate of one of the two - as we shall see.

The ships were financed by a loan of £2,600,000 at a highly preferential interest rate of two and three quarters per cent, and in addition an annual subsidy of £150,000 was to be paid to Cunard for 20 years to take account of the Admiralty's costly specifications. Since the Company was valued at £1,600,000 such a huge loan at half the normal interest rate indicated the government's desperation for a fast and flexible merchant fleet.

The government's generosity to Cunard was no gift. Not only were the two ships to be available as armed merchant cruisers whenever required, but so was the entire fleet - and any plans Cunard may have for future vessels capable of more than 17 knots had to be submitted for Admiralty approval.

Such measures, largely agreed before his death in 1901 by Lord Inverclyde for Cunard, were announced by Prime Minister Arthur Balfour in 1902, and effective from 1903. They reflected not just the government's concern about Pierpoint Morgan's new company with its vast capital reserve of £34 million, but also the increasing pressure on the North Atlantic of aggressive German competition. First there had been the *Kaiser Wilhelm der Grosse*, which outstripped all other ships on the route, but this was followed by the even faster *Deutschland*. These ships were massively subsidised by upwards of $750,000pa by the German government. Cunard's new ships, capable of 25 knots for a sustained period and carrying huge reserves of coal, would be able to elude every vessel they wanted to escape and overtake every vessel they wanted to engage.

Four yards tendered for the work - John Brown and Fairfields on the Clyde, Vickers in Barrow and Swan Hunter on the Tyne. However, tests to assess the optimum dimensions for the 30,000 ton ships determined that a breadth of 85 feet would be required - wider than anticipated. Both Fairfields and Vickers were now in some difficulty as the new stipulated dimensions exceeded those with which their facilities could cope. Therefore one contract, for the ship which was to become the *Lusitania*, went to John Brown, and the other, for the ship which was to become the *Mauretania*, was awarded to the Tyne.

For those who have difficulty with the spelling of the *Mauretania*, and involuntarily tend to 'Mauritania', there is good news; for three months in 1906 they were right! The Admiralty had asked Cunard to settle on names in November 1904, but a year later the Board was still dithering over three pairs of names: 'Britannia' and 'Hibernia', 'Britannia' and 'Hesperia', and 'Albania' and 'Moravia'. Finally, at a Board meeting on 15th February 1906 they agreed on a totally different pair – the *Lusitania* and *Mauritania*, with an 'i'. On 17th May the *Mauritania* was changed to the *Mauretania* – the

Caronia. (University of Liverpool Cunard archive)

Carpathia. *(University of Liverpool Cunard archive)*

the greatest ship ever to come out of the North East.

The ships were very similar sisters externally, though there were differences that allow those who know what they are looking for to tell them apart, but the interiors were created by different designers - the best of their day. What they shared internally, however, was opulence undreamed of by the Cunard of old, with First Class at least resembling a cross between a country house and an ornate royal palace.

At this stage it was intended that both ships would have traditional steam reciprocating engines, but Cunard had been subject to a barrage of persuasive approaches since 1901 from Sir Charles Parsons, another Tyneside entrepreneur, to adopt the revolutionary turbines which he had developed. As recently as 1902 the Cunard Board had rejected the option.

Parsons had very effectively drawn the attention of the public and the Admiralty to the superiority of turbines in June 1897 when his prototype, the *Turbinia*, appeared uninvited and unexpectedly at Queen Victoria's Diamond Jubilee Review at Spithead and zipped, at an unprecedented 30 knots, up and down the static lines of warships being reviewed by the Prince of Wales. As *The Times* reported the following day, "the patrol boats which attempted to check the adventurous but unlawful proceeding were distanced in a twinkling".

Cunard's problem though, was that the two ships were to be of 70,000 hp - five times greater than any ship powered by turbines to date. But it was persuaded, probably with some Admiralty 'guidance', after a detailed committee review, and the bold decision to use turbine propulsion was made in 1904 after construction had begun.

correct spelling for the Roman province in North Africa after which she was named.

Swan Hunter was thus poised to take on a much bigger job than it had ever undertaken before, and one which would stretch its resources beyond their limit. Its response, however, was not to withdraw as Fairfields and Vickers had done, but to seek a merger with Wigham Richardson, also on the Tyne, and to secure an interest in the Wallsend Slipway - thus creating a major shipbuilding force. Swan Hunter and Wigham Richardson began work on immense facilities capable of accommodating the new ship - including covered berths with roofs 150 feet high. New railway sidings linked to the North Eastern Railway were built to bring in the required raw materials, and a 140-ton floating crane was acquired along with new workshops for rolling steel. Tyneside was rising to an unprecedented challenge in an admirably determined way - a determination which went on to produce

Fortuitously, Cunard was at the same time building two 19,000-ton ships at the John Brown yard. This pair, to be named the *Caronia* and *Carmania*, were virtually identical except for the means of propulsion. In order to 'compare and contrast', Cunard had taken the sensible step of giving the *Caronia* traditional steam quadruple expansion engines and twin screws while the *Carmania* was fitted with three turbines and triple screws. When this pair came into service in 1905 it was clear that the *Carmania* was both more efficient and faster - though not

From left to right: John Pierpoint Morgan and Prime Minister Arthur Balfour.

Kaiser Wilhelm der Grosse.

Deutschland.

significantly so. But she gave Cunard two years in which to become accustomed to this new form of propulsion, first installed in a ship as recently as 1901.

Over on the East Coast, eighteen months had elapsed from keel-laying to launch, in which time the *Mauretania* and *Lusitania* had become ranked among the wonders of the world. The *Mauretania* was 790 feet long, 88 feet wide, and with capacity for 560 First Class passengers, 500 in Second Class, and 1,400 in Third - together with 800 crew. As *The Shipbuilder* reported after fitting out, "when spaciousness and beauty are taken into account, (the *Mauretania*) certainly justifies the use of the extravagant term "a floating palace"'. Cunard had got there at last!

The *Mauretania's* launch, performed by Sir Winston Churchill's aunt, the Dowager Duchess of Roxburghe, was an enormous affair with excursion trains carrying 80,000 spectators to Wallsend. And Cunard set out to impress all 80,000. The dignitaries, led by the Dowager Duchess, were driven from lunch to launch in new-fangled motor cars two abreast through three of the ship's four funnels lying on the dockside waiting to be hoisted into place after the launch.

Launching ships then was very different from now. Now

ships are constructed in blocks, often in different parts of the yard, and then the blocks are lifted into place and welded. Then the whole hull was built on a sloping slipway from the keel upwards, and the metal plates of the hull were riveted onto the frame rising up from the keel; once the hull was complete it was 'launched' into the river by the simple expedient of sending it sliding down the slipway into the water. The superstructure and interiors were completed once the hull was afloat, which is why there was usually a 12 month delay between launch and maiden voyage.

The operation of launching was a remarkably delicate process considering the size of many of the ships. There was a need for the ship to slide easily down the slipway once the blocks holding it in place had been knocked away, simultaneously it was hoped, with the bottle smashing on the bow, but not so easily or speedily that it could not be stopped before thundering out of control and hitting the far bank of the river. The first requirement was met by the free application of 290 hundredweight of tallow, 12 hundredweight of train oil and 22 hundredweight of soft soap to the slipway; and the second requirement, to halt 17,000 tons of steel in accelerating motion, was achieved by

*The **Aquitania** compared to the Capitol in Washington. (Cunard)*

*The **Lusitania** in New York in 1907. (Cunard)*

six drag chains, each of 1,000 tons, on each side of the ship.

On 17th September 1907 after fitting out, the *Mauretania* left the Tyne without fanfare for the first time on her way to yard trials off Flamborough Head. The trials were so secret that performance reports were sent back to the yard by homing pigeon rather than by more modern but less secure methods.

The *Mauretania* finally left her birthplace on 22nd October 1907 - the only four-funnelled liner to be built in England.

She was the pride of the Tyne which went on to hold the Blue Riband Atlantic speed record for 22 consecutive years; in so doing, she became the pride of Britain.

Meanwhile, on the Clyde, work on sister ship the *Lusitania* was progressing as planned, slightly ahead of the efforts on the Tyne. She was launched on 7th June 1906 by Lady Inverclyde, widow of George Burns, the second Lord Inverclyde who had succeeded his father as Cunard's chairman, but who had died prematurely only the year before. In September 1907 the

*The **Mauretania** leaving the Tyne on 17th September 1907. (Cunard)*

Lusitania undertook her maiden voyage from Liverpool to New York, and on the second crossing - in October - she took the Blue Riband from the Germans. But not for long.

The *Mauretania* proved to be slightly faster than her sister, even on sea trials, and in November 1907 she took the Blue Riband from the *Lusitania* with an average speed of almost 24 knots and kept it for two decades. She surpassed even her own record in 1909 when new four-bladed propellers were fitted, achieving an average speed of 26 knots. And age did not weary her; in 1929 she managed an average of 27.48 knots, followed in 1933 - just two years before being

withdrawn from service - by a 112-mile run at 32 knots.

It is worth noting that these two large vessels caused many problems for the Mersey Docks and Harbour Board. Firstly, in order to accommodate them over 20 square miles of the river had to be dredged to allow the ships to go alongside; more than 200,000 tons of rock, clay and sand had to be removed.

But they also demonstrated the inherent unsuitability of the Mersey for these large ships, which, when awaiting space at the landing stage, had to tie up at two Cunard Buoys in the Sloyne, a stretch of water out of the way of traffic. But the

*The **Lusitania** sailing down the Clyde on 22nd June 1907.*

*First Class Smoking Room on the **Lusitania**. (University of Liverpool Cunard archive)*

*Above & Below: Deck scenes on the **Mauretania** taken early (above) and later (below) in her career. (Cunard)*

river on an ebb tide could race at 5 knots at this point, making tying up difficult – sometimes impossible. When such efforts failed, the ships would anchor – but often both ship and anchor would be dragged downriver by the tide, and then the ship would need to steam back up river and drop anchor again. Such difficulties and the anxieties they caused foreshadowed the eventual move to Southampton, which began tentatively in 1911.

In 1914, despite the agreement with the government under which the two ships had been built, neither was requisitioned on the outbreak of war. This may seem odd in view of the huge sums of money expended by the government on developing these ships as armed merchant cruisers to be called upon in war. But it soon became evident

*HM King George V and HM Queen Mary, accompanied by HRH Prince Edward, board the **Mauretania** in the Mersey from the Mersey Docks and Harbour Board's tender **Galatea** on 11th July 1913. (Newall Dunn Collection)*

that large ships were not suitable for the purpose. Apart from the expense of running them – the *Mauretania* and *Lusitania* consumed 1,000 tons of coal a day, at a time when coal was in restricted supply – they were also too large to enter small ports for bunkering; the number of ports able to handle them was thus limited, and bunkering at sea left these large ships helpless and exposed. The lesson was learned from the fate of Germany's the *Kaiser Wilhelm der Grosse*, the ship which in part had led to the development of the *Mauretania* and *Lusitania*. She was armed and sailed as an auxiliary cruiser, but shortly

*The launch of the **Aquitania** on 21st April 1913. (University of Liverpool Cunard archive)*

afterwards she was spotted rebunkering at sea off the coast of West Africa, and was sunk by an obsolete cruiser, the *HMS Highflyer*. How are the mighty fallen.

However, the hostilities understandably caused a significant reduction in transatlantic traffic, so the *Mauretania* was laid up; her sister ship, at the insistence of the Admiralty, continued on the Liverpool to New York service - with eventual disastrous consequences.

In 1915 the *Mauretania* was finally requisitioned and took 10,000 soldiers in three voyages to Gallipoli, and later the same year she became a hospital ship. In 1916 she carried Canadian troops to Europe, followed in 1918 by the transport of US troops when the Americans entered the war; no sooner

had she brought them over, of course, than she had to take 34,000 back again after the Armistice was signed. This might seem flippant, but it was literally true. The *Mauretania* took on her last consignment of US troops in New York on 7th November. On 11th November, at sea, official confirmation of the Armistice was received – confirmed obliquely by a German 'U' boat overtaken travelling eastwards on the surface which signalled 'I have no hostile intentions' – but

*The fourth funnel is hoisted onto the **Aquitania**. (University of Liverpool Cunard archive)*

Franklin D Roosevelt.

The **Aquitania** *departs Liverpool on her maiden voyage on 30th May 1914. (Cunard)*

orders were for the troops to be taken to Liverpool so taken to Liverpool they were. On arrival they were dispatched to Knotty Ash Camp, and after a few hours they were returned to the *Mauretania*, and re-embarked for the return journey to New York. They were the last American troops to leave New York, and they were the first to return – to be greeted with garlanded streets, huge crowds and a civic welcome. But no doubt to most in the crowd, Knotty Ash sounded just as foreign and menacing as anywhere on the Western Front.

In February 1923 she operated her first cruise, from New York to the Mediterranean, which became an annual event right through to 1930 when the Depression put an end to such frivolities. The Depression also affected transatlantic traffic greatly, and Cunard was reduced to operating the ship on short 'booze cruises' out of New York.

In 1929 she lost the Blue Riband to the German liner the *Bremen*.

The last indignity came in 1933 when the *Mauretania* was painted white and transferred permanently to cruising. But this role did not last long and in 1934 she was withdrawn from service, making her last voyage from New York on the day the *Queen Mary* was launched. the Queen is dead, long live the Queen.

In April 1935 Cunard sold the *Mauretania* for scrap, and at 9pm on Monday 1st July 1935 she left Southampton for the last time. She was waved off by thousands, including her most illustrious master, Commodore Sir Arthur Rostron who,

emotionally, could not bring himself to step aboard and see the old lady in her stripped down condition. She progressed slowly up the East Coast under the command of Captain A.T. Brown, master for the final voyage only. Passing his home town of Scarborough at 10pm on 2nd July, he paused in the South Bay. There, as elsewhere, thousands lined the cliffs, ferried to the town by special trains which had been laid on to vantage points all along the Coast, intent on saying

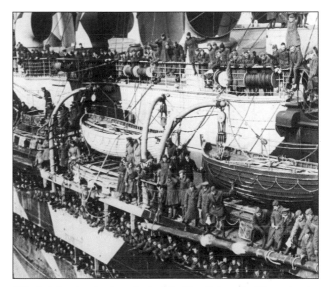

*The first American troops arrive back in New York on the **Mauretania** in November 1918 – from Knotty Ash! (University of Liverpool Cunard archive)*

*The **Aquitania** departs Liverpool on her maiden voyage on 30th May 1914. (Cunard)*

goodbye to the most famous ship of the age.

She arrived at her birthplace, the Tyne, on 3rd July where she lingered offshore for an hour to be visited one last time by local dignitaries. On departing she sent The Lord Mayor of Newcastle, Councillor R.C. Dalglish, a final message to the city of her birth:

"For 28 years I have striven to be a credit to you, and now my day is done. Though I pass on, may Tyneside ever reach out to further and greater triumphs. With pride and affection, I greet you. Farewell, *Mauretania*".

And so, on the following day, Wednesday 4th July 1935 - Cunard's 95th anniversary - the company's greatest ship to date passed under the Forth Bridge, her masts cut down to allow it, and reached her final resting place at Rosyth on the Firth of Forth where she was to be broken up.

But even in death she attracted attention on a grand scale. When the ship breakers set aside one day for the public to visit her before demolition began, 100,000 people turned up. Even after queuing for five hours, 80,000 had to be turned away disappointed.

The *Mauretania's* end caused great sadness, and not just in Britain. The American President, Franklin D. Roosevelt, wrote: "Neither size nor speed alone could have given *Mauretania* her fame. That rested on something more secure and intangible - on her personality; for *Mauretania* was a ship with a fighting heart".

He went on: "If ever there was a ship that possessed a thing called a 'soul', *Mauretania* did.....very few ships have earned the right, and *Mauretania* has earned it, to be remembered 100 years hence."

The last of the trio of four-funnelled liners that led Cunard majestically into the world of floating palaces, of country house refinement (for First Class, at least) was the *Aquitania*. Frequently referred to as 'the ship beautiful', a phrase so divorced from normal English syntax it can only have been dreamt up by the marketing department, the *Aquitania* certainly was beautiful. There seems to be consistent agreement that her external lines were superlative, and that her interiors - the *Mauretania* and *Lusitania* plus some - while

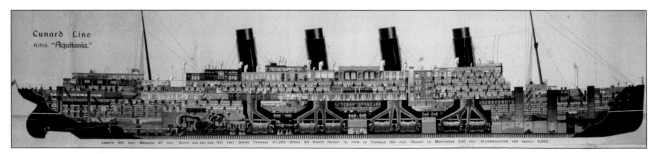

*Cross-section of the **Aquitania**. (Cunard)*

Aquitania

Interior views from different times of her career. **Aquitania** *is still regarded by many to be the most beautiful ship ever built.*

Left: The Palladian Lounge.(University of Liverpool Cunard archive)

Above: First Class Bedroom. (Cunard)

Below: Tourist Class Dining Room. (Cunard)

Above: The **Aquitania** *leaving Newcastle after her conversion to oil in 1920. (University of Liverpool Cunard archive)*

Right: Preparing the **Aquitania** *for another crossing. (Cunard)*

Overleaf: Cross-section of the **Aquitania**. *(Cunard)*

more subjectively a matter of taste were certainly palatial.

The 45,647 ton ship, considerably larger than her two earlier quadruple screw sisters, was launched at the yard of John Brown and Co on the Clyde in May 1913, and entered service just one year later - nicely timed to be taken up for active service in the Great War after just three commercial voyages. To get the ship ready for war service 5,000 men were employed to remove her valuable fixtures and fittings mere months after they had been installed. Two thousand lorry loads of finery, from furniture to ornate plasterwork, were removed in just 48 hours and dispatched for safe keeping to warehouses around the North West.

During that war she steamed over half a million miles and carried 400,000 troops.

The *Aquitania*, apart from her opulence and elegance has three claims to fame: the first being that in 1919, after war service, she became the first Cunard express Atlantic liner to sail from Southampton to New York (though a service to Montreal had been inaugurated in 1911), and the second being that this long-lived ship was the only major passenger vessel to serve in both world wars. Her third claim to having been involved in an event of historic significance came in 1926 when the leaders of Britain's four biggest chemical companies – Brunner Mond, Nobel Explosives, United Alkali and British Dyestuffs - met on board during a transatlantic crossing. There they agreed that the best way for them to prosper in the global economy would be to unite and form a huge chemical combine. And so, in December 1926, ICI – for many years Britain's biggest chemical manufacturer – came into being.

The *Carpathia*:
Guided by a greater hand

At the same time as negotiations were proceeding for the construction of the superlative Tyneside liner the *Mauretania* by an expanded Swan Hunter and Wigham Richardson consortium, another little ship was being built for Cunard by Swan Hunter and Wigham Richardson at Wallsend.

Mediterranean ports of Trieste and Fiume to New York and a new life. This role was secured in the long term for her, the *Slavonia* and the *Pannonia* in 1904 when Cunard obtained the Hungarian government contract to carry emigrants. She began that duty in November 1904, plodding tenaciously backwards and forwards, year in year out, without incident, carrying

Carpathia *by Odin Rosenvinge. (Cunard)*

The *Carpathia* was a workhorse; she wasn't one of the glamorous express transatlantic liners built to compete for the Blue Riband and designed to resemble Versailles. Only once was she met by hordes of reporters and photographers, flashbulbs popping, as she chugged into New York. For the *Mauretania* it was to happen every time.

She was launched with no fuss on 6th August 1902. At 13,603 tons and capable of just 14 knots, she was intended to carry Hungarian emigrants from the

emigrants westbound at a fare of just £5 10s, and American tourists and returning émigrés eastbound.

On Thursday 11th April 1912, she left New York unnoticed just after noon bound as usual for Trieste on a journey she, for momentous reasons, was destined never to complete. But it was a journey which would take her from insignificance to celebrity.

At about the same time on the other side of the Atlantic, an already celebrated ocean greyhound was leaving Queenstown on her maiden voyage to New

The *Carpathia*: Guided by a greater hand

*The deck crew of the **Carpathia** involved in the rescue of the **Titanic** survivors. (University of Liverpool Cunard archive)*

York; she was the *Titanic*, brand new pride of the White Star fleet. Commanded by Captain Edward Smith, on his last voyage before retirement, the *Titanic* had on board many rich and famous socialites, the celebrities of the day, and her departure from Southampton had been as feted as the *Carpathia's* from New York had been unremarked.

In command of the little *Carpathia* was 42-year-old Arthur Rostron, an officer with Cunard since 1895 and master of the *Carpathia* for just three months. With him were 700 passengers, 150 of them mainly elderly American tourists and the rest former emigrants making a visit home.

Also on board was Second Officer James Bisset, later to be Commodore Sir James Bisset, master of the *Queen Mary*; it is fortunate that he was because he made contemporary notes of the unfolding drama of that voyage which he publicly recorded in Volume 2 of his autobiography. It is largely thanks to him that we know what we know.

Just before midnight on 14th April, Captain Rostron made his customary last visit to the bridge before retiring to bed, and Second Officer Bisset advised him of ice warnings that had been coming in. Rostron called the wireless operator, Harold Cottam, and asked him what ships were within range. "The *Titanic*, sir" replied Cottam... "Then there's the *Californian*. She's stopped engines for the night as she is surrounded by ice."

"It must be thick, then" commented Rostron. "I suppose the *Titanic* will have to slow down or steer a more southerly course". She did neither.

He then turned to Bisset and remarked, "You may sight the *Titanic* if she bears southward to avoid the ice. I don't suppose she will try to run through it when (the ice) is so thick the *Californian* has stopped for the night." But she did.

With this, the Captain went off to bed.

At a quarter past midnight on the morning of 15th April, Harold Cottam was untying his shoelaces in readiness for bed. He was late, some ten minutes later than he would normally be turning in and, providentially, his earphones were still clamped to his head; had he not

The *Carpathia*: Guided by a greater hand

been, and had they not been, there may not have been any *Titanic* survivors at all. For at that moment he received the first distress call from the liner.

Cottam immediately awoke Captain Rostron who, after a moment of disbelief, ordered a change of course. The *Carpathia* was 58 miles from the *Titanic*; at 14 knots it would take her over four hours to get there.

The Chief Engineer was ordered to turn off all the heating and hot water so that every ounce of steam could be directed to power the engines. All off-duty stokers were roused from their beds to shovel coal into the furnaces as fast as they were able.

Next, Rostron instructed his First Officer to begin specific preparations - the lifeboats were to be slung out ready to be lowered, lighting rigged along the ship's sides, all shell (hull) doors were opened, slings made to haul up children and the infirm, ladders and rigging lowered and the forward cargo crane made ready to lift on board luggage, belongings and lifeboats.

Meanwhile, all remaining crew were summoned to

Captain Arthur Rostron. (University of Liverpool Cunard archive)

duty and preparations were made to receive potentially 2,000 *Titanic* passengers in the public rooms; blankets and warm clothing were gathered to distribute; tea, coffee and soup prepared.

*A rare photograph of some of the hotel staff of **Carpathia** who took part in the rescue. (University of Liverpool Cunard archive)*

The *Carpathia*: Guided by a greater hand

*The **Olympic** (left) and **Titanic** seen at the Harland & Wolff Shipyard in Belfast. (Ferry Publications Library)*

First aid posts were established in the three dining rooms, with a doctor in charge of each.

And when all this was ready, the ever thoughtful Rostron ordered his crew to take refreshment in anticipation of a long and arduous night ahead.

The ship, meanwhile, strained and shuddered as, with every stoker piling fuel into the furnaces, she edged beyond her maximum speed. Fifteen, sixteen and finally seventeen knots were achieved as the little ship surged through a calm and placid sea in the dark without radar. Rostron's team of lookouts were denied the usual benefit of a line of white surf breaking against the ice cliff as the sea was so still; the glistening icebergs were visible only by the reflection of the stars. As the ice thickened, the ship slowed and Rostron zig zagged through the bergs that dwarfed her.

At 4am the *Carpathia* reached the *Titanic's* last known position, and the engines were stopped as crew and passengers (awoken not just by the hubbub of preparations, but by the increasing cold in their cabins) strained to see any sign of the great ship. There was none. Then suddenly, in the distance, they saw a soaring green flare fired by the *Titanic's* lifeboat number 2. The search was over and Rostron moved slowly forward. The first survivors began to board at 4.10am, and at 8.30, Charles Lightoller, the final person to be rescued, stepped

*A lifeboat alongside the **Carpathia**. (author's collection)*

The *Carpathia*: Guided by a greater hand

Commodore Sir Arthur Rostron with Prime Minister Ramsay McDonald on board a Cunard ship. (University of Liverpool Cunard archive)

aboard the *Carpathia*.

Now carrying double her original complement after rescuing 703 survivors, the *Carpathia* steamed slowly among floating wreckage seeking more survivors. But none was found.

Rostron's next decision was where to go. Halifax was the nearest port, but the passage would involve travelling through more ice and he felt that his new passengers had had enough of that; the Azores were the best destination to keep the ship on course and incur the least cost to Cunard, but he had insufficient supplies for such a journey with the greater numbers to feed. So Rostron turned back whence he had come - New York.

The *Carpathia's* passengers and crew did what they could, giving up beds and clothing to those who had survived freezing temperatures, often inadequately dressed. But most of the rescued were grieving widows, inconsolable whatever creature comforts were supplied.

The ship was besieged by messages from anxious relations, and the survivors were equally anxious for messages to be sent. Aided by a surviving radio officer, Harold Cottam worked without sleep for three days and nights to cope with the deluge. It is interesting to reflect here that most ships at the time, the *Carpathia* included, had only one radio officer and when he was asleep or at meals, the ship was without communication. Little did those survivors know just how fortunate they were that Cottam was late to bed that fateful night.

The *Carpathia* was also besieged by calls from the press, which Captain Rostron ordered to be ignored, and when she finally arrived back in New York on the morning of 18th April she was accompanied upriver by reporters on a fleet of fifty tugboats shouting questions through loudhailers. They even tried to board from their tugs as the ship was under way and had to be physically repelled; one feigned a fit by putting soap in his mouth in order to gain sympathy and access, and others waved $100 bills at the crew by way of unaccepted bribes.

Never in her decade of arrivals and departures had the *Carpathia* made such an entry into New York.

At 9.30am she berthed at Pier 54, from which she had set out seven days earlier.

Although widely praised and decorated for his calm and exemplary conduct, Rostron was reluctant to speak about the *Titanic*; even his autobiography written decades later is self-effacing and devoid of sensation. But in response to a journalist querying how the *Carpathia* could have negotiated an ice field in the dark, and at a speed of which she was supposedly incapable, the profoundly religious Rostron replied "A hand other than mine was on the wheel that night".

The now famous *Carpathia* returned to her Mediterranean duties until 1915 when she was requisitioned for war. And on 17th July 1918 just three months before the Armistice, she was torpedoed by the *U55* 120 miles south west of Ireland. Two and a half hours later, she sank.

Many vessels were lost to torpedoes in that war and the next, but unlike most that little ship from the Tyne will be forever remembered.

For King and country

When, to paraphrase Sir Edward Grey's famous aphorism, the lamps started going out all over Europe on 4th August 1914, Cunard was going about its business.

The *Mauretania* was en route for New York, but on declaration of war was diverted to Halifax; the *Lusitania* was already in New York, and left on 5th August for Liverpool; the *Aquitania*, already in Liverpool, was immediately requisitioned, as were other vessels of the fleet when they returned to their home port. In theory, all three of the company's great liners were ready for the purpose for which the Admiralty had originally conceived them and towards the construction of which the government had so generously contributed.

Meanwhile, the company was already advanced on its new headquarters being constructed on The Pier Head, and destined to become one of the world-famous Three Graces - a move that reflected Cunard's return to dominance on the Atlantic.

As already noted in the preceding chapter, the *Aquitania* was immediately stripped of her finery and put to sea on 8th August, fitted with six 6 inch guns, as an armed merchant cruiser. Almost immediately damaged in a collision with her naval escort off Anglesey, she returned to port. It was decided that she, and the *Mauretania* and *Lusitania*, were too large, unwieldy and expensive to run to serve as auxiliary cruisers. The *Aquitania*, like the *Mauretania*, was laid up until 1915 when she took 30,000 troops to the Dardanelles, followed by a year as a hospital ship ferrying 25,000 injured from the Turkish war zone. She was laid up for most of 1917, and then in March 1918 began the first of nine voyages bringing 60,000 US troops to Europe - before, just months later, assisting in the task of repatriating them.

This pattern followed a very similar one to that followed by the *Mauretania* during the war, as we saw in the previous chapter.

Other Cunard vessels converted successfully to armed merchant cruisers included the *Laconia*, *Carmania* and *Caronia*. The *Carmania* had the distinction of being the first British armed merchant cruiser to sink a German armed cruiser in single combat when, in September 1914, she took on and sank the disguised and brand new German liner the *Cap Trafalgar* off the coast of South America. The *Cap Trafalgar*, bizarrely, had had one of her three funnels removed and the remaining two painted in Cunard's red and black colours. She looked remarkably like the *Carmania*.

And the *Ascania, Ivernia* and *Saxonia* were used to house

The story of
CUNARD'S
~*175*~
YEARS

Sir Edward Grey, Foreign Secretary at the outbreak of the First World War.

German prisoners of war throughout 1915, but later became transports - as did most of the fleet - carrying both men and supplies to wherever they were dispatched.

The *Campania*, which just after the outbreak of war had been sold for scrap, was recalled by the Admiralty and converted into the country's first ever 'aircraft carrier'. One of her funnels was removed, and a rather short flight deck constructed. In April 1915 she became the first ship to launch a plane while under way.

In the course of undertaking war duty, of course, many ships and lives were lost. The most famous was the *Lusitania* - of which more later - but in addition the *Caria*, *Veria*, *Franconia*, *Alaunia*, *Ivernia*, *Lycia*, *Laconia*, *Folia*, *Thracia*, *Feltria*, *Ultonia*, *Volodia*, *Vinovia*, *Andania*, *Aurania*, *Ausonia*, *Vandalia*, *Carpathia* and *Flavia* were all lost to torpedoes and mines. And, inevitably, many Cunard crew lives were also lost.

It is often said that the sinking of the *Lusitania*, with its loss of over 120 American lives, drew the United States into the war. While it may have hardened American attitudes against Germany, it was not until two years later that the USA joined the war - so simple cause and effect is not evident. But much less noted, though probably more significant, was the sinking

*The **Mauretania** in dazzle paint. (University of Liverpool Cunard archive)*

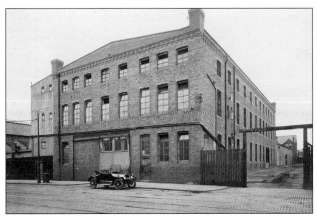

The National Shell Factory at Bootle. (Cunard)

*The **Kaiser Wilhelm der Grosse** in battle with HMS
Highflyer, 26th August 1914.*

of the *Laconia* by U50 in February 1917.

The *Laconia* had returned to normal commercial
transatlantic service between Liverpool and New York in
September 1916 and on the day of the sinking was
homeward bound to Liverpool. Out of the 292 persons on
board only six passengers and six crew survived. The sinking,
almost unremarked in the UK where sinkings had become the
norm, caused outrage in America and was a more likely

catalyst for a change in President Wilson's stance than was the
much earlier *Lusitania*.

With demands on them getting greater, but their capacity
reduced by losses, Cunard was forced to buy new tonnage -
the *Royal George* and the rechristened *Folia*, *Feltria*, *Flavia*,
Vinovia, *Valeria*, *Velodia*, *Valacia* and *Vandalia* – most of which
were themselves lost before the war's end.

A further burden was placed on the company in 1917

Carmania. (Cunard)

CUNARD LINE

vessels of all kinds and from all trades. This burden became even greater after America joined the war and the company was responsible for the rapid transportation of 900,000 troops from the US. 900,000! A column of 900,000 men marching four abreast without stopping would take six days to pass a single point. It was some task.

Between the outbreak of war in August 1914 and the armistice in November 1918, the company's ships - not including the managed - sailed almost 3.5 million miles in war service and carried almost 9 million tons of foodstuffs, munitions and general cargo - mainly from the US and Canada, but also from the UK to Mediterranean outposts and to the far north of Russia. They also moved those 900,000 troops.

It is often not realised that requisite for a large ocean going company is a large and sometimes multi-faceted shore-based organisation. At the time of the First World War the Cunard empire included repair shops, laundries, engine works, and furnishing departments as well as the army of clerks and administrators - almost all of them based in and around Liverpool. So, on the outbreak of war, as well as continuing to repair and service the company's own ships, the repair shops and engine works were also given over to military use servicing and maintaining naval craft; the laundries, hitherto dealing with all the linen taken from ships now also gave themselves over to dealing with laundry from military hospitals.

when the government appointed a Shipping Controller; under this scheme, designed to deploy the nation's diminishing tonnage where it was best employed, all British shipping came under the control of the government which in turn appointed established companies as managers. Consequently Cunard found itself not only deploying its own fleet, but being responsible for the management of a large number of other

But these were activities you might expect. What you would not expect, was the establishment of a Cunard aeroplane factory at Aintree in 1917. This was an enormous undertaking, not least for a company with no experience whatever of building planes. But by 1918 the factory employed 5,000 people and was turning out 100 planes a month.

Similarly, one of the company's vast warehouses in Bootle was given over to the manufacture of shells, and became the Cunard National Shell Factory. Employing over 1,000 people, 900 of them women, the factory worked 24 hours a day, seven days a week in three shifts, from October 1915 until November 1918 when it closed down within a week of the Armistice being signed. All told, the factory produced 410,302 shells.

Ausonia. *(University of Liverpool Cunard archive)*

The Third Grace

Cunard's imposing Headquarters on Liverpool's Pier Head. (Cunard)

From its inception in 1839 until 1967, Cunard had its headquarters in Liverpool - firstly at 14 Water Street and then, in August 1857 as the fast growing business outgrew the premises, at 8 Water Street on the corner with Rumford Street.

The later Water Street premises were to become the hub of an enormous business, concerned not just with shipping across the Atlantic to the United States and Canada, but also with routes to ports in the Mediterranean and Middle East. Just 20 years on from the move to 8 Water Street the company had 46 vessels - 12 of them in the Mediterranean. But, of course, a shipping company is not just the ships - there is a vast back room operation ordering supplies from food to coal, coordinating repairs and servicing, dealing with Customs

and the administrative requirements of the countries served, planning and executing the construction of new ships and so on and so on.

And by this time emigration to the USA and Canada had begun to develop, and although Cunard was not a major participant at the beginning, travel arrangements of amazing complexity had to be engineered through the Water Street office. As noted earlier it was possible for a potential emigrant to walk into a Cunard agent's office in, say, Vienna and make travel arrangements for a journey through to California - rail to the North Sea Coast, ferry to Hull, train to Liverpool, crossing to New York and onward rail to California - together with any accommodation required on the way.

At the same time Americans had - even at that stage -

The Third Grace

General Office. (Cunard)

begun to develop a taste for crossing the Atlantic on a Cunard liner and at Liverpool transferring to one of the Mediterranean fleet and undertaking a European Grand Tour - all for £40.

Following a further half century of persistent if erratic growth into one of the notable companies of the world, Cunard was ready in 1914 to begin construction of its magnificent landmark building - a shoreside palace to match the palaces at sea.

The Cunard Building, still so called though the company vacated it in 1967, is the middle building of the Three Graces that constitute Liverpool's World Heritage site Pier Head.

All three of the Graces - the Mersey Docks and Harbour Board, the Cunard Building and the Royal Liver Building - occupy the site of the former George's Dock. Built in 1767, by 1898 the dock had become too small for

the new generation of steamships and was closed. It was divided into three sites by the extension of both Water Street and Brunswick Street across it to the river frontage, and was destined to transform from a workaday dock to one of the finest waterfronts in the world.

The Mersey Docks and Harbour Board Building was the first to rise, as would be expected, followed soon after by the Royal Liver Building. As ever, Cunard moved slowly though surely and was the last of the three to build.

The old dock walls were reinforced with 700,000 cubic feet of concrete to prevent the Mersey from seeping in, and the floor of the dock became the floor of the lower level of the new building's two basements.

The first problem to be tackled was one of external design. The two buildings on either side were both massive and ornate. Should the central edifice be even more massive and more ornate? In tune with the belief of Sir

The Third Grace

South side of General Office. (Cunard)

Samuel Cunard in plain and simple, just like his first ship and his grave in London's Brompton Road Cemetery, the Board opted for understated - though the building, designed by Willink and Thicknesse of Liverpool, still delivered some awe inducing statistics.

The design, while relatively simple and devoid of flounces to a degree that would have made Sir Samuel proud, was based on the Farnese Palace in Rome - only much, much bigger. Big enough, in fact, for 250,000 people to stand inside - and over 1,000 worked on its eleven floors.

Altogether, 180,000 cubic feet of Portland stone was used on the exterior, and 50,000 cubic feet of finest Italian marble on the interior; the massive public rooms, corridors and stairways, lavishly adorned with marble columns and floors, were largely the creation of Arthur Davis, who also designed the interior of the *Aquitania*.

The Cunard empire was ruled from the fifth floor, with its Board Room and pivotal naval architects' department. Apart from the battalions of clerks making bookings, ordering supplies, managing the to-ings and fro-ings of a large fleet, the building was also home to hydrographers mapping out the world's tides and an experimental chef whose job it was to try out new recipes on the staff before unleashing them on a doubtless more discerning clientele.

On the ground floor was the enormous pillared ticket hall and lounge for First Class passengers. Second and Third Class were dealt with in the first basement - including, for emigrants, compulsory medical examinations.

Shields on the riverside elevation acknowledged the troubled times in which the building was conceived, bearing as it does the arms of countries allied during the

The Third Grace

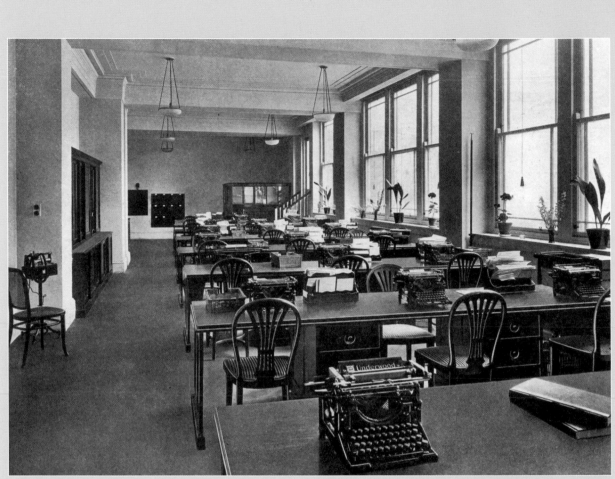

Stenographers' Room. (Cunard)

Great War - Britain, France, Russia, Italy, Japan, Belgium, Serbia and Montenegro. The United States is missing as the building was completed before America entered the war. At each corner is the shield of the Cunard company supported by an eagle - each weighing 43 tons. And above each third floor window are the arms of the principal passenger ports in the United Kingdom - Liverpool, Bristol, Southampton, Plymouth, Falmouth, Hull, Portsmouth, Newcastle, Glasgow, Leith, Dundee, Aberdeen and Queenstown (Ireland not being an independent country at that time).

It was clearly the headquarters of a company that mattered.

Staff moved in in June 1916 and remained there for the next 51 years.

While the Cunard Building was perfect in every way, not just for the reassurance its air of permanence and

Manager's Office. (Cunard)

The Board Room where many momentous decisions were taken. (Cunard)

solidity gave to nervous passengers, and not just from the efficiency inherent in having all the staff on one site, but because the directors could look out of their fifth floor Boardroom window and see all the cohorts of their empire - the ships - coming and going from the Mersey. It truly was the centre of the Cunard world.

But change was afoot. After the First World War, both the *Aquitania* and the *Mauretania* began services from Southampton - much to the relief of captains, who found the vagaries and vicious tides of the Mersey a constant trial, but simultaneously to the dismay of Liverpudlians.

In 1936 the *Queen Mary*, despite having Liverpool emblazoned on her stern like every other Cunard ship since 1878, never even visited - not just in her maiden year, but ever. All her sailings were from Southampton (or, during the Second World War, from the Clyde); she was simply too big. And her later sister, the *Queen Elizabeth*, was even bigger. An inexorable shift had begun.

The Cunard Building's walls could speak of many momentous decisions and the debates that led to them; there would have been the decision first to build the *Queen Mary*, and then the *Queen Elizabeth*. The detailed planning took place here, as did the agonising decision to suspend construction of the *Queen Mary* as the company's revenues collapsed during the Depression. Here too the *Queen Elizabeth's* secret dash to the USA was planned, and the colossal troop movements that followed were coordinated.

The arguments over the replacement tonnage for the *Queen Mary* and *Queen Elizabeth* took place here, and the eventual decision to build the revolutionary *Queen Elizabeth 2* - the ship that became the company's most successful ever.

So, although it is almost fifty years since the company made its principal shift from Liverpool and vacated the Cunard Building, Cunard history and that of Liverpool will remain permanently intertwined.

The *Lusitania*: Casualty or conspiracy?

On 5th October 1914, Alfred Booth - then Chairman of Cunard - was 'required' to meet the Secretary to the Admiralty, Sir William Graham Greene, in the Smoking Room of the Reform Club in London's Pall Mall. There Booth was given instructions he did not want to hear: rather than being laid up, as Cunard wanted, and as the *Aquitania* and *Mauretania* had been once their unsuitability as armed merchant cruisers became evident, the *Lusitania* was to continue in commercial transatlantic service crewed by Cunard but under the direction of the

if that were not enough, the Admiralty took over the entire area of the ship forward of number two funnel for its own purposes, and the area was sealed off from the rest of the ship.

It was soon evident that the *Lusitania* was being used to carry 'contraband', mainly in the form of small armaments for use in the war in Europe, and it is doubtful if this was strictly legal in international law. However, the amounts were relatively small and were declared, after a fashion, on the manifests.

The **Lusitania** *arriving in New York by Odin Rosenvinge. (Cunard)*

Admiralty. Indeed, the involvement of the Admiralty was comprehensive; not only was it to give the ship's master the designated route for each crossing, but Cunard - including Booth himself - was forbidden to contact the master except with the permission of, or through, the Admiralty.

Booth could not demur; such powers for the Admiralty had been established in the agreement of 1903 which had led to the construction of the *Lusitania* in the first place. As

Common sense dictates that there was some official duplicity going on, although the extent of it is not clear. But the Admiralty was using the *Lusitania* to carry cargo she should not have been carrying, and this could not have been done without the knowledge of officials in the United States - a neutral country at that stage, and one that wished to be seen to be so. But the war in Europe was also a lucrative business for America, and over $1,100,453, 950

*From left to right: Winston Churchill-First Lord of the Admiralty, Admiral Jackie Fisher, First Sea Lord and Lord Mersey, Chairman of the Inquiry into the sinking of the **Lusitania**.*

worth of war related goods were bought from the US in the space of one year.

And so the *Lusitania* continued her transatlantic duties under a senior Cunard master, Captain Daniel Dow. But on 8th March 1914 Captain Dow resigned from his position because, he said, he was no longer prepared to mix innocent passengers with armaments. He was, however, retained by Cunard; perhaps they felt he had a point. He was replaced as master of the *Lusitania* by the notoriously grumpy and taciturn Captain William Turner, who made up for what he lacked in tact and diplomacy with an excellent and unblemished record as a seafarer.

On the day the *Lusitania* was due to make her 101st crossing, 1st May 1914, a notice appeared in New York newspapers and in other major cities signed by the Imperial German Embassy in Washington. It advised would be passengers that vessels flying the flag of Great Britain or of any of her allies "are liable to destruction", and that travellers did so at their own risk. The intention was clear enough.

On the same day, Captain Turner made his way to see Sir Courtney Bennett, the British Consul General in New York, to receive his Admiralty instructions for the voyage he was about to undertake to Liverpool. There were none. He was told by Sir Courtney simply to follow his previous

course and to rendezvous 10 miles south of the Fastnet Rock off the south west coast of Ireland with his escort, for the final leg of the voyage, the Royal Navy cruiser the *Juno*.

Turner took the ship down the Hudson and out into the open sea that afternoon. There was some nervousness on board, partly as a result of the German warning in that day's papers - though few passengers had cancelled - and Turner shared with passengers the reassurance he himself felt that the ship was to be in the hands of the Royal Navy once it got to the area where U boats were reputed to be. Until that point he knew he could rely on the ship's speed as the best defence against attack. The *Lusitania* had been built to travel at 25 knots, but with a coal consumption of 1,000 tons a day at that speed one boiler had been closed down to save fuel, but her top speed was still a healthy 21 knots. No ship travelling at over 14 knots had ever been torpedoed by U boats capable of only nine, and Turner took some comfort in that too.

Back at the Admiralty in London there was quite detailed knowledge of U boat positions and movements; this was based not just on regular reports of attacks that came in, but on the fortuitous and crucial fact that the Admiralty was in possession of all the German transmission codes. Every message that passed between

The *Lusitania*: Casualty or conspiracy?

German naval headquarters and its entire fleet of U boats was intercepted and decoded; the British were as aware of what U boats were up to as was Kaiser Wilhelm himself. They put this to good use when, for example, the Cunard liners the *Ausonia* and *Transylvania* (at the time under the command of Captain Turner) were ordered into Queenstown (now Cobh) in order to avoid the malign intentions of U21 lurking just off the Irish Coast. But, for the *Lusitania* in May 1914 no such beneficial use of valuable knowledge seems to have been made.

Indeed, in 1927, some 12 years after the event, a Commander Joseph Kenworthy - who at the time of the *Lusitania* sinking had been a member of Naval Intelligence - published a book. In it he refers to a meeting which took place on 5th May 1914, two days before the *Lusitania* went down, at which were present the First Lord of the Admiralty, Winston Churchill, and Admiral Jackie Fisher, the First Sea Lord. In front of them was a large map on which were marked the positions of shipping off the South Coast of Ireland. There was the *U20*, just north west of Fastnet; and there was the *Lusitania*; and there too was the *Juno*.

And in his reflections on the meeting in 'The Freedom of the Seas', Kenworthy had this to say: "The *Lusitania* was sent at considerably reduced speed into an area where a U boat was known to be waiting, and with her escort withdrawn". Her escort withdrawn! No-one thought to tell Captain Turner that the *Juno*, rather than acting as escort from Fastnet, had been ordered back to Queenstown.

And, also as the Admiralty knew, the *U20* was not just sitting there doing nothing. On 5th May she torpedoed and sank a small coastal vessel, the *Earl of Lathom*; on 6th May she sent to the bottom two steamers, the *Centurion* and *Candidate*. And the Admiralty knew of all this activity by the *U20* on the course the *Lusitania* was to take the following day. But did they tell Captain Turner? They did not.

By breakfast time on 7th May the loss of these three vessels was common knowledge in Liverpool, and Albert Booth was seriously disturbed by them. Forbidden to contact Captain Turner himself, he immediately called Admiral Stileman, the senior naval officer in Liverpool, to do so urgently. Booth was satisfied that the *Lusitania*, like the *Ausonia* and the *Transylvania* earlier, would be diverted to Queenstown. She was not.

Instead the Admiralty simply sent out a general warning to all shipping that U boats were 'active' in the area. No more.

By now, on board the *Lusitania*, Captain Turner realised that the naval escort he had relied on so much to ease the minds of anxious passengers was not there. He comforted himself with the thought that he may just have missed her in the fog.

At about the same time, back in London, the British Foreign Secretary Sir Edward Grey was meeting another Edward, Colonel Edward House, special adviser to US President Woodrow Wilson. "What would America do", asked Grey, "if the Germans were to sink a passenger ship with Americans on board?" And House, according to his own memoirs, replied, "It would be sufficient to carry us into war." Strangely, just a few hours later House met the King at Buckingham Palace; "And what," asked the King "would the Americans do if the Germans were to sink the *Lusitania*?" There was clearly a train of thought among the British political establishment, an establishment that although fully aware of the danger into which the *Lusitania* was sailing did absolutely nothing about it.

At Fastnet, in the absence of the *Juno*, Captain Turner might have expected a message directing him up the west coast of Ireland, away from submarine activity, to approach Liverpool from the north. No such instruction arrived, and without it Turner had no option but to proceed on the course he was taking. In the meantime he followed standard instructions for ships in a zone of U boat activity to the letter: he swung out the lifeboats, closed watertight doors where possible for a ship under way, increased lookouts and ordered portholes to be closed. Many were not, but the order was issued nonetheless. Having sighted the Irish Coast, but being unsure of his exact position (there being no sophisticated positioning instruments on the bridge in those days) he ran parallel to the coast at about 11 miles distant to achieve an accurate bearing. And then, once he was sure of his position, he calculated that in order to time his arrival at the Mersey so that he did not have to wait for the tide to be right to enter, something which would have made the ship an easy target, he needed to reduce his speed to 18 knots. That would allow him a straight run into the Mersey without need to loiter in the dangerous waters outside, but still, he thought, gave him sufficient speed to thwart a U boat attack.

At 2.10pm Kapitanleutenant Walther Schweiger, commander of the German submarine the *U20*, could plainly see and identify the *Lusitania* through his periscope. He ordered one torpedo to be fired, which within seconds had struck the *Lusitania* on the starboard side just aft of the bridge. He noted three important things in his log, and sent messages back to base relaying the same information - which the British received and decoded: he reported he

sold at a shilling each, with the proceeds going to St Dunstan's. Very rapidly Germany's demonstration of U boat supremacy was turning into a public relations catastrophe. The medals, incidentally, bore the wrong date of 5th May on both the German and British versions, and the British version has the additional error of spelling 'May' in the English manner rather than the German.

Naturally, the circumstances surrounding the loss of the *Lusitania* have generated an entire tribe of conspiracy theories. Some people believe the British government, and notably Churchill, engineered the sinking of the *Lusitania*

*The **Lusitania** at full speed. (Cunard)*

had fired one torpedo, that after the explosion caused by that torpedo there was almost immediately a second, larger explosion, and that the ship sank in under twenty minutes. Of 1,275 passengers on board, 785 died, of which 128 were neutral American citizens including the multimillionaire Alfred Vanderbilt. Of the 702 crew, 413 died; 94 of the 129 children on board died, as did 35 of the 39 babies. So did three unidentified stowaways. The world was outraged.

But Germany was ecstatic, to the extent that Karl Gotz, a jeweller, designed and produced just 44 samples of a medal to celebrate the sinking of the ship. Unfortunately for Germany, one got into the hands of the British and Gordon Selfridge, of department store fame, paid for 300,000 of them to be produced and distributed. They

to bring America into the war and his case is not helped by injudicious comments he made to the effect that the sinking of neutral shipping, and notably American-flagged ships, was necessary to bring the non aligned into the war on the side of the allies; others insist that as the *Lusitania* was carrying armaments, and even Canadian troops, she was a fair target - although there is absolutely no evidence that the *Lusitania* ever carried troops or that the armaments were of such significant scale to warrant the sinking of an unarmed passenger ship; others, because the *Lusitania* had gun placements fitted below the decks when built, maintain that she was armed whereas all the evidence, from passengers, crew and photographs clearly indicates that she was not; yet others puzzle over the second explosion and ask was there a second torpedo, or did the

The death of **Lusitania***, 785 passengers and 413 crew. (Painting by Ken Marschall)*

The *Lusitania*: Casualty or conspiracy?

first ignite contraband explosives, or did the boilers blow up or was coal dust ignited? Certainly such a large hole was blown into the starboard side that she listed immediately and sank in just 18 minutes - the list and the speed of sinking being the cause of many deaths. And three other puzzles remain: why, even today, does the Admiralty warn against diving to the wreck and why are so many official files relating to the *Lusitania* 'missing'? And, perhaps most puzzling of all, why was the Admiralty so utterly determined to blame Captain Turner that it put immense pressure on Lord Mersey, who led the official enquiry, to find against Turner, that it failed to produce all the requisite documents at the enquiry, that it carefully selected witnesses who would give an agreed line, and that it wrote crew members' witness statements for them?

Admiral Lord Fisher, the First Sea Lord at the time commented "I hope Captain Turner will be arrested immediately after the enquiry whatever the verdict or finding may be" and "I am absolutely certain Captain Turner is a scoundrel and has been bribed". Churchill weighed in with "we shall pursue the captain without check".

The first enquiry into the sinking took place the day after at Kinsale, where many survivors and bodies had been landed, and was presided over by John Horgan, the local coroner. The chief witness was Captain Turner, still in a slightly damp uniform which had endured four hours in a cold sea only the day before. At the end of his evidence the coroner commented, "We express our appreciation of the courage you have shown which is worthy of the high traditions of the service to which you belong". At this, Captain Turner burst into tears.

The verdict of the coroner was that Germany, and Germany alone, was guilty of "wilful and wholesale murder". It was fortuitous that Mr Horgan acted as expeditiously as he did, for no sooner had the verdict been given than word arrived from the Admiralty forbidding the holding of an inquest and demanding that Captain Turner should not appear in public. They were as late with that as with everything else concerning the *Lusitania*.

The full enquiry, under the chairmanship of an accomplished lawyer, Lord Mersey, who had also presided over the *Titanic* enquiry three years earlier, was held in London some months later. He sat with four expert assessors, one of whom, Admiral Sir Frederick Inglefield, represented the Admiralty. He was the Admiralty expert whose solution to the U boat threat was for ships' crews to place bags over periscopes.

In the course of the enquiry Lord Mersey received a note from the Admiralty stating, "It is considered politically expedient that Captain Turner of the *Lusitania* be most prominently blamed for the disaster". But Mersey was a fair man, and he was having none of that. He was even more upset by the behaviour of the Admiralty when he discovered that they had knowingly withheld from the enquiry copies of messages which they had sent to the *Lusitania*, and denied sending others of which there was a clear record.

Lord Mersey and three of the assessors absolved Captain Turner of blame. Only Inglefield, from the Admiralty, dissented.

Mersey himself was so outraged by the manner in which the enquiry had been pressured that he wrote to the Prime Minister refusing to accept any fee, and stating he wished to be excused from presiding over any future such enquiries.

So, who was to blame?

Well, clearly the German submarine commander and the regime whose instructions he followed must bear blame for what the Kinsale coroner called 'wilful and wholesale murder'. Had the torpedo not been fired, no-one would have died.

But were they justified in sinking an unarmed merchant ship in a time of war? The Germans argued that the ship was carrying contraband, and there is some evidence for this, but she was emphatically not armed and was not carrying troops.

Both the British and American governments must take some blame as it is clearly fact that the *Lusitania* was carrying 4 million rounds of ammunition and unprimed shells of which both were aware. But it has also been established that the quantities were modest, and most certainly would not have resulted in the massive second explosion which was reported by Schweiger and many witnesses. It is far more likely that was caused by the torpedo striking the boiler room.

But was the sinking engineered by the Admiralty to draw America into the war? There is certainly superficially attractive evidence to suggest this, such as the fact that the Admiralty knew where the *U20* was and what it was doing and yet no attempt appears to have been made to divert the *Lusitania*, or the fact that the *Juno* was withdrawn as an escort for whatever reason. The remarkably similar conversations Sir Edward Grey and the King had with Colonel House that very morning look suspicious, as does Churchill's recorded wish that neutral shipping should be attacked. Most suspiciously of all were the concerted and strenuous efforts to blame the entirely blameless Captain Turner.

But much of this, if not all of it, could equally well be explained by sheer incompetence rather than malice. Even the attacks on Turner have the stench of desperate attempts to blame 'anybody but us'.

So, then, was Captain Turner to blame? On that it is possible to say 'most emphatically not'. What exactly was he accused of? Well, firstly of sailing into an area known to be frequented by U boats - and yet he had no choice as he was forbidden to divert except by express authority, which he did not receive. Secondly, he was accused of disobeying a general advice to mariners to keep away from land; but, having emerged from fog it was clearly necessary for him to take a bearing using landmarks - and even so he was 11 miles from land when the torpedo struck. It is interesting to note that just three months later White Star's Arabic was torpedoed more than 50 miles from land, so the advice seems to have been little more than guesswork from the desk bound. Thirdly he was criticised for not zig zagging in order to confuse the U boats but in fact he never received any instruction to do this, and as he himself pointed out at a later enquiry in the United States (which directed those making claims against Cunard to send them to the German government) his command after the *Lusitania* was the *Ivernia*, which was torpedoed with Turner on the bridge while zig zagging!

It is certainly true that there was much confusion on the ship as it sank, though Turner can hardly be blamed for that; in those days passengers were not allocated specific lifeboats (as crew were) and there was no tannoy system with which to transmit instructions. And, of course, the speed of the sinking and the ship's list rendered lowering the lifeboats almost impossible. Many of those who died were victims of hypothermia or of placing their life jackets on the wrong way up - again hardly the fault of the man who stayed on the bridge till his ship sank beneath him, and then survived in an icy ocean for four hours.

Cunard, that most conservative of companies which since its inception had walked hand in hand with governments and had striven to be at one with the establishment, knew Captain Turner was entirely innocent of the crimes of which the Admiralty wished him to be condemned. In a magnificent piece of understated thumbing of the corporate nose, they not only refused to sack him, as Admiral Fisher demanded, but in 1917, on the retirement of Commodore Barr, they elevated Captain Turner to Fleet Commodore. Such a subtle snub to the Admiralty bully boys must have given Alfred Booth quiet satisfaction. And it possibly even brought a smile to the lips of the maligned and taciturn Captain Turner.

Captain Turner in Queenstown on 8th May 1915. (University of Liverpool Cunard archive)

Chapter Six

Three 'Queens'

In the aftermath of the First World War, and indeed during it, Cunard set about repairing the damage and preparing for the future by means of acquisition - such companies as Anchor Line, Commonwealth and Dominion Line and Brocklebank were subsumed but continued under their established names and as separate companies, so they need not detain readers here. The post war years also saw the construction of thirteen new ships, eight passenger liners and five dual purposes, some of which replaced ships sunk in the latter part of the war which had themselves been bought to replace vessels lost in the early part.

But most importantly, Cunard received in 1919, as part of

Imperator. *(Ferry Publications Library)*

war reparations, the German liner the *Imperator*, which had been launched in 1912 by Kaiser Wilhelm himself. That gives the ship the distinction of being one of only two Cunard vessels ever to have been launched by a man and, perversely, the first Cunard ship to be launched by a monarch. The other ship to be named by a man was *Royal Viking Sun*, by actor James Stewart.

In 1921 the *Imperator*, by now in Cunard service, was renamed the *Berengaria*. This name conveniently conformed to the traditional 'ia' ending given to many Cunard ships, starting with the *Britannia*, and which over the years resulted in some spectacularly unwieldy and ugly names. But whereas

The story of
CUNARD'S
175 YEARS

Ascania. (*University of Liverpool Cunard archive*)

the others were named after Roman provinces, the *Berengaria* was not. The Berengaria after whom the ship was named was the wife of Richard the Lionheart, and so a Queen of England, thus giving the ship her second 'first': she was the first Cunard ship to be named after a Queen and so was, arguably, the first of Cunard's famous 'Queens'.

With her heavy Teutonic decor, the *Berengaria* attracted many admirers, notably the Prince of Wales, later Edward VIII, and became the company's flagship.

The *Berengaria* also carried the Prince of Wales' younger brother, Prince George, in 1928 when he was travelling back to the UK in response to his father, King George V, being taken seriously ill. Prince George's birthday fell on the penultimate night of the crossing, and he was presented with a cake – which he asked to be auctioned off among the passengers to raise money for the Welsh Miners' Fund. The cake was sold for £200, and the purchaser immediately handed it back to be re-auctioned. Prince George suggested it be cut and sold in slices; he cut it himself. As a result, his cake raised a total of £2,069.13s.4d (£2,069.80p).

And the *Berengaria* didn't just carry the glamorous living, but also the glamorous dead; in 1930 she brought back to Britain the body of noted author Edgar Wallace.

But again, Cunard was losing out to foreign competition with fancier ships and faster ships; by comparison Cunard's premier transatlantic liners, the *Mauretania*, *Aquitania* and

Berengaria, were beginning to look tired. They had their loyal fans, but much new business - and especially luxury loving business - was going elsewhere.

So, in October 1929, it was decided that Cunard would build a new liner, ostensibly to replace the ageing *Mauretania*.

Cunard New York office at 25 Broadway. (*Cunard*)

Aurania

The **Aurania, Andania** and **Alaunia** were sister ships. The last of the series, the **Aurania,** was due to serve Canada and Europe. She was ordered in 1913 but did not enter service until 1917 due to the First World War. She was torpedoed and sank on 4th February 1918.

(All photos University of Liverpool Cunard archive)

Laconia. *(University of Liverpool Cunard archive)*

In December of the same year a contract was signed with the yard of John Brown and Co in Clydebank for a vessel of over 80,000 tons and capable of well over 30 knots. Destined to become one of the world's most celebrated ships, almost equal to the *Mauretania* in both celebrity and affection, she was at that time simply *yard number 534*.

Newspapers and magazines were quick to familiarise their readers with the statistics graphically. The 'Modern World of Conquest', for example, reported that if you could pick up the new ship and set her down next to St Paul's Cathedral, you could climb up to the crow's nest (centrally heated, of course) and look down on the cross at the top of the dome. Or, if you were so minded, you wedged her stern into The

Strand the bow would nicely fit into Pall Mall.

At a cost of £4.5million, the *534* was to be built using Cunard reserves and revenue without the benefit of subsidy. Almost alone at the time, Cunard operated on the North Atlantic on a commercial basis; every other major line was subsidised in some way by its national government.

In one way, however, government assistance was immediately required and rendered. It became clear that the value of the *534* constituted a risk which could not be covered by the insurance market in the normal way, and so Cunard proposed to the government that it might absorb whatever risks, either in construction or in operation, that the British insurance market proved unable to bear. It agreed, and in

*The **Berengaria** compared to Tower Bridge in London.*

Berengaria

Despite the best attempts of Cunard, the German roots of **Berengaria** were perhaps always in evidence on board but her First Class public areas remained spectacular.

Above: First Class Dining Saloon.

Right: First Class Palm Court.

Below right: The Pompeiian Swimming Pool.

Below left: Bedroom of suite.

(All photos Cunard)

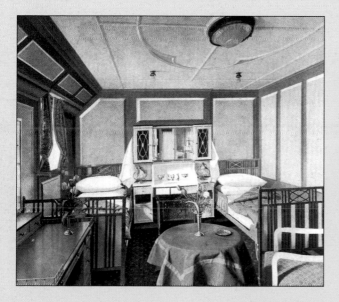

December 1930 the Cunard Insurance Act was passed.

Shortly before Christmas 1930, work began. The first rivet was hammered home on 27th December by yard manager Donald Skiffington, and for 12 months it continued apace. And then, exactly one year later, it stopped. Cunard had been derailed by the Depression and the fall in annual revenues from £8.3 million in 1922 to just £2.6million in 1928 says all that needs to be said. Despite staff, on shore and at sea, taking a pay cut to assist the company in its financial distress - a distress felt by most businesses at the time - the construction of the *534* was halted just before Christmas, a most inopportune time, in 1931. Immediately 3,640 men in Clydebank - a town where half the wages came from the *534* - were put out of work. But the ripples were felt by another 10,000 ancillary workers much further away. They were felt in Stoke on Trent, fashioning 200,000 items of crockery; in Sheffield where 100,000 pieces of cutlery were in production; in Walsall, producing 400 tons of tubes; in Rugby, manufacturing seven turbo generators; in Wallsend, where

Top: **Berengaria**. *(Cunard)*

Left top: **Queen Mary** - *An artist's impression of a corner of the main tourist lounge. (Cunard)*

Left: **Queen Mary** - *A colourful artist's impression of the Third Class garden lounge. (Cunard)*

*Three locomotives pass through one of the **Queen Mary**'s funnels. (University of Liverpool Cunard archive)*

Parsons' was providing the four turbines, each with 257,000 blades fitted by hand; in Liverpool, milling 2,500 square feet of toughened glass; in Millwall, casting four 20 foot propellers; in Darlington, forging a 190 ton stern frame, the largest ever made; in Belfast, working on the 5.5 ton gear wheels; in Halifax, weaving ten miles of blankets; in St Albans, turning out 600 clocks; and in Kidderminster, also weaving - but this time six miles of carpets. The list goes on and on as in other towns up and down the land supplying curtains, anchor chains, furniture, kitchen machinery, lifts and light fittings, work stopped. The impact of Cunard's unavoidable decision was not just a crisis for Clydeside, it was a crisis for Britain; and it was not just an economic crisis for the directly affected, it was also a crisis of confidence and prestige for the whole country.

The construction of the ship was, as can be seen, a truly national effort – and one that produced many logistical challenges. Moving the stern frame from Darlington necessitated the closing of entire railway lines, and the propellers could only be transported from Millwall to the Clyde by sea.

The rusting ribs of the *534*, with 80% of the rivets – made just down the road in Coatbridge and Airdrie - in place, 2,000 portholes cut and £1.5 million already spent, seemed symbolic of the financial disaster which had engulfed both Britain and America.

It was so graphic a symbol, and one of which the general populous was so aware, that members of the public sent Cunard thousands of unsolicited donations of money in an effort to get the work restarted.

The Prince of Wales, later Edward VIII, was so concerned by the plight of Clydeside that he paid a 3-day visit in March 1933 to see the situation – and *534* – for himself. It was to be his first encounter with the ship – the first of many.

Ramsay MacDonald's government was implored to lend Cunard the money to complete the ship and get so many back to work, but the government was steadfast in its refusal for the next two and a half years. Stalemate prevailed.

But in an echo of the situation back in 1902 when the government of Arthur Balfour had looked to Cunard to sustain British dominance on the Atlantic, so in the early thirties a similar scenario was developing. This time the threat came not from an American multimillionaire, but from the French and Germans who were launching fast and powerful liners that were dominating the Atlantic trade. Meanwhile, Britain's two principal transatlantic shipping companies were languishing. Cunard, despite its famous fleet, was again looking rather dowdy and, as a consequence of the *534*, financially squeezed. Meanwhile White Star, once the pride of America but bought by Lord Kylsant's British company, Royal Mail Group, in 1926, was in an even worse position, with a fleet of outdated ships busy making a loss and in the hands of

Queen Mary

Construction of what would become Queen Mary - "The stateliest ship now in being" according to King George V at her launch

(All photos University of Liverpool Cunard archive)

*Above: The launch of the **Queen Mary** on 26th September 1934. (University of Liverpool Cunard archive)*

*Left: King George V views the **Queen Mary** on the slipway just prior to the launch. (University of Liverpool Cunard archive)*

Queen Mary

Fitting out of the **Queen Mary**.

(All photos University of Liverpool Cunard archive)

Above: Final work being undertaken to the **Queen Mary**.

Left: The **Queen Mary** in dry dock at Southampton.

Below: Giant castings for the **Queen Mary**. *A special train and steamer were used for the transport of eight castings, weighing approximately 625 tons, for the construction of the frame of the new Cunard liner being built at Clydebank. Owing to their extraordinary dimensions an entire railway track from Darlington to Middlesbrough was used for the purpose.*

(All photos University of Liverpool Cunard archive)

82

Above: The **Queen Mary** *leaving the Clyde on 24th March 1936. (University of Liverpool Cunard archive)*

Opposite page: The **Queen Mary** *undergoing annual overhaul. It was an immense task, employing some 2,000 workmen during her five weeks out of service. (University of Liverpool Cunard archive)*

a tottering parent company whose accounting seemed to be a triumph of smoke and mirrors.

The solution in the eyes of Neville Chamberlain, at that time Chancellor of the Exchequer, was for Cunard and White Star to merge in order to form one powerful combine. Cunard did not favour this at all, not only because it was confident that it would survive its temporary embarrassment without difficulty, but because White Star was, in the words of Chairman Sir Percy Bates, "a worthless asset". But the government proposed a deal, which while not ideal for Cunard nonetheless gave it the opportunity to resume work on the *534* faster than would have been the case, and made the prospect of a sister ship much more certain - a prospect which, if realised, would enable Cunard to achieve its long held dream of a weekly transatlantic service in each direction using just two ships. The government proposed to loan Cunard - loan, not give - the sum of £9.5 million, of which £3 million would guarantee the completion of the *534*, £5 million to be available if a second ship were built, and £1.5 million as working capital.

It is frequently said, even by those who should know better,

that Cunard and White Star did merge; they did not. Instead, a totally new company was set up called Cunard White Star, to which ten ships of White Star's transatlantic fleet were transferred together with Cunard's transatlantic fleet. The Cunard Steamship Company owned 62% of the new company, which was thus in effect a subsidiary of Cunard Steamship, and the remainder was owned by White Star's creditors - notably the government of Northern Ireland and Harland & Wolff. White Star's non-transatlantic fleet was either sold off to other shipping companies or for scrap, while Cunard's non-transatlantic fleet, the four Mediterranean ships, continued as before.

As Sir Percy had said, White Star was a worthless asset and by 1933 was effectively bankrupt. Three of its ships, the *Baltic*, *Vedic* and the *Megantic* went to the breaker's yard just before the new company was instituted, the *Gallic* and *Delphic* were sold to Clan Lines, and the *Ceramic* to Shaw Savill and Albion. And, of the ships that transferred to Cunard White Star, three - the *Adriatic*, *Albertic* and *Calgaric* - were immediately sent for scrap without entering service for the new company. The *Olympic* and the *Doric* were scrapped in

1935, with the *Homeric* and the *Majestic* following a year later. By the end of 1936 only two of the ships White Star contributed to the new fleet were still in service.

The bill necessary to allow the government to make the proposed payments, the North Atlantic Shipping Bill, was passed on 16th March 1934 and Cunard White Star formally came into being on 9th May 1934.

Although the new company did not give John Brown's shipyard formal notification to restart work on the *534* until 26th May, the workforce in anticipation marched to the yard on 3rd April to begin the preparatory tasks of removing 130 tons of rust and dozens of nesting crows from the dispiriting skeleton.

Just one problem remained. The name *Queen Mary*, intended for the *534*, was already in use by a Clyde steamer owned by Williamson Buchanan Steamers, and two ships of the same name are not permitted on the British register. Naturally, the steamer company was reluctant to part with the name, but eventually was 'persuaded' by Sir Percy Bates personally to change the name of their vessel to the *Queen Mary II*.

Just five months later, on 26th September 1934, Queen Mary wife of King George V became the first British monarch to launch a merchant ship, a job she accomplished with a bottle of Australian wine rather than the traditional French champagne. As she said the words, broadcast over the radio, "I am happy to name this ship *Queen Mary*; I wish success to her and all who sail in her", millions of the King's subjects heard his wife's voice for the first time.

As well as King George V and the Prince of Wales, two hundred thousand spectators watched the launch - and many, on the opposite bank of the dredged and widened Clyde, got wet up to the knees as an eight foot wave surged across the river when the enormous hull entered the water.

The nation was ecstatic as the launch of what King George called "the stateliest ship now in being" seemed to symbolise Britain's emergence from the years of economic hardship. The launch, just like the maiden voyage two years later, dominated the front pages of every newspaper in the land. The Poet Laureate, John Masefield, was moved without coercion to poetry:

"...this, a rampart of a ship

Long as a street, and lofty as a tower

Ready to glide in thunder from the slip

Opposite page: The front cover of the Christmas edition of the Cunard Magazine in 1931.

And shear the sea with majesty and power."

A popular story has it that Cunard White Star's Board had not intended to name the ship the *Queen Mary*, but instead, clinging to the traditional Cunard 'ia' ending prevalent among its transatlantic fleet - the most recent being the *Berengaria* - they despatched one of their number, Lord Royden, to ask his friend the King for permission to name the ship the *Queen Victoria*. As is often the case when Royalty is addressed, Lord Royden was respectfully circumspect with his request and indicated that the Board wished to name the new ship after Britain's most illustrious Queen.

"My wife will be delighted" the King supposedly replied, "I will go and tell her now".

A good story, but not true. The board had already decided, after much tempestuous internal argument, that since the ship was the first to be launched for the new Cunard White Star company, neither the Cunard 'ia' ending nor the White Star 'ic' ending should prevail. The ship needed to break with those traditions, and the *Queen Mary* it was intended to be.

Royalty, though, did take a keen interest. King Edward VIII visited the ship in the fitting-out basin on 5th March 1936, and, on seeing the kennels and the dogs' walking area, suggested there was a need for a lamppost. One was installed. He visited again the day before the ship left Southampton on her maiden voyage, and as Duke of Windsor, became a regular passenger – he and the Duchess of Windsor always occupying Suite 58 on Main Deck.

The journey on 24th March 1936, from the fitting-out basin in Clydebank down the narrow and meandering River Clyde was both difficult and slow. The ship was pushed and pulled by seven tugs – three astern, three in front and a spare 'just in case'. A particularly powerful tug, the *Romsey*, had been brought up from Southampton to assist – and her assistance was certainly needed. On the tortuous four-hour journey, the *Queen Mary* was grounded on mud banks twice, and was officially recorded by Lloyds as a 'casualty' before she had even seen the sea. Nevertheless, as she passed the birthplace of James Watt, perfector of the steam engine, her whistle sounded a mighty blast of salute.

And soon she was on her way to Southampton under her own steam, where she was gently eased into the King George V Dock - specially built for her, under protest, by the Southern Railway Company - for a final check before her maiden voyage. At her speed trials, over a measured mile, she achieved a remarkable 34 knots.

The maiden voyage began in Southampton on 27th May

Queen Mary

While not as dramatic as the public rooms on her great rival the
Normandie *the passenger spaces on the* **Queen Mary** *were certainly grand but more comfortable – one reason the* **Queen Mary** *was preferred by travellers.*

Above: Cabin Class Main Lounge.

Left: Starboard Gallery

Below: Cabin Class Children's Playroom.

(All photos University of Liverpool Cunard archive)

Above: Another view of the Starboard Gallery.

Left: Lifts to C Deck.

*Overleaf: Cabin Class Main Lounge on the **Queen Mary**.*

(All photos University of Liverpool Cunard archive)

*Cabin Class Dining Room on the **Queen Mary**. (University of Liverpool Cunard archive)*

*The Verandah Grill on the **Queen Mary**. (University of Liverpool Cunard archive)*

'Piccadilly Circus' Shopping Area on the **Queen Mary**. *(University of Liverpool Cunard archive)*

Cabin Class Bedroom on the **Queen Mary**. *(University of Liverpool Cunard archive)*

Life on board Cunarders

Days spent on board Cunard ships offered all types of entertainment from tug of war matches to boxing on the upper deck. For those wanting just to take in the sea air a steward was always at hand for drinks or tea. Evening dress, cocktails and food made for that special Cunard evening.

From left to right: Captain John Townley; Sir Percy Bates, Chairman of Cunard and Neville Chamberlain, Chancellor of the Exchequer in 1933.

1936, and the *Queen Mary* left to the sounds of bands and ecstatic crowds. The day before a whole phalanx of Royals visited, led by the King, Edward VIII. They included Queen Mary, the Duke and Duchess of York (soon to be King George VI and Queen Elizabeth), the Duke and Duchess of Kent, the Duchess of Gloucester and the Princesses Elizabeth and Margaret.

On board, as well as 3,500 mailbags, were the famous bandleader, Henry Hall, scheduled to give a series of live radio broadcasts during the crossing; virtuoso harmonica player, Larry Adler; and a popular singer at the time, Frances Day, who performed a song composed especially for the *Queen Mary* by Henry Hall, 'Somewhere at Sea'. But much as Miss Day may have enjoyed being at sea, she did not trust the ship's eggs to be fresh by the end of the voyage so she took along her own chickens. The crossing was one long party, but uneventful save for the discovery that the overhead gangway at the purpose-built Gare Maritime in Cherbourg was six feet too short, and the ship could not take the Blue Riband because of fog.

A rapturous welcome in New York on 1st June marked the completion of the first voyage, which should have been the start of a long and glamorous career. But things didn't quite turn out like that.

It soon became clear in that year's Atlantic October storms that the *Queen Mary* had a propensity to roll very badly indeed. On one occasion she rolled to an angle of 44 degrees! And while that was a dangerously extreme incident the problem was nonetheless general and acute. Because no

significant movement had been anticipated in so large a ship, the companionways lacked handrails, as a result of which passengers breaking limbs was not uncommon; the ship was met at the end of one crossing by waiting ambulances to take away the 12 passengers who had been injured. Enough crockery was smashed to keep Stoke on Trent busy, and occasionally public rooms had to be closed off while heavy furniture and even secured pianos wrenched themselves free and careered around the room smashing fittings as they went. But that wasn't all; the ship also had a tendency to vibrate, and the company received a host of claims from passengers whose clothes had been marked by deposits from the funnels. In the December of her first year she had to be withdrawn from service for six weeks and stripped down internally. The vibration was tackled with the addition of steel stanchions, and the rolling by adding weight higher in the ship. It worked. It was also a repeat of the same problem that had afflicted the *Lusitania* 30 years earlier, and which had been solved in the same way.

Once the problems were rectified, the *Queen Mary* began that truly glamorous career in which the orchestra played until the last passenger left – which often meant all night. Until, that is, the intervention of the war just a couple of years later.

Just a year after the *Queen Mary's* maiden voyage, Cunard laid the keel for a new two funnelled liner of 35,739 tons - the *Mauretania* - at the Cammell Laird yard in Birkenhead. She was built without subsidy as Cunard's fortunes recovered, and was launched in July 1938. She bore the name of Cunard's

*Cunard advertising for the **Queen Mary** in 1937.*

The **Queen Mary** and **Aquitania** in Southampton on 8th April 1936. (University of Liverpool Cunard archive)

The **Queen Mary** arrives in New York on her maiden voyage on 1st June 1936. (University of Liverpool Cunard archive)

Cunard ephemera

*Band Leader Henry Hall who broadcast live from the **Queen Mary**'s maiden voyage. (Cunard)*

hitherto most celebrated liner, and on her maiden voyage to New York in June 1939, she was under the command of Captain A.T. Brown, who had taken the original *Mauretania* on her melancholic last voyage to the breaker's yard. Despite the mantle of so famous a name, however, the new *Mauretania* never achieved the celebrity and affection heaped on the original.

At the same time as the *Queen Mary* was beginning her working life, her sister ship the *Queen Elizabeth* was stirring. The contract was signed with John Brown and Co on 6th October 1936. The yard had thoughtfully set aside yard number 535 for the ship, as a logical consequence of the *534*, but the government intervened taking the view that sequential yard numbers made the *Elizabeth* contract seem like a

Painting from Robert Lloyd of the Queen Mary arriving at New York on on her maiden voyage. (by kind permission Frank Trumbour)

Mauretania

Forever in the shadow of her famous predecessor and understudy to the 'Queens' the **Mauretania** *was a fine ship in her own right.*

Above: Cabin Class Smoking Room. (Cunard)

Left: Cabin Class cabin. (Cunard)

Below left: Cabin Class Dining Room. (Cunard)

Below: The onboard branch of Midland Bank. (Cunard)

*Above: The **Mauretania** in Southampton Water. (FotoFlite)*

*Below: In October 1962 the **Mauretania** became the second ship to be painted in Cunard's cruising green and is seen here in New York. (Cunard)*

Queen Elizabeth

*As war clouds gathered over Europe construction continued on **Queen Elizabeth** - the largest liner in the world and the biggest passenger ship ever built until **Carnival Destiny** took that distinction from her in 1996.*

*This page and next page: Various views of the **Queen Elizabeth** under construction at John Brown shipyard.*

(All photos University of Liverpool Cunard archive)

Top: The launch of **Queen Elizabeth** *on 27th September 1938.*

Above: The Royal party and assembled crowd admire the great ship on the slipway.

Left: Fitting out the **Queen Elizabeth***.*

(All photos University of Liverpool Cunard archive)

foregone conclusion - a fix, in other words. So the *Queen Elizabeth* became yard number 552. The keel was laid on 4th December 1936, and work progressed without any two year interregnum interrupting the schedule as it had with the *Queen Mary*.

The *Queen Elizabeth* never quite achieved the status of the *Queen Mary* in the public eye, despite her being a significantly superior ship technically, generating the same power with half the number of boilers, and with her two funnels she looked altogether more modern and sleek. She even had the distinction of a Captain's cabin panelled in wood taken from the foundations of the original nineteenth century Waterloo Bridge. But, as we shall see, the *552* was denied a maiden voyage replete with crowds, bands, fanfares and acres of publicity; she got off to a much more subdued start than her sister.

The *Queen Elizabeth* was launched on 27th September 1938 by Her Majesty Queen Elizabeth, wife of King George VI and later The Queen Mother, accompanied by the Princesses Margaret and Elizabeth.

The usual preparations were made for a faultless launch, along the lines of those described for the *Mauretania's* splash into the Tyne over thirty years earlier, only much more complex. But, despite the best laid plans the ship had a mind of her own and decided to move when the Queen was only part way through her speech. "Quick, Ma'am, she's going - launch her now!" hissed the Yard Director, and the Queen managed to release the bottle just in time to catch the hull before it disappeared down the slipway out of reach.

The King himself was unable to attend, being detained in London by the unfolding crisis in Czechoslovakia - events which were eventually to deny the *Queen Elizabeth* her maiden voyage or, at least, to delay it for five years. On 3rd September 1939, war was declared.

In 1940 the ship was in the process of being fitted out, a singularly obvious target for the Luftwaffe. But in addition, she was also taking up valuable yard space required for military purposes. The government decided she had to move, unfinished though she was.

And so, the *Queen Elizabeth* disappeared. In late February 1940 she slipped out of the fitting-out basin under the command of Captain J.C. Townley with a crew of 500 signed on for a voyage to Southampton. On board was a Southampton pilot, and in Southampton officials were busy studying the ship's docking plans. The dockside was littered with packing cases containing equipment and fittings marked for the *Queen Elizabeth*. It was deliberately no secret that the

HM Queen Elizabeth accompanied by HRH Princess Elizabeth (left) and HRH Princess Margaret (the hat below the right microphone!) and Stephen Pigott, Managing Director of John Brown & Co. Glasgow Herald. (Cunard)

Queen Elizabeth was Southampton bound.

But on the day she was due to arrive there, a day on which Luftwaffe activity over Southampton was curiously heavy, the ship was still moored off Gourock, and her crew was informed that her destination was New York. The few who could not undertake such a trip were taken off by tender and held in Gairloch until the ship was under way. On 2nd March, incomplete and bare though she was, she slipped out of the Clyde and headed at full speed for New York, with some of her launch gear still attached, in a dash for safety from U boats and bombers. Her untried engines worked perfectly.

She appeared out of the mist to the surprise of New York, and moored alongside her sister the *Queen Mary* which had been there since the outbreak of war six months earlier. Then, in concert with the old stalwart the *Aquitania*, two ships built to operate in tandem in time of peace began to do so to incalculable effect in time of war.

*The **Queen Elizabeth** leaves the shipyard on 26th February 1940. (Cunard)*

Chapter Seven

Through dark days to the sunlit uplands

With the two 'Queens' safely in New York, the decision had to be taken on what role they could best serve. And even before America joined the war, when they performed the greatest service of them all, it was clear that mass trooping movements were required to take the military from various parts of the Commonwealth to where they were needed. The Queens and the *Aquitania*, the latter reprising an earlier role, were perfectly suited.

On 1st March 1940 the *Queen Mary* was officially called up. She was painted grey in New York and despatched on the long and dangerous journey to Sydney. Once there she was stripped of all the refinements associated with a luxury liner, and converted into a troopship; by dint of building bunks in every available space, her passenger capacity was increased from 2,000 to 5,000. If that sounds rather claustrophobic, a lot worse was to come.

She began by carrying a full complement of Australian troops to the UK by way of Simonstown and Freetown. But the *Queen Mary* was not built for the heat of the tropics, and the lack of air conditioning - an unnecessary frivolity on the North Atlantic run for which she was designed - resulted in cabin temperatures of 125 degrees Fahrenheit; those in turn resulted in a number of soldiers deserting when the ship docked in South Africa.

After trooping in the Middle East from the Clyde, she returned to Sydney in April 1941 to be reunited for the first time since New York with her big sister which had been converted for trooping in New York and Singapore. She made several voyages carrying Australian troops to reinforce the war effort in North Africa, and on the return journeys carried Italian prisoners of war back to Australia. As the Japanese moved down the Malay Peninsula and Australia appeared to be under increasing threat, she carried over 8,000 American GIs to Sydney to bolster the Australian defence effort.

The *Queen Elizabeth* followed a similar career path, and in February 1941 she began trooping Australians to North Africa - with the same discomfort of heat suffered by those on her sister. In 1942 she too was refitted, as the *Queen Mary* had been, to give her the capacity to carry a far greater number of troops.

In 1942 the *Queen Mary* and the *Queen Elizabeth*, along with the *Aquitania*, began their most notable task of the war - ferrying American troops to Europe. The numbers carried on each trip were colossal - in summer over twice the number carried on each trip from Australia. In winter the two 'Queens' carried 10,000 a trip, but in summer that number rose to 15,000. In July 1943 the *Queen Mary* carried the largest

*The **Mauretania**, **Normandie**, **Queen Mary** and **Queen Elizabeth** in New York on 7th March 1940 after the latter's secret Atlantic dash. (University of Liverpool Cunard archive)*

number of people ever recorded on any ship anywhere - ever; 16,643. The record stands today.

After leaving American waters, in which they were afforded protection from the air, the ships travelled alone across the Atlantic at full speed - in excess of 30 knots; speed, together with zig zagging, was their protection against U boats and torpedoes. Even though Hitler offered any U boat captain who sank either ship the equivalent of $250,000 together with Germany's highest honour, the Knight's Cross of the Iron Cross with Oak Leaves, there were no takers. In November 1942 Horst Kessler, a U boat commander, reported to his headquarters that he had fired a torpedo at the *Queen Elizabeth* which had struck. He maintained he heard an explosion and the liner's propellers had stopped. Some GIs on board later reported hearing a detonation and that the ship stopped for 15 minutes - something the Captain was under strict orders not to do. Whatever did happen and

whatever the explanation for this alleged incident, the *Queen Elizabeth* was unharmed and she arrived at her destination with a full complement. Horst Kessler, however, arrived back at his base in St Nazaire convinced he was in line for the big prize; he was a disappointed man.

But even though the *Queen Mary* and *Queen Elizabeth* escaped the unwanted attention of U boats, many ships did not: U boats were worryingly effective. In the first four months of the war alone 221 Allied ships – 750,000 tons in total – were sunk. Over the period of the war as a whole, September 1939 to May 1945, 2,500 ships equating to 3 million tons were lost.

The American troops were landed at Gourock on the Clyde, and the approach was made along the North Coast of Ireland. Both ships, which had travelled at over 30 knots zig zagging across the Atlantic, were met off the coast of Donegal by six or so naval cruisers which escorted them into

the Firth; the risk of torpedo attack was greatest here and the zig zag pattern employed by the liners was also adopted by the escorts. There were various patterns, and the one to be used was agreed between the liner and the escorts. On the bridge was a clock, the zig zag clock, which was set to the pattern required - number eight was the favoured pattern of the *Queen Mary's* Captain Illingworth. When a directional change was required the clock would ring to alert the helmsman, and the change made.

But on 2nd October 1942 an error of judgement occurred which resulted in the *Queen Mary* slicing right through one of her escort ships, the *HMS Curacoa* - which sank within minutes. The *Queen Mary*, with almost 11,000 GIs on board was forbidden to stop, and the rescue operation was carried out by the remaining escorts which were some way distant. The speed of the sinking meant considerable loss of life, with 338 men of the Royal Navy being lost. Only 101 of the *Curacoa's* crew survived, including the Captain who remained on the bridge until his ship sank beneath him.

Despite 'a hole as big as a house' in her bow, the *Queen Mary* was able to reach Gourock and discharge her cargo of troops. The incident, which it was feared would affect wartime morale, was hushed up until after the war. There were three enquiries in all; the first placed all the blame on the warship for cutting across the liner's bow, but the Admiralty would not accept the finding and appealed. The second hearing apportioned blame - two thirds resting with the cruiser, and one third with the *Queen Mary*. Cunard then appealed against that, but the finding was upheld.

In the Cunardia museum on board the *Queen Victoria*, passengers may not even notice a small, plain clock on the wall; it is labelled simply as being from the bridge of the *Queen Mary*. But it is a much more significant artefact than just 'a clock'; it is in fact THAT clock, the zig zag clock, and most who see it are unaware of its significance or poignancy.

The operational labyrinth of carrying 15,000 passengers at a time was a daunting one. To begin with, virtually none of the young GIs had ever been on a ship before, and a substantial number had never even seen the sea. It would have been easy for the whole exercise to dissolve into chaos, and so strict rules were applied and rigorously enforced.

Opposite page: The **Queen Mary** *in Boston's dry dock for emergency repairs to the bow damage caused by her collision with HMS* **Curacoa**. *The new stem section was constructed from templates rushed over from Britain. (University of Liverpool Cunard archive)*

HMS **Curacoa**. *(University of Liverpool Cunard archive)*

The ship was divided into three sections, each denoted by a colour. Boarding soldiers were given a coloured badge at embarkation which indicated their section, and they were required to wear it at all times. They were not permitted to stray from their section.

A strict one-way system was enforced; those moving forward used the starboard companionways, and those travelling aft kept to the port side.

Life jackets had to be worn at all times; anyone, regardless of rank, found without one had his left shoe removed - and he didn't retrieve it until he reported back duly life-jacketed.

The kitchens, of course, providing 30,000 meals a day worked 24 hours a day. There were two meals served daily, each with six timed sittings - and because of the significant gap between meals, the troops were allowed to eat as much as they wanted and take bread and cold meats away with them. But on some significantly rough days, they didn't get much in the way of food at all.

Most of the men slept in what were called 'standee bunks' which were rigid hammocks that pulled down from a central metal frame. They were everywhere - even in the drained swimming pool where they were seven high. Other troops were packed into cabins - some of them, meant for a couple, were occupied by 21 soldiers. Even so, there wasn't room for all so all the bunks and beds were shared on a shift basis. In addition in summer, every man had to sleep on deck for two nights, and inside for two nights.

For the Americans, if a long sea voyage was a novel and unsettling experience, the prospect of being in Britain - of which they knew little - and in a foreign country for the first time, was even more unsettling. But the US authorities, ever thoughtful, compiled a book of useful hints which was distributed on board; it told the GIs what to expect, what to do - and, more particularly, what not to do.

It included some gems:

The **Queen Mary** and **Queen Elizabeth** were built to carry around 3,000 passengers and crew. Their heroic service in the Second World War saw both carry up to 15,000 troops at a time. In July 1943 the **Queen Mary** carried 16,643 people from New York to Gourock – a standing record for the most passengers ever transported on one vessel. (University of Liverpool Cunard archive)

*The **Queen Mary** in Sydney in March 1940. (University of Liverpool Cunard archive)*

- Don't assume a woman with a medal got it for knitting more socks than anybody else in Ipswich.
- If invited to a meal with a British family, don't eat much; you might wipe out their ration for the week.
- Don't criticise the King.
- Don't claim the Yankees won the First World War.

While these strictures may have had an effect, one matter where all attempts at persuasion failed was getting the GIs to accept that the *Queen Mary* was a British ship. The vast majority refused to believe that any country except America could create something so huge, so impressive and so fast.

But while the *Queen Mary* was busy on eastbound crossings she undertook with American troops, she was hardly idle on the return journeys. She regularly carried 5,000 German prisoners of war to North America and once the Americans were fully engaged in the war in Europe both she and the *Queen Elizabeth* carried back home 2,000 wounded at a time.

The *Queen Mary* was also, on three occasions, the hub of the war effort when Winston Churchill travelled on board to both the USA and Canada. The first occasion was in May 1943 when he and a large retinue sailed to confer with President Roosevelt, sharing the ship with several thousand German prisoners - kept suitably separate, of course, and quite unaware of whom was travelling with them.

The second time was in August 1943 to Halifax, Nova Scotia, to thrash out the details of the D-Day landings.

And the third time was in 1944 for the second Quebec Conference, which was primarily to determine action in the Far East.

On these journeys Churchill and his entourage had need to send many messages back to London and elsewhere as the *Queen Mary* was, temporarily, the centre of operations for the war effort. These messages, of course, could not be radioed in the normal way or the ship's position would have been revealed to the enemy. Instead, a cruiser would travel alongside and the messages transmitted by Morse lamp; then the cruiser would speed away and transmit the messages by radio, sometimes as many as 200 in a day, when safely far removed from the *Queen Mary*.

All told, the *Queen Mary* made 30 return transatlantic crossings, and the *Queen Elizabeth* 32, and between them they carried during the war period a total of 1,250,000 troops, over a million on the Atlantic alone.

The importance of these two ships to the war effort cannot be exaggerated because by carrying whole divisions at a time they were freeing up other ships for other duties and executing their tasks far faster than other vessels could have done. For example, as Daniel Allen Butler points out in *'The Age of Cunard'* when in 1942 the US 34th Infantry Division was sent from New York to Belfast, it required a convoy of 21 ships and took 11 days. A short while later, the *Queen Mary* carried the entire 1st Infantry Division on her own in six days. For 3 years the *Queen Mary* and *Queen Elizabeth* ferried 30,000 US and Canadian troops a month to Europe. More than half the Allied Divisions in the 'D' Day landings – 26 in all – were brought to the UK by just those two ships. It has been said,

Come, friendly bombs

Captain Rudolph Sharp OBE RD RNR, like Captain Turner of the *Lusitania*, who was torpedoed twice, had the grotesque misfortune to command the *Lancastria* when she sank with the greatest ever British loss of life at sea, and the *Laconia* which resulted in the second greatest loss. Captain Sharp survived the burning sea that engulfed the *Lancastria*, and with remarkable stoicism and fortitude he went back to sea to be given command of the equally unfortunate *Laconia*.

On 12th August the *Laconia*, which had been

slowly, and Hartenstein speeded things up by firing a second. He could see that many of those on board had taken to the boats and so, in accordance with the rules issued by German High Command he surfaced in order to ascertain from the ship's captain his cargo and destination and to relieve him of any papers he had chosen to save. He was wasting his time on two counts - firstly because all Allied ships were supplied with a weighted bag in which to throw papers overboard in the event of an attack to ensure the Germans could not glean any information of value; and secondly because

Laconia*.   (University of Liverpool Cunard archive)*

converted to an Armed Merchant Cruiser and so carried obvious gun placements, left Port Tewfik in Egypt and headed down the East Coast of Africa. Her job was to take 1,793 Italian prisoners and their 103 Polish guards, together with 820 civilian expatriates - mainly women and children - and 286 military personnel via Cape Town to the UK. By 12th September the ship had rounded the Horn and was about 250 miles North East of Ascension Island - as was the *U156*.

Kapitanleutnant Werner Hartenstein, observing through his periscope that the *Laconia* was armed, determined that the ship was probably a troop carrier and thus a legitimate target. He fired his first torpedo at 8pm. That torpedo struck home and killed most of the Italian prisoners in Hold 2. But the ship sank painfully

Captain Sharp had remained on the bridge as his ship sank just as he had at St Nazaire, but on this occasion he did not survive.

What Hartenstein found surprised him; instead of British troops he was surrounded, in boats and in the sea, by women, children and Italians.

Immediately, and without authority, he began to take those in the sea on board his submarine - both British and Italian, and 193 in all.

He provided them, crammed onto the deck of the sub, and those in the surrounding lifeboats, with bread and butter, jam, coffee and soup. Those who required medical attention were taken inside the sub to receive it, and his crew surrendered their bunks to them. He even dried the clothes of women who had been in the sea.

Captain Rudolph Sharp

Hartenstein then despatched a message to Admiral Donitz of German High Command seeking permission to broadcast, in English, his position and to request assistance; he received permission, and additionally Donitz ordered two further U boats, the *U506* and the *U507*, to rendezvous and assist. This they did.

The U boats took the overcrowded lifeboats in tow, and proceeded slowly towards the West African Coast. Their message had been intercepted by two French vessels, Gloire and Annamite, and the intention was to

Kapitanleutenant Werner Hartenstein.

meet the two ships and offload the survivors.

But the message had also been intercepted by the American base on Ascension Island, and a US Liberator bomber was despatched to investigate. By this time Hartenstein had erected a large Red Cross symbol on his sub, and that, together with the sight of 200 survivors huddled on deck and others in lifeboats being towed, shouldn't have left the reconnaissance plane in any doubt. The pilot reported this back, and the base commander, Captain Richardson - later to become a US senator - issued the stark order, "Sink the sub!"

The Liberator dropped four bombs in all, one of

Some of the survivors on U506.

which damaged the U boat's conning tower, another of which destroyed a lifeboat and everyone in it, and a third overturned a lifeboat and cast all the survivors again into the sea.

Hartenstein had no choice but to place the survivors on and in the badly damaged sub back into lifeboats, cast off the boats and dive.

The *U506* with 142 survivors on deck was also bombed, and had to dive with some of the *Laconia* survivors on board; eventually, with the *U507*, she met up with the French ships and 1,041 survivors were transferred. Most of those who had been with the *U156* and who had been bombed perished, though a small number managed to reach the African Coast. 1,275 died.

The sinking of the *Lancastria*; Britain's biggest loss of life at sea

Lancastria. *(University of Liverpool Cunard archive)*

While the focus of Cunard's wartime contribution tends to be on the 'Queens' and the *Aquitania*, high profile and individually of huge value to the war effort, other ships in the Cunard fleet were valiantly plugging away moving foodstuffs, armaments and people as required.

One such was the *Lancastria*.

Just two weeks after the evacuation of the British Expeditionary force from Dunkirk had been achieved it was revealed that not all of them had arrived home. Some 150,000 men were left behind, about 30,000 of them grouped around Nantes and the port of St Nazaire. An attempt had to be made to rescue them too.

Thirty ships were sent to effect the rescue, of which the largest was Cunard's 16,000-ton *Lancastria*, newly returned from service in the Arctic. Under the command of 62-year old Liverpudlian, Captain Rudolph Sharp, she anchored in the estuary of the River Loire and immediately began to take on board the departing soldiers.

The men were ferried out to the waiting ships on anything that would float, and the imperative was to load as many as possible as quickly as possible onto the waiting ships rather than bureaucratic good order. It is not known exactly how many were on board the *Lancastria*, but it is known that the Purser stopped counting when he reached 6,000; so the number was certainly above that.

As the ship was preparing to depart she was attacked by German Junker bombers, and hit at least four times. One particularly effective bomb went down the funnel and caused huge damage internally which caused the ship to sink within twenty minutes. Thousands were either trapped inside the sinking vessel, or thrust into a sea of burning oil. Captain Sharp and his third officer Harry Grattidge, who went on to command both the *Queen Mary* and the *Queen Elizabeth*, waited on the bridge as the water lapped around them - and then stepped into a burning sea. They survived, but at least 3,500 - and possibly many more - did not.

*The **Queen Elizabeth** crossing the Atlantic. (University of Liverpool Cunard archive)*

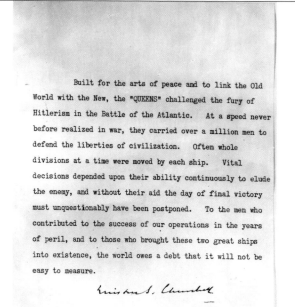

> Built for the arts of peace and to link the Old World with the New, the "QUEENS" challenged the fury of Hitlerism in the Battle of the Atlantic. At a speed never before realized in war, they carried over a million men to defend the liberties of civilization. Often whole divisions at a time were moved by each ship. Vital decisions depended upon their ability continuously to elude the enemy, and without their aid the day of final victory must unquestionably have been postponed. To the men who contributed to the success of our operations in the years of peril, and to those who brought these two great ships into existence, the world owes a debt that it will not be easy to measure.
>
> *Winston S. Churchill*

*Letter from Sir Winston Churchill to Cunard Chairman Sir Percy Bates acknowledging the services of the **Queen Mary** and **Queen Elizabeth** in the war. (University of Liverpool Cunard archive)*

*On 29th September 1946 the **Queen Mary** arrived in Southampton prior to her renovation back to passenger ship and met with the **Queen Elizabeth** being readied for her commercial maiden voyage the following month. (John Hendy collection)*

and it bears repeating: the Allies relied on Cunard; and Cunard did not let them down.

Sir Winston Churchill was in no doubt as to the value of their contribution to the war effort, and in a letter to Sir Percy Bates he noted "without their aid the day of final victory must unquestionably have been postponed". Sir Percy always interpreted that to mean the ships had shortened the war by a year - and in all probability they had.

The *Aquitania* for her part made 53 transatlantic crossings and travelled half a million miles, carrying 400,000 troops – not bad for a ship which was to have been scrapped in 1940 if the war hadn't intervened.

The Cunard fleet as a whole carried 2,473,000 people and nine million tons of cargo in the war years.

The end of the war, of course, didn't end the war service of Cunard ships. There were thousands of troops to be repatriated and, in what came as something of a surprise to the Americans, this was not just a matter of getting GIs home. British troops were scattered all over the place, not just a ferry ride from Dover but in North Africa, the Middle East and the Far East. And, of course, the Commonwealth troops, notably from Australia, Canada, India, New Zealand and South Africa needed to be returned home. One of incoming

*The **Queen Elizabeth** on sea trials in October 1946. (University of Liverpool Cunard archive)*

*Above left: HM Queen Elizabeth takes the helm of the largest liner in the world during the **Queen Elizabeth**'s sea trials on 8th October 1946. (University of Liverpool Cunard archive)*

Left: Sir Winston Churchill on the bridge with Commodore Sir James Bisset. (University of Liverpool Cunard archive)

*Above: HRH Princess Elizabeth monitors the stop watch given to her to time the **Queen Elizabeth**'s speed over the measured mile on 8th October 1946. (University of Liverpool Cunard archive)*

Premier Clement Attlee's first battles was to advise the Americans that they could not commandeer the two 'Queens' and the *Aquitania* to return the GIs home as there were other troops, just as important and just as longing to be back where they belonged, to be considered. An eventual compromise was reached where the *Queen Mary* remained on the GI run, and the *Queen Elizabeth* and the *Aquitania* tackled the rest.

In February 1946 the *Queen Mary* began the pleasant duty of taking the British brides who had married American soldiers, along with their children, to start a new life with their husbands. The ship had to be amended yet again to deal with the new influx, including an abundance of cots and nursery space. In 1946 the ship carried almost 13,000 GI brides and their children to New York, and a further 9,000 to Canada. For the British brides, the journey must have been as strange and unsettling as it was for their husbands when they sailed into the unknown two or three years earlier. But the welcome the brides received on arrival must have compensated for any doubt and distress.

On 29th September 1946 the *Queen Mary* arrived back in Southampton and was officially demobbed - slightly behind her bigger sister which experienced that welcome day back in March of that year. The refitting of the ships was carried out largely by workers from Clydeside - over 1,500 of them - who were accommodated in camps in Southampton while the refurbishments went on. Furniture, fixtures and fittings which had been in store for years - some of it in Sydney - were returned to their intended place. Despite having by now been at sea under strenuous circumstances for years, the *Queen Elizabeth* was still required to undertake sea trials which had never been carried out before her dash to New York in 1940. She undertook the trials in the Firth of Clyde with HM Queen Elizabeth, and the Princesses Elizabeth and Margaret on board - and, as might be expected, her performance was exemplary.

A specially-commissioned portrait by Robert Lloyd of the first Queen Elizabeth in New York for the Queen Elizabeth in 2010.

Queen Elizabeth

*By the time the **Queen Elizabeth** entered service in 1946 her Art Deco interiors were perhaps dated but certainly provided luxurious comfort to passengers.*

Above: First Class Main Hall. (University of Liverpool Cunard archive)

Left: London-based Simpson Piccadilly shop front. (University of Liverpool Cunard archive)

Above: Second Class Dining Room. (University of Liverpool Cunard archive)

Right: First Class Dining Room. (University of Liverpool Cunard archive)

Below: First Class Observation Lounge and Cocktail Bar. (University of Liverpool Cunard archive)

The **Queen Elizabeth** First Class Main Lounge. (University of Liverpool Cunard archive)

*The **Queen Elizabeth** in the English Channel. (FotoFlite)*

The *Queen Elizabeth* left on her maiden voyage from Southampton on 16th October 1946 – an event clouded by the death the same day of Sir Percy Bates, who had been chairman of Cunard, and had guided it through many difficult events. But for him there would have been no *Queen Mary* or *Queen Elizabeth*. There were many well-known travellers on that maiden voyage, but one stands out for his incongruity: Comrade Molotov.

And so began the glory days, a brief visit to the sunlit

*Loading cars onto the **Scythia**. (University of Liverpool Cunard archive)*

uplands. In its history Cunard has had three peaks that combined dominance on the Atlantic with commercial success and the reputation for luxury and service for which the company became famous. Firstly, the period from 1907 to the outbreak of the Great War in 1914 when the *Mauretania* and *Lusitania*, Cunard's first real Grand Hotels afloat, dominated the market and public awareness - a period which, at seven years, was agonisingly short. There followed the *Queen Mary's* solo career from 1937 after her initial problems had been addressed, until the outbreak of the Second World War in 1939 - an even shorter period of glory which was marred by the absence of her sister, the *Queen Elizabeth*. And lastly came the post-war era, from 1947 until the end of the 1950s, when Cunard provided a glamorous, fast and luxurious weekly shuttle across the Atlantic where standards were exemplary and have become legendary and the ships were home from home for royalty, moguls, film stars and statesmen. But again, it was a maddeningly short period and once the number of people crossing the Atlantic by air became greater than those crossing by sea - a crunch point reached in 1958 - the decline was rapid and relentless.

But for a dozen years from July 1947 the two ships shuttled back and forth, always in the news, always met at each terminus by a phalanx of press photographers anxious for a picture of a disembarking Queen Mother, or Winston Churchill, or the Duke and Duchess of Windsor, or Noël Coward, Elizabeth Taylor, Laurel and Hardy - or any other of

Life on board the Queen Elizabeth

*Above: Games deck on the **Queen Elizabeth** as she crosses the Atlantic. (University of Liverpool Cunard archive)*

Left: Telephone switchboard - a far-cry from communications today. (University of Liverpool Cunard archive)

Above left: Doctors' Room with two officers, one preparing medicine.

Above Right: Tourist Class Laundromat.

Right: Print Room - July 1965.

Below left: Sir James Bisset and the Bell Boys.

*Below right: On the bridge wing of the **Queen Elizabeth**.*

(All photos University of Liverpool Cunard archive)

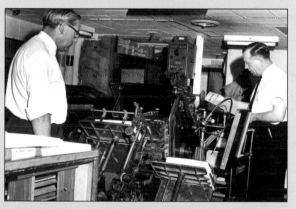

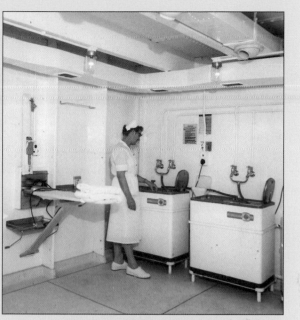

*The **Queen Elizabeth** at the Ocean Terminal in Southampton. (FotoFlite)*

*The **Caronia** arrives in New York on her maiden voyage on 11th January 1949. (University of Liverpool Cunard archive)*

the Hollywood aristocracy for whom a crossing on either ship was a regular event. Of course there were competitors, and sometimes Cunard regulars would defect as the Windsors did to the *United States*, which seized the Blue Riband in 1952. But broadly speaking it was Cunard's triumphant twins that swept the board, making the company great profits in the process – each round trip producing a surplus of £100,000. There was no hint then of a rapidly approaching doom, and both ships were fully booked for months in advance for year upon year.

And it wasn't just celebrated people who travelled on the 'Queens'. Both ships still carried the Royal Mail and cargo, and in 1946 Sir James Bisset carried a very rare cargo indeed - the Lincoln Cathedral copy of Magna Carta, which had been in the USA for the duration of the war and was to be returned. It was delivered to the ship in a large sealed metal box, and the Captain was asked to sign for the receipt of a box "containing Magna Carta". Bisset had no doubt that was what the box did contain, but as it was sealed and could not be opened he amended the receipt to read "allegedly

*The Duke and Duchess of Windsor on **Queen Elizabeth** in 1953. (Cunard)*

125

Parthia

Unusually for Cunard **Parthia** *and her sister* **Media** *were large cargo carriers with accommodation for 250 First Class passengers. The pair became quite popular with certain celebrities as they offered more privacy than the 'Queens'.*

Above: The **Parthia** *on sea trials prior to entry into service.*

Left: One of three London buses being loaded aboard the **Parthia** *at Liverpool. The buses were sent to New York on an 8,000 mile tour of the United States, sponsored by the Travel Association .*

Below left: Dining Room.

Below right: Smoking Room.

(All photos University of Liverpool Cunard archive)

Caronia

Affectionately known as the 'Green Goddess' thanks to her unusual green livery the **Caronia** *was perhaps one of the most luxurious liners/cruise ships ever built and was also known as the 'millionaires' ship.*

Above: The **Caronia** *fitting out at John Brown & Co.*

Right: Fitting what was the largest funnel in the world at the time.

Below left: Cocktail Bar

Below right: Theatre.

(All photos University of Liverpool Cunard archive)

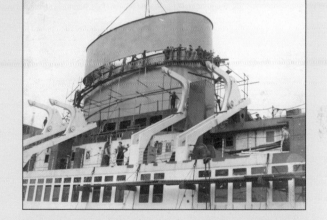

The **France** (top) and **United States** were the Cunard ships' greatest rivals on the Atlantic. (FotoFlite)

containing". He made the crossing with the box tucked under his bed.

The following year, 1947, the Cunard Steamship Company Limited took control of Cunard White Star by buying from White Star's creditors the 38% share they owned, and by the end of 1949 all the assets of Cunard White Star were transferred to Cunard Steamship - and Cunard White Star ceased to exist.

The most significant ship of Cunard's post-war re-construction period was initially intended to be a running mate to the pre-war *Mauretania*, but this new ship was ahead of her time. The *Caronia* was launched by HRH Princess Elizabeth on 30th October 1947 on her last public engagement before her marriage. The ship was one of the first built for a dual-purpose role of cruising as well as Atlantic crossings. Unusually painted four shades of green - mainly as a marketing gimmick - she quickly became known as the 'Green Goddess'. A rich clientele spent months on board her cruising the world. One, Clara Macbeth, lived on board for 14 years!

By 1950 it was time for the grand old *Aquitania* to go. She had originally been intended for scrapping in 1940 when the *Queen Elizabeth* was to have been in service, but the war put paid to that idea – and the *Aquitania* went on to do magnificent service in war for the second time. But by 1946, her repatriation duties done, she was a weary ship and, as the last four-funnelled liner in the world, looking distinctly old fashioned. She then spent three years carrying the dispossessed of Europe, the bombed out and refugees of a ruined

*The **Queen Elizabeth**, now known as the **Seawise University**, arrived in Hong Kong on 15th July 1971 for her conversion to a floating university and cruise ship. (University of Liverpool Cunard archive)*

continent, to new lives in Canada. On 15th February 1950 she was taken out of service, and in March of that year she made the poignant journey from Southampton to the breaker's yard in Inverkeithing.

By the early sixties the ships were making severe losses. Not only was the aeroplane making inroads but new ships, such as the *France*, were creaming off much of the luxury traffic on which Cunard depended. Both ships were expensively refitted and moved from purely transatlantic transport to cruising leisure. They had limited success, but they were both looking dated; as one passenger remarked, it

*'The Queen That Never Was', a painting of the projected **Q3** by Mervyn Pearson. (David Williams)*

*The **Queen Mary** departs Southampton for the last time on 31st October 1967. (John Hendy)*

 *The **Queen Mary 2** and **Queen Mary** meet for the first time in Long Beach on 23rd February 2006. (Cunard)*

*The **Seawise University** being destroyed by fire in Hong Kong on 9th January 1972. (University of Liverpool Cunard archive)*

was like spending five days in the foyer of an Odeon. Eventually the ships were losing Cunard £4 million a year, and on some of the crossings the passengers were hugely outnumbered by the crew. Something had to be done.

But what? In an act of lunacy the Board decided to replace two very large, fast, quadruple screw, all steel and expensive-to-run transatlantic liners that were losing millions with - two very large, fast, quadruple screw, all steel and expensive-to-run transatlantic liners! The first, codenamed *Q3*, would replace the *Queen Mary* and the second, codenamed *Q4*, would replace the *Queen Elizabeth*. And, as if they were completely oblivious to the company's balance sheet, the Board proposed to do it without any external assistance.

Once they had been advised of the potential cost - £40 million - and reconciled this with the fact that Cunard revenues in 1957 were £6 million down on the previous year, a bout of common sense broke out and they realised they would need a government loan. The government was amenable - after all, the US government had effectively subsidised the *United States* and the French government feather bedded the liner the *France* - but they were astute enough to see that replacing like with like was not an option. As governments always do, they set up a committee - this one

under Lord Chandos - which reported in 1960. It recommended that support should be given for just one ship and not two, and that it should be multi-purpose and flexible. Cunard harrumphed and said such a thing could not be done. But the new Cunard chairman, Sir John Brocklebank, was less immovable than his colleagues and certainly more forward looking; he felt he could do things with the proposed £18 million loan.

Tenders were invited for an 80,000 ton, 30 knot, all steel, quadruple screw transatlantic liner, and the successful bidders - a consortium led by Swan Hunter on the Tyne - won the

*The **Queen Mary** arriving in Long Beach on 9th December 1967. (Cunard)*

day with a quote of £28 million. But, in a move that saved Cunard and ultimately damaged Swan Hunter, they also suggested that Cunard may consider a slightly smaller twin screw ship, still capable of a service speed of 28.5 knots, but with a much lighter aluminium superstructure that would save massively on both fuel and engine room crew.

Brocklebank was convinced, and the Board cancelled *Q3* and pursued instead the Swan Hunter proposal, which became *Q4*. And, as we shall see in the next chapter, *Q4* became the most famous Cunard ship of them all - and was built by John Brown on the Clyde, not by Swan Hunter which had proposed the idea in the first place

But for the *Queen Mary* and the *Queen Elizabeth* the day which had to come some day came on 8th May 1967, when the then Chairman, the splendidly named Sir Basil Smallpeice, announced that the *Queen Mary* would be withdrawn later that year and the *Queen Elizabeth* in 1968.

The *Queen Mary* was put up for sale and a number of significant cities, including Philadelphia and New York, put in bids. But the successful bidder was the relatively small city of Long Beach in California which put in a bid of $3.45 million. Part of the deal, against the advice of Cunard which could remember the difficulties encountered by Australian troops in equatorial heat on the ship early in the war, Long Beach insisted that the final voyage should be sold as a cruise. Since the ship was too big for the Panama Canal this involved going round Cape Horn and crossing the tropics twice. The *Queen Mary* left Southampton for the last time on 31st October 1967, an emotional departure marked by hundreds of small

boats and thousands of spectators. On board were 1,000 passengers and two red double decker buses, earmarked to be tourist attractions in California. As predicted, as the ship moved south it got hotter, until - just as Australian soldiers had deserted in Simonstown - some passengers went AWOL in Rio. But the vast majority, including Tessie O'Shea, stayed with it, sure in the knowledge that the voyage would never be repeated; and nor would the opportunity to round Cape Horn in a double decker bus.

The ship reached Long Beach on 9th December to a stupendous welcome and on 11th December the ship's master, Captain John Treasure Jones, formally handed over his ship to the city. So started an entirely new career, as a building rather than as a ship, as a result of which she is still a great attraction even today.

The *Queen Elizabeth* was less lucky, and was sold initially to a consortium in Fort Lauderdale. She left Southampton for the last time on 29th November 1968. The venture was not a success and she was sold on to the Chinese magnate CY Tung who intended she should be a floating university - Seawise University (geddit?). She received a £5 million refit in Hong Kong, but in January 1973 a number of mysterious fires broke out simultaneously; both the fire and water from fire hoses destabilised the ship and she turned over and sank - though still visible. Eventually she was cut up and what could be removed was removed. A sad end for the *Queen Elizabeth* - but by then a new Queen Elizabeth was being fitted out on the Clyde. Yet again, the Queen is dead! Long live the Queen!

*The **Caronia** at Southampton just prior to her sale by Cunard in 1967. (John Hendy)*

*The **Ivernia** in the Clyde. (University of Liverpool Cunard archive)*

Stars Aboard

Above left: Bing Crosby.

Above right: Burt Lancaster.

Left: Cary Grant.

Below left: Clarke Gable.

Below right: David Niven.

(All photos Cunard)

Above left: Ginger Rodgers.

Above right: Liz Taylor.

Right: Duke Ellington.

Below left: Gracie Fields.

Below right: Jackie Onassis with Robert Kennedy.

(All photos Cunard)

Stars Aboard

Above left: *Judy Garland.*

Above right: *Mae West.*

Left: *Rita Hayworth.*

Below left: *Shah of Persia.*

Below right: *Sir Noel Coward.*

(All photos Cunard)

Above left: **Vera Lynn.**

Above right: **Walt Disney.**

Right: **Fred Perry.**

Below: **Viscount Montgomery.**

(All photos Cunard)

Chapter Eight

Sir Basil
and
his 'Queen'

"We battle for our survival" was the blunt message delivered to shareholders by Sir Basil Smallpeice at the 1966 Annual General Meeting in one of the frankest statements given by a Cunard Chairman at such an occasion.

Several Chairmen stand out in the history of Cunard for their vision, their influence and their personalities. For his ambition to establish the line in the first place: Samuel Cunard. John Burns, the first Lord Inverclyde who rescued Cunard in the 1880s and was responsible for the *Lusitania* and the *Mauretania* though he died before work started on them. Sir Alfred Booth who at the age of 26 became the youngest-ever Chairman and had to guide his company through the First World War. Sir Percy Bates who in 1926 had the

*Re-conditioned for cruising, as seen by the new lido and swimming pool built in 1965, the **Queen Elizabeth** departs New York. (Cunard)*

foresight to create the two-ship weekly express service which would eventually become the *Queen Mary* and the *Queen Elizabeth* - "the smallest and slowest ships which could accomplish such a service" is how he diffidently described them when plans began. And Sir Basil Smallpeice, who, unbeknown at the time of his appointment, would become the last Chairman of an independent Cunard and the man who changed the company forever to ensure its survival.

Originally a chartered accountant, Basil Smallpeice spent 13 years in the airline business before joining the Board of The Cunard Steamship Company Limited in April 1964. He then became Deputy Chairman in June 1965 and Chairman in November 1965 after ill health forced Sir John Brocklebank, who had been reluctant to take on the Chairmanship in the first place, to resign.

Sir Basil (from 1961) entered shipping from BOAC after Cunard took to the air.

In 1958 aeroplanes carried more passengers across the Atlantic than passenger liners and the number taking to the air rather than crossing by ship would increase yearly thereafter. Cheap air travel by the early 1960s threatened Cunard's future as a transatlantic carrier so the old adage 'if you can't beat them...' came into play when in March 1960, not wanting to miss out on the new boom in air travel, the Cunard Steamship Company bought a 60% shareholding in Eagle Airways Ltd. On 28th July 1960 Cunard Eagle Airways was formed and the new airline became the first British independent airline to operate pure jet planes. In June 1961 Cunard Eagle became the first independent airline in the UK to be awarded a licence by the newly constituted Air Transport Licensing Board (ATLB) to operate a scheduled service on the prime Heathrow-New York JFK route at a frequency of one round-trip per day. The licence was valid for 15 years from 31st August 1961 to 31st July 1976.

On 6th June 1962, the British Overseas Airways Corporation (BOAC) and Cunard formed BOAC-Cunard Ltd to operate scheduled services to North America, the Caribbean and South America. BOAC provided 70% of the new company's capital and eight Boeing 707s. The independent Cunard Eagle Airways, of which Cunard still held a 60% shareholding, provided two more 707s. Cunard called the new partnership "...probably the most significant development in sea-air co-operation which has yet been achieved by two major operators".

Harold Bamberg was appointed Chairman to the Board of BOAC-Cunard but after becoming disenchanted with Cunard's corporate culture he resigned from the Board in 1963 while continuing as Managing Director of Cunard Eagle Airways. His growing disenchantment with BOAC-Cunard resulted in the decision to reconstitute Eagle by buying back control from Cunard. The BOAC Managing Director, Sir Basil Smallpeice resigned from the airline in December 1963 and joined Cunard a few months later.

The initial losses of the air venture were turned around and 1964 and 1965 saw profits but the National Union of Seamen's strike of 1966 cost Cunard £4 million and once again assets had to be sacrificed and, despite Cunard at one point seriously considering leaving the shipping business and

Sir Basil Smallpeice, Chairman of Cunard. (Cunard)

going solely into the airline business, the BOAC-Cunard operation was dissolved in September 1966 which resulted in Cunard obtaining £11.5 million in cash giving it a profit of £3 million on the original deal. However joint selling arrangements would continue for a time as sales outlets and booking procedures for the two companies had been rationalised when they joined forces and both agreed to strengthen the sea-air packages that had been developed.

The British-built Super VC10 were operated by BOAC Cunard.

*The **Carinthia** in the Mersey. (Ian Collard)*

After becoming Chairman, Sir Basil's biggest challenge was the successful construction, delivery and entry into service of the new ship whose keel was laid in July that year - a ship many were already saying was a huge gamble and a "white elephant" that would probably have to be laid up after six months in service. But Sir Basil also had to fix Cunard and before that new ship even finally appeared the company would have to go through a prolonged and difficult period of "do or die".

At this time the Cunard passenger fleet consisted of the *Queen Elizabeth*, the largest passenger ship in the world (a distinction she would hold until the introduction of the *Carnival Destiny* in 1996), the *Queen Mary*, the *Caronia* (the 'Green Goddess'), the *Mauretania* (her withdrawal from service in November 1965 had already been announced), the *Carmania* (formerly the *Saxonia*), the *Franconia* (formerly the *Ivernia*), the *Carinthia* and the *Sylvania*.

The latter four had been built between 1954 and 1957 and known as the 'Canadian Quartet' as built for the Liverpool to Canada service. They were only a moderate success given the fact they did not have any cruising features such as swimming pools built into them and they were too small with too little cargo capacity. The *Saxonia* and the *Ivernia* had been expensively and heavily rebuilt for cruising in 1963 while the other pair were sent cruising with minor refitting.

Sir Basil firmly believed that Cunard was "fighting for its life" and could only survive and flourish by "selling floating holidays instead of just a form of transport". He was committed to his mission to "save Cunard, not only for its stockholders but even more for the sake of those who worked in it". His challenge was a daunting one as Cunard's total volume of business had remained static for the previous ten years or so and between 1961 and 1964 the company's passenger business had lost £16 million leaving it to live off its capital.

When, in the spring of 1966, Cunard started selling Mediterranean and Canary Island cruises outside the peak transatlantic season, Sir Basil travelled to see *Queen Mary* in Cannes. The French Line's *France* was anchored a few hundred yards away and as he had never been aboard *France* he asked if he could visit the ship. The *France*'s Captain replied that the President of the French Line, Edmond Lanier, was on board and would like to meet him. Sir Basil had been told that no Cunard Chairman had ever before met a French Line President and, whether that was true or not, Sir Basil and his rival hit if off from the start. Both had common problems in the changing pattern of Atlantic shipping and both agreed to meet again. In 1968, with both companies reduced to one large ship only, the *Queen Elizabeth* and the *France*, it made good business practice for both companies to arrange their timetables so that each sailed out of New York on alternate weeks and maintain a joint service throughout the summer season. Both also agreed to pool revenue and undertake joint sales and advertising with Cunard representing both lines in Britain and the French Line doing the same in France. While the possibility of a full-scale merger of the two lines' Atlantic operations could not be excluded, this agreement would result in big savings in overheads.

Within months of running Cunard, Sir Basil had put together a new management team of six, with an average age of 43, before he appointed consultants Urwick Orr and Partners to improve the organisation with a widespread brief. The Economic Intelligence Unit was asked to thoroughly review the cruise market. As he swept through the troubled company with the intention of leaving no stone unturned, Sir Basil told shareholders: "The time has come to give younger men their heads – men who realise that for them it is do or die".

Figures revealed at the end of 1966 showed for the first time that Cunard ships collected £24 million a year from passengers. Sir Basil claimed that to wipe out the yearly losses of between £2.5 and £3 million "…all we need is a 12.5% improvement. In other words, if the passenger side can cut costs by 2s. 6d. in the pound or make an extra half-crown profit on every pound earned – the losses would go. There ought to be little doubt that this, and more, can be achieved".

The main recommendations of the combined management team and outside consultants were acted upon immediately. The fleet would be dramatically reduced with the sale of the *Mauretania* in 1965, the *Queen Mary* in 1967 and the *Queen Elizabeth*, the *Caronia*, the *Sylvania* and the *Carinthia* in 1968. The greatest passenger fleet on the Atlantic in 1957 had been reduced to two, the *Carmania* and the *Franconia*, by the end of 1968.

In 1968 the Cunard Building in Liverpool was sold for £3 million and the management of ships moved to Southampton with the main decisions being taken in New York - in July 1968 the Head Office at 25 Broadway was closed and a new Head Office opened on Fifth Avenue. Offices in London, Sydney, Paris, Le Havre and Dublin were closed and staff numbers in London, Liverpool and Southampton were reduced. Overall the company was split into five divisions: commercial, hotel, technical, personnel and accounting.

Cunard was going into the 'holidays at sea' market. The new Cunard marketing was certainly different, with the new 'Go Sun Hunting' slogan replacing the revered 'Getting there is half the fun!' but while the new marketing was bold,

innovative and fun, the reality was limited success in the cruise market because the ships themselves were not bold, nor innovative and lacked fun. Attempts to modernise the *Caronia* and the *Queen Elizabeth* in 1965 and 1966 with new outdoor swimming pools and the earlier transformations of the *Saxonia* into the *Carmania* and the *Ivernia* into the *Franconia* to make them more cruise-friendly were lacklustre at best and failed to appreciate that the future of cruising lay with purpose-built cruise ships.

In 1966 the passenger fleet carried 104,262 passengers, which was more than any other shipping line, and Cunard was able to keep its position at the top of the transatlantic league despite the six-week seamen's strike which had crippled the shipping industry. Its position was also maintained despite 49 fewer sailings than in 1965. Thirty-seven cruises were operated in 1966, 10 from British ports and 27 from North America and of the 22,962 cruise passengers carried 6,620 sailed on a cruise from the UK and 16,342 from North America.

Ivernia. (*University of Liverpool Cunard archive*)

The Building of *QE2*

As mentioned earlier Sir Basil's biggest challenge was the construction of Cunard's new ship, the *Queen Elizabeth 2*. Sir John Brocklebank should always be remembered for his role in cancelling the *Q3* and initiating what would become the *QE2* while Sir Basil should be remembered for getting her built and put into service. The determination shown by both men in succeeding are their long-standing gifts to Cunard.

Shortly after cancelling the proposed *Q3* Project a new

exercise was implemented which among other things, reduced the number of boilers originally planned, and to raise extra cash Cunard mortgaged five passenger and six cargo ships.

The Times reported: "What Cunard has embarked on is a unique compromise between express liner and cruise ship. No one has attempted it before. It remains to be seen whether the two are commercially reconcilable. This ship is genuinely an act of faith and courage. The country will applaud both owners and builders and wish them well".

At this time both Cunard and John Brown were badly

ship, the *Q4*, was announced by Cunard in 1963. The new ship was designed as a dual-purpose liner / cruise ship that would speed across the Atlantic in the summer months and follow the sun in the winter and access ports denied to her predecessors despite her size (65,000 tons) making her one of the world's largest passenger liners. She would be capable of transiting both Panama and Suez Canals and this new concept in ship design, or "resort hotel" as Cunard would call her, was a complete break for the company which was sailing unchartered territory. At this stage Cunard still planned for three classes. The government eventually agreed to loan £17.6 million at 4.5 % over ten years from the delivery date.

Initially Cunard had estimated that the *Q4* would cost £22 million but when the contract was signed with the John Brown shipyard on 30th December 1964 the cost had risen to over £25 million. Immediately the company set about to reducing the cost of the ship and a dramatic cost-cutting

*Top and below: Two models depict the **Q3** in various stages of her prolonged design period.*

managed and practically bankrupt organisations about to embark on the building of very special ship indeed that was scheduled for delivery in May 1968.

The keel for the *Q4* was to be laid on Friday 2nd July 1965, just two days before the 125th anniversary of the maiden voyage of the *Britannia* – Cunard was unable to wait and lay it on 4th July because the keel had to be laid before the shipyard closed for the annual summer holiday. The keel for No. 736, the shipyard's order book number for the *Q4*, was to be laid at No. 4 slipway in the East Yard of John Brown and Co, the same slipway on which the *Queen Mary* and the *Queen Elizabeth* and other famous Cunarders had been built.

As the process began, in front of a score of television cameramen and about 30 journalists from London and Glasgow, it rapidly became clear that something was wrong. Although the keel section initially moved a few inches it then stuck and refused to move further. Seemingly the weight of the keel was greater than the two cranes could manage, and the strain on the winch threatened to tear its concrete base out of the ground. This was not what Prime Minister Harold Wilson had in mind when he said the ship should be "a showcase for modern Britain". The embarrassing ceremony ended abruptly and the guests were quickly taken away where they were entertained; fortunately press coverage was sympathetic. After such an initial high-profile disaster, the keel section was moved without fanfare into position onto the building blocks on Monday 5th July.

The debacle with the keel was perhaps indicative of problems to come, with each new problem creating huge publicity. The *Q4* would prove as difficult to build as the *Queen Mary* had before her on the very same slip – but for different reasons.

Within months of July 1965, Cunard had concerns over the progress the yard was making in terms of completion of drawings, the progress of steelwork, the shortage of workers and the fact that John Rannie, Managing Director of John Brown, was being allowed to manage the build entirely by himself. The entire build period would see owner and shipyard endure a strained relationship, and a battle of blame between the two escalated into total war evidenced by a series of acrimonious meetings and exchanges of correspondence.

In March 1966 the yard conceded that the new liner was already six months behind schedule. The launch was now rescheduled from April 1967 to September 1967, with delivery in November 1968, which lost Cunard the lucrative summer 1968 season – a great blow as transatlantic revenue would have been in the region of £200,000 per week. This delay did allow for the resolution of one of the biggest issues in the design of the new ship – the number of classes. Sir

Basil was finally able to reverse the company's insistence that the ship should offer three classes. The layout was re-drawn for two classes in perhaps one of the most important decisions to be taken about the new ship.

Three thousand men would work on the construction of the *Q4* – a figure that would increase by another 500 at the peak fitting-out period. Such numbers would inevitably invite trouble from unions and problems with work demarcation. Water supplies on ships had traditionally been delivered by zinc pipes, which, being water pipes, were fitted by plumbers. But on the *Q4* there was a move to copper pipes which, because they were copper, had to be fitted by coppersmiths, thus denying work to plumbers. The compromise reached was that coppersmiths would do the work, and each would be accompanied by a plumber – who would be paid to do nothing.

Then owner and builder had to deal with what seemed endless strikes. The first major one came in March 1967, when the Draughtsmen's and Allied Technicians' Association began a dispute that was to last over ten weeks. In June, the plumbers walked out, rapidly followed by 286 electricians. Many other trades went on strike in July and August. Such stoppages continued throughout the entire time the ship was on the Clyde, each union apparently calling a strike of its members without any regard for the overall effect on the progress of the ship or on its brother unions. So it went on and on; strike and dispute piled one on top of the other, serving only to compound the already serious delays. But it was – and is – difficult to determine to what degree the strikes

*The **QE2** under construction on the Clyde. Cunard decided against calling their new ship Ian S! (Cunard)*

*The **QE2** on the slip with her launch approaching as seen by the scaffolding being erected for the launch platform. (University of Liverpool Cunard archive)*

Above: The launch of **QE2** *on 20th September 1967. (Cunard)*

Left: John Brown & Co Managing Director, John Rannie, calls for hush as HM The Queen prepares to name and launch **QE2**. *(Cunard)*

Below: The **Queen Elizabeth 2** *in the Caribbean in 1970. (Cunard)*

*The lower section of **QE2**'s funnel is lowered into position on 18th April 1968. (University of Liverpool Cunard archive)*

*The Bridge of **QE2** being hoisted on board on 5th April 1968. (University of Liverpool Cunard archive)*

resulted from genuine grievance, from archaic demarcation, from the political motivation of a few – or whether they were just a means of causing delay, to keep the job, and hence paid employment, going longer. The Minister of Technology, Anthony Wedgwood Benn, would visit the yard and claimed in a rousing speech that he was there to take the steam out of the argument and put it into the turbines.

But strikes and acts of God were only part of the toxic mix conspiring to compound the delays. Another was a Clydebank hobby known euphemistically as 'squirrelling' but which most people would recognise as theft. In August 1967 Bob Arnott, later to become the *QE2*'s longest-serving captain, was appointed chief officer, and his initial duties before the ship came into service were to oversee aspects of construction on Cunard's behalf. He soon became aware of the practice of 'squirrelling', which was explained to him as not just being a lucrative perk but, rather like some of the strikes, a means of keeping a good job going longer. That was not how he saw it, though, preferring as he did the epithet 'larceny on a grand scale'. He later recalled: "Some of the yard workers were stealing the ship faster than the others could build it."

There was a thriving trade around Glasgow of materials removed from the ship, a trade which was so organised and prevalent that items even had a fixed retail price including delivery. Paint was £1 a gallon, light fittings (including shades) from the cabins just 5 shillings (25 pence) and Formica sold at 10 shillings (50 pence) for 2.4 x 1.2 metre sections. When rolls

of carpet for the public rooms were laid out, they were found to have front room-shaped sections, complete with window bay, cut out of them as if by a giant pastry-cutter. There were certainly some cosy and expensively carpeted living rooms in Clydebank that winter. By way of example, Arnott cited one electrician whose home was raided by the police, who was found to have removed from the ship 27 metres of carpet, two chests of drawers, a wall cabinet, three bookcases, three lounge stools, 55 metres of fibreglass, five lamps, 36 litres of paint, plus crockery and soft furnishings. In mitigation the man's solicitor implied such activity was the norm. "My client just walked off the ship with the stuff," he said.

It was regular practice for workers to walk out of the yard concealing items beneath their clothes – items ranging from copper piping to towels. Ironically, Bob Arnott noted, most of the stolen material had to be carried past the police station adjacent to the dock gates, but the prevailing attitude of the police was that although an ocean liner was being stolen piece by piece in front of them, there was little they could do about it.

On 21st July 1967 the Prime Minister, Harold Wilson, visited the yard to inspect progress on the new ship before having lunch with the directors of Cunard and the yard. The man who coined the phrase "the white heat of the technological revolution" could not fail to be impressed with the *Q4*.

Cunard's financial situation had worsened during 1967 and the company forecast a further £3.5 million loss on the passenger ships for that year. This was compounded by the news from John Brown in July that the contract price for the *Q4* of £25.5 million would probably be increased by a further

'Queen Elizabeth 2' about to be applied.
(University of Liverpool Cunard archive)

£3 million. Even if the *Q4*'s cost had not risen, the additional losses on the passenger ships would mean that the government's financial aid would not be adequate. Cunard warned the Board of Trade that the project was in danger of being abandoned, with major political repercussions, unless the government agreed to increase the loan.

Cunard and the Board of Trade met to discuss a new loan to cover the increases in shipyard wages and materials since the £25,500,000 contract for the *Q4* was signed in 1964. A new loan, to cover 80 per cent of the estimated cost of the hull and machinery, was arranged but it did not take into account a substantial escalation in cost levels.

There then followed a period of intensive negotiations between Cunard and the government throughout August and September. Cunard stressed that a final decision had to be made by the time of their next board meeting on 14th September 1967 – if the news was bad the company felt it would have to give The Queen at least five days' notice of the cancellation of the launch on 20th September!

On 19th September, on the eve of the launch, Cunard announced that agreements had been reached in the discussions with the Board of Trade. The existing loan agreement under which the government would make available a loan of £17.6 million on delivery of the ship by the shipyard to Cunard was to be replaced with a new arrangement. Under it the government was now prepared to lend in the neighbourhood of £24 million.

Simultaneously the future of the John Brown yard itself had to be decided when, after the collapse of the Fairfields yard in October 1965, the Board of Trade established the Shipbuilding Inquiry Committee to decide the best course of action for shipyards on the Clyde and the resulting Geddes Report recommended the amalgamation of smaller yards on the Clyde into two larger groups. Thus in January 1968 the name John Brown disappeared from shipbuilding, and the yard became part of Upper Clyde Shipbuilders. The engine works, meanwhile, was separated and became John Brown Engineering and that organisation later joined Cunard under Trafalgar House ownership.

The Queen had her first view of the liner as she flew overhead on 20th September. At precisely 14.28 hours on a sunny afternoon, in front of 30,000 Clydesiders, Her Majesty stepped forward on the launching platform and said: "I name this ship *Queen Elizabeth the Second*. May God bless her and all who sail in her."

There had been much speculation about what name the *Q4* would be given. Cunard had privately decided to name

'E Stairway' takes shape on the **QE2**. *(University of Liverpool Cunard archive)*

her the *Queen Elizabeth* but the addition by The Queen of "the Second" caused uproar in Scotland where she is the first Queen Elizabeth there. To diffuse the argument Cunard announced that the new ship would be known as the *Queen Elizabeth 2* (Queen Elizabeth Two) and not the *Elizabeth II* (Queen Elizabeth the Second): in other words she was merely the second ship to be called the *Queen Elizabeth*. An unusual argument for Cunard given the second *Mauretania* or the second *Laconia* had not been named as such. The *QE2*, as she became universally known, would always cause debate over the exact origins of her name throughout her life. The use of 2 was obvious whenever the *QE2* was berthed alongside the Queen Elizabeth II Terminal in Southampton - the Terminal was named after The Queen. Even today lazy radio presenters or journalists talk about traffic congestion on the *QE2* Bridge at Dartford which is incorrect - they should announce traffic congestion on the Queen Elizabeth the Second Bridge as the Bridge is named after The Queen. The same mis-naming applies as well today to that Terminal, the Queen Elizabeth II Conference Centre or the Queen

Above: The Midships Lobby on the **QE2**. *(University of Liverpool Cunard archive)*

Below: The Double Room (lower level) on the **QE2**. *(University of Liverpool Cunard archive)*

QE2

'The Queen Elizabeth Two is something new and exciting for the holiday market, not only of today but of tomorrow' John Whitworth, Cunard Managing Director in 1969.

Top left: The Double Room.

Right: The Juke Box Room and Teenage Area.

Below left: Suite on Two Deck.

Below right: Entrance to the 736 Club.

(All photos University of Liverpool Cunard archive)

Elizabeth II Hospital in London.

In July 1968, as the first wisps of smoke were to be seen emanating from the funnel, Cunard by now was resigned to even more delay and to the fact that the earliest possible date on which the *QE2* could satisfactorily be completed, would be 19th December. Cunard still felt that the ship would be reasonably complete for her maiden Atlantic voyage scheduled to depart on 17th January 1969.

The ship had the first of many royal visits on 19th November 1968, when Prince Charles was on board as the ship left her birthplace for the first time – Cunard was shrewd enough to realise that a forthcoming royal visit would ensure the yard remained focused. A special holiday had been declared for the locals and thousands assembled on the fields and shores along the Clyde. Six tugs eased her from the fitting-out berth, where she had been since her launch, and she moved ahead, using her own engines for the first time.

Cunard continued to express its concern at the volume of outstanding work and pressed for improved organisation and supervision on the part of the builders but the situation deteriorated rapidly after the arrival in the dry dock. The builders arbitrarily dismissed 500 tradesmen in the key trades (joiners and electricians), which precipitated a ban on overtime working, and meant that the ship was desperately short of labour on her return from technical trials.

Delays caused by strike action were further compounded by wholesale vandalism, which served no purpose other than to delay completion and so preserve jobs in Clydebank a little longer. On one occasion the First Class Queen's Room was deliberately flooded with oil, and on another, leather walls

Captain W. E. Warwick and President of Cunard in North America, Nick Anderson, chat on board the **QE2**. *(University of Liverpool Cunard archive)*

covering 'D' Stairway were slashed.

The *QE2*'s preliminary sea trials commenced two days later than planned on 26th November 1968, but these had to be abandoned because of contamination of the steam and feed system by oil fuel. Her main trials to the Canaries, due to start on 4th December, were postponed. The first of the 'mini-maiden voyages' that had been scheduled for the new ship, the Christmas charity cruise in aid of Cancer Research, was now cancelled and her arrival in Southampton and Handover delayed until 1st January 1969. Cunard still maintained that the maiden commercial voyages commencing with the 10th January 'mini maiden' preview cruise were not affected in any way.

The **QE2** *limps into Southampton on her maiden arrival on 2nd January 1969. (University of Liverpool Cunard archive)*

The **QE2** *approaching the Ocean Terminal in Southampton. (University of Liverpool Cunard archive)*

*HM The Queen and Captain W. E. Warwick inspect 'Britannia' in the Britannia Restaurant of the **QE2** on 1st May 1969. (Cunard)*

On 23rd December, the *QE2* quietly left the Clyde and headed for what were to be comprehensive sea trials. On the technical side the main and auxiliary machinery would be tested including simulated breakdowns and damage conditions. On the hotel side the 570 'passengers' would have to simulate a full ship so they were put into groups and asked to turn up at specific times for particular functions.

So sensitive was Cunard about the unfinished state of the

*The **QE2** arrives in New York for the first time on 7th May 1969. Note the break with Cunard tradition with the black and white funnel and, for the first time on any passenger ship, the name of her owner on the superstructure – a practice common in the air industry. (Cunard)*

ship that the 'strictest secrecy' was to be enforced and all communications between the ship and the UK were to be sent in code for the chairman's attention. The use of the radio telephone was to be avoided as far as possible.

It was now apparent to the company that it would be unrealistic to maintain the 10th and 17th January voyages. This was not only due to the extent of the uncompleted work but also the fact that many items of the ship's equipment had not been properly commissioned by the builders and when put into operation were found to be defective. A press party of 71 was due to join the ship in Las Palmas on 28th December and great difficulty was experienced in finding sufficient cabins in which they could be accommodated regardless of the number of defects these rooms contained.

Earlier problems on trials paled into insignificance when on Christmas Eve both turbines experienced trouble starting, with vibrations and then serious overheating. After four days of problems, on 28th December, the *QE2* limped into the port of Las Palmas where Sir Basil and Anthony Hepper,

Chairman of Upper Clyde Shipbuilders, joined the ship. The next day Sir Basil announced that Cunard would not be taking delivery of the *QE2* on her return to Southampton because of the degree of uncompleted builders' work in the passenger spaces and because of the technical problems which had arisen with both sets of main machinery during the trials.

The *QE2* had broken down and technical people from both Cunard and the yard still did not know what had caused the damage let alone how to cure it. The Pametrada turbines which were approved by Cunard for the *QE2* were a well-known design and had been well proved in many other ships. The *QE2*'s previous speed trials demonstrated that these turbines were fully capable of achieving their required performance. The fault was major, could not be rectified at sea and would take some time to repair. To take the ship back to the Clyde was just not practical – Southampton was the nearest port so the *QE2* headed 'home' and the 'splendid arrival' that had been organised was cancelled.

The engineering difficulties did prove to be a blessing in disguise for the yard as it now gave them extra time to complete the unfinished passenger accommodation. The turbines were opened, and it was revealed that blades in both rotors had sustained damage – hundreds of blades had been stripped from the main body of the rotor hub. It was immediately clear that a major repair, requiring entirely new blades, would be needed.

An investigating team, under the leadership of Sir Arnold Lindley, President of the Institute of Mechanical Engineers, was established to assess the cause of the damage and find a solution to the problem.

Upper Clyde Shipbuilders remained responsible for the ship during this completion period. Cunard Line Limited, acting as agents for and on behalf of the builders, undertook the care, maintenance and security of the ship including the operation of the ship's machinery in accordance with the builder's requirements, using the ship's crew and shore personnel for these purposes with all costs and liabilities attributable to the builders.

The examination showed, in simple terms, there were design faults in the blades, and that steam supply nozzles which directed steam to the blades were both too numerous and of inadequate quality. The resulting vibration caused blades to crack or shear, and each one so affected that it damaged its immediate neighbours. Once identified, the problem was rapidly remedied and the rotors were re-installed by early March.

Questions about the *QE2* were raised in the House of Commons with MPs asking for an enquiry into all the troubles and delays. The Minister of Technology, Anthony Wedgwood Benn, responded that he did not believe a formal enquiry would serve any purpose at all. Reports of widespread pilfering during the building of the liner were raised in the House of Lords and the government spokesman, Lord Beswick, responded that that was a matter for the management.

Finally on 3rd March 1969, Cunard announced that the *QE2* would make her maiden voyage from Southampton to New York on 2nd May. In making the announcement Sir Basil said: "*Queen Elizabeth 2* will more than fulfil the promises made to her prospective passengers as to her performance. She will be the most superb example of the shipbuilder's craft the world has yet seen. The *QE2* is certainly a new place to visit between New York and London or Paris."

On Friday, 18th April, the *QE2* officially became a Cunard ship when she was finally handed over to her owners by a simple exchange of letters reserving all rights or claims on both sides. Unusually the handing-over took place in London at a private ceremony because Sir Basil was 'flying out of the country immediately afterwards'. With three triumphant blasts on her whistle, the Cunard flag was hauled up by coxswain Andrew McGregor at 13.15 hours as the Upper Clyde Shipbuilders' flag – which had been flown over the liner since her arrival in Southampton on 2nd January – was lowered. The flag-raising was at first scheduled for 12 noon, but because of a delay in the London ceremony the UCS flag remained in place on the *QE2* for another hour.

Everything depended on the *QE2* being a success and Cunard was determined to distance itself from all that had gone before in terms of marketing and the ships themselves. In order to sell the *QE2*'s modernity, a marketing and advertising campaign the like of which had never been seen before was devised that compared cruising on the *QE2* to space travel under the provocative slogan 'Ships Have Been Boring Long Enough'. Other shipping companies were horrified and thought Cunard was insulting rivals and the industry as a whole, but Cunard was also distancing itself from its own past and the new campaign underlined this radical change of direction.

The designation RMS (Royal Mail Ship) proudly assigned to every Cunarder since the *Britannia* in 1840 would not be applied to the *QE2* as it was seen as too old-fashioned and at odds with the new image being forged.

Cunard's Managing Director in 1969, John Whitworth, proclaimed: "This is *Queen Elizabeth Two* year – the most flexible and sophisticated ship ever to come into service. She represents a complete transformation in Cunard thought. We are not decanting old wines into new bottles, but ruthlessly transforming our image from the 'aspidistra and public bar' image which the dear old ships have carried since 1840. We are getting rid of the images of 'dukes and duchesses' on the other hand, and the 'knees Up, Mother Brown' type on the other. We want something more sophisticated but still retaining the Cunard tradition with the same high standards. The *Queen Elizabeth Two* is something new and exciting for the holiday market, not only of today but of tomorrow."

The fact the *Carmania* and the *Franconia* were "old wines into new bottles" did not sit well with the 'new' Cunard, but the *QE2* was something new and her 1960s interiors of Formica, plastic, vibrant colours and moulded wood appalled some of the Cunard regulars (the "dukes and duchesses") when they first boarded in 1969, but Cunard had changed by then.

155

The *QE2* had cost £29 million and in terms of stress, worry, anxiety, frustration, heartache, sleepless nights and anger for all those concerned, probably a great deal more. But was she worth it?

At the annual shareholders meeting in London in June 1969, where a profit of £3 million was announced, Sir Basil reported that the *QE2* was right on target, making the profits Cunard expected from her. He had confirmed the day before the meeting that passenger numbers were increasing and that the *QE2* had brought 1,868 passengers from America to France and the UK, earning a total gross revenue on this single one-way voyage of over $700,000.

The painful "do or die" initiative had, by now, to some extent resuscitated the patient and Cunard had a wonderful new flagship, but staffing numbers reflected the harsh reality of decisions taken. The three years leading to 1969 had seen sea staff reduced from 7,344 to 4,867 – one in three. And the number of shore staff had been cut by almost half, from 2,332 to 1,311. Remarkably these reductions had been achieved without a single strike.

It was at this time that Cunard brought in consultants McKinsey & Co to undertake a review of the company. The subsequent report was very critical of the prospects for the *QE2*. McKinsey recommended that serious consideration should be given to laying up the *QE2* as the vessel was forecast to lose £1.7 million in 1972 and approximately £4.4 million by 1975. Fortunately, Cunard paid not the slightest attention and continued to make profits from the *QE2*. At the

same time McKinsey had advised another client, Denmark's Maersk Line to not enter the container shipping business.

By the start of the 1970s it was clear to Cunard that it had to invest in purpose-built cruise ships as the heavily-rebuilt *Carmania* and the *Franconia* were not totally suitable for that role and were struggling against ships built purely for the cruise business, plus they were no match for the *QE2* and the facilities she offered.

Overseas National Airways had announced plans for a series of eight purpose-built small cruise ships and Cunard purchased a 50% share in this new undertaking. ONA soon ran into financial difficulties and Cunard took over the entire project and reduced the number of ships to two. The 14,000-ton mass-market cruise ships the *Cunard Adventurer* and the *Cunard Ambassador* entered service in 1971 and 1972 respectively and were placed on New York to Bermuda and San Juan to the Caribbean cruise service in the winter and Alaskan cruising from Vancouver in the winter. They were unusual little ships to say the least and even having James Gardner, who had produced the external styling of the *QE2*, assist with their external profiles, and his painting the funnels white and black just like the *QE2*, did little to enhance their overall appeal and the ships were not a success. The ships were simply too small and inefficient and had suffered from mechanical problems from the start. The *Cunard Ambassador* caught fire in September 1974 while on a re-positioning voyage without passengers and declared a total loss before being sold to Danish owners to become the sheep carrier the

*The **Cunard Adventurer** on sea trials. (Newall Dunn Collection)*

The **Cunard Ambassador** in the Caribbean. (Newall Dunn Collection)

Linda Clausen. The *Cunard Adventurer* was sold in 1976 to Norwegian Caribbean Cruises and re-entered service as their *Sunward II*.

A poignant meeting took place in Aruba in mid-March 1971 when the *QE2* met, for the first and only time, her namesake the *Queen Elizabeth*, by now renamed the *Seawise University* and about to undertake her voyage to the Far East and eventual destruction in Hong Kong. Both vessels exchanged farewells as the *QE2* sailed away, an act the then Managing Director Lord Mancroft described as "painfully moving".

About the same time, Sir Basil faced his own Battle of Trafalgar when he received a call from Nigel Broackes, Chairman of Trafalgar House Investments, and Victor Matthews requesting a meeting with them that afternoon. Trafalgar House was an aggressive young company specialising in property and construction and wanting to expand and diversify its business into other industries – the Cunard Head Office happened to be in their building. By 1970 Cunard's fortunes had taken a downturn, with losses of £2 million forecast by the accountants, and Sir Basil would later claim the Mckinsey Report "proved to be our Achilles heel".

On 29th June 1971, Cunard shares increased in value and the next day Trafalgar House announced a bid for Cunard, having valued the company at around £1.85 per share. Despite doubts being expressed that a company like Trafalgar House with over 260 subsidiary companies could manage Cunard appropriately and profitably, the bid, after being increased to £2.10 per

share, succeeded in July.

Nigel Broackes described the meeting with Sir Basil in a hotel room in Nice where he took Cunard: "He had a portfolio of threats combined with inducements for a better price; I added a few pennies per share, and we shook hands... I drove Basil on to La Violetta for lunch with Joyce (Mrs Broackes) and our three children, and then back to Nice airport where he collected his Hawker Siddeley HS 125 and flew back to London. I wrote the memorandum of our agreement in pencil on a notepad, we both initialled it, and Basil took it with him to get it typed. I was absolutely thrilled with the acquisition".

And so he should be for Trafalgar House had bought Cunard after an independent existence of 131 years, for just £27.3 million – less than the *QE2* had cost to build – and acquired assets of £39 million.

The last meeting of the Board of Cunard as an independent company took place on 25th August 1971. By then most of the senior management which had struggled and achieved so much the previous six years had left Cunard. Nigel Broackes, Victor Matthews, the new Chairman and Chief Executive of Cunard and Eric Parker, Financial Director of Trafalgar House, would now be responsible for the future of Cunard.

Sir Basil stayed on the Trafalgar House Board for another five months and then "...with sadness in my heart, I let myself quietly over the side and went ashore".

Chapter Nine

The jewel
in different
crowns

Trafalgar House was at pains to stress, right from the start of their ownership, that they were not intending to break Cunard up or seek to capitalise on any financial opportunities or tax implications that may have arisen thanks to the purchase. Trafalgar was in it for the long term but a great deal still depended on the *QE2*.

When she entered service, the *QE2* had been acclaimed as the great hope for the passenger shipping industry and, while much of her original design proved highly successful, certain aspects, most notably her galley arrangements, were not as effective as Cunard had hoped. This resulted in service levels in the *QE2*'s first few years in service being disappointing in terms of the number of complaints received from passengers. In North Atlantic service, complaints from First Class passengers centred on the menus, food and service (particularly the lack of special orders) while in cruise service, the cruising passenger capacity meant Cunard had to provide a two-sitting operation in the Britannia Restaurant in what was supposed to be a one-class experience. The *QE2* was not helped by the fact that her main rival, the *France*, was seen as offering a more superior product plus one-sitting dining while cruising.

The *QE2* was acknowledged by Trafalgar House as a potential money-maker and, given time, she would prove to be a winner. In the first six months of their ownership, they undertook a complete survey of the liner, looking at the services she could provide and how she could be reconfigured so that more money could be made from her.

Trafalgar House was determined to maximise Cunard profits and a wide-ranging refit was planned for the *QE2* at the end of 1972 which would produce dramatic changes on a young ship. Additional accommodation was added, public spaces were modified to allow for one-sitting dining, more lucrative shop space was added and a casino was built. This would be the first of several major refits for the *QE2* which would be 'updated' every few years to reflect the times and changes in society as well as ensure that the *QE2* continued to offer what passengers wanted - she was too important to Cunard and so her owners had to keep investing in her. So much so that over 15 times the amount she cost to build was ploughed into her over her career. Additional Penthouses were added in 1977 and in the mid-1980s, health facilities were dramatically expanded, the ship featured the first Computer Centre at sea, more shops were added, and additional restaurants were built to increase her luxury offerings as well as to satisfactorily offer single-seating dining for all passengers. This is something she would do several times for a few years and then revert to two-sittings in the largest of the restaurants.

Some things would remain the same and the magnificent wood-panelling found throughout her cabins and corridors on One, Two and Three Decks would creak and comfort occupants of those decks the same way in 2008 as they would in 1969. The *QE2* was the last Cunard ship to offer classes - 'First and Tourist' was replaced with 'First and Transatlantic' on crossings while she was one-class on cruises, but fixed classes were done away with completely in 1994. She was also the first to introduce the current Cunard system when dining - the

Atlantic in order to board the *QE2* and search for bombs that did not exist. President Anwar Sadat of Egypt revealed in a BBC Panorama interview that he had personally countermanded an order to torpedo the *QE2* after being woken in the early hours one morning by a telephone call. The *QE2* was on a private charter to Israel to mark the 25th Anniversary of the founding of that State in 1973, and the caller asked for confirmation of orders issued by President Gaddafi of Libya, with whom Egypt was sharing a political and

cabin booked determines where the passenger eats. Passengers would use US dollars on the Atlantic and pound Sterling on cruises from the UK and the cocktail menus, wine lists and tills would change over with no hassle in the days before fancy computer systems were put in charge.

The *QE2* was never far from the news in her first years. In January 1971 she received an SOS call from the French liner the Antilles and rescued 500 passengers from that ship which sank after grounding and catching fire. In May 1972, while she was mid-Atlantic, Cunard received a call saying there were bombs on board that would be detonated if a ransom was not paid. A bomb disposal team of four was parachuted into the

*The **QE2** in her short-lived post-Falklands livery (August 1982 – June 1983). (FotoFlite)*

military alliance under a temporary unification of the two countries. Sadat rescinded the orders immediately when he found out Gaddafi had ordered an Egyptian submarine to go and sink the *QE2* to avenge the Libyan airliner shot down by Israel over Sinai late in 1972, killing more than 100 passengers. In April 1974 a fractured pipe in a heat exchanger resulted in all of the *QE2*'s passengers having to be transferred to the *Sea Venture* which was drafted in by Cunard.

In early 1972, the *Carmania* and *Franconia* were withdrawn

*The **Cunard Countess** seen with her short-lived white and black funnel livery. (Cunard)*

after several issues including grounding and problems with obtaining safety certificates. Both ships were sent to be laid up in the River Fal in Cornwall where they would remain until finally sold in August 1973 for £1 million each. They would eventually become the Russian *Leonid Sobinov* and *Fedor Shalyapin* and enjoy long careers before being scrapped 1999 and 2004 respectively.

Trafalgar House set about acquiring or constructing hotels that operated under the Cunard name so from the early-1970s to the mid-1990s Cunard not only operated 'hotels at sea' they also took on an interesting collection of hotels in the UK and USA as well as three resorts in the Caribbean. The first one, The Hotel Bristol, on Berkeley Street in London opened in 1972. Then the Cunard International Hotel on Cromwell Road London was followed by the Cunard International in Hammersmith opened in June 1973. Outside London the company purchased and opened The Cunard Cambridgeshire Hotel and then in 1976 came the most significant purchase when the world-famous Ritz Hotel was bought for £2.75 million. By now Cunard had 1,342 hotel bedrooms in the UK, all but 100 in London and by the mid-1970s the company had purchased and was operating three resorts in the Caribbean: The Montego Beach Hotel in Jamaica, The Paradise Village and Beach Club in Barbados and Hotel La Toc and La Toc Suites in St Lucia. They had wanted to add The Savoy in London to the portfolio but never managed to purchase it.

The Hotel Bristol and the two Cunard International Hotels were sold by the mid-1980s but Cunard was still keen to add to its hotel portfolio so The Stafford and The Dukes, both in St James's, London, were acquired followed by The Hotel Atop The Bellevue in Philadelphia while Cunard took on the management of the infamous Watergate Hotel, overlooking the Potomac in Washington DC. By the mid 1990s all of the hotels had been sold.

Rumours throughout the summer of 1972 were rife that Cunard and P&O were to join forces in the US cruise trade. It was even suggested that there was to be a merger between the two companies and that the *Canberra* would enter the transatlantic market alongside the *QE2* with Cunard marketing the two ships for cruises on the east coast of the USA.

According to Chairman Victor Matthews the talks between the two companies were: "Only a straight honest endeavour to reduce our overheads in the States and help P&O with their marketing problems. Beyond that nothing is contemplated at the moment, but from a working relationship other things can develop".

Cunard produced a brochure marketing the *Canberra*'s 1973 inaugural cruise programme from New York after becoming the General Agents for P&O in the United States and press releases about the *Canberra* were issued on Cunard-headed paper. In the end the *Canberra*'s US programme was poorly booked and the fact that much of her accommodation did not have private facilities did not endear her to American passengers.

The dramatic and immediate withdrawal from service of the *France* in 1974, after the French government withdrew her subsidy, left the *QE2* alone on the Atlantic and made Cunard

*Her Serene Highness Princess Grace of Monaco names the **Cunard Princess** in an historic first for New York on 30th March 1977. Closer examination of the photograph reveals the ship's previous name, the **Cunard Conquest**, and how crudely it had been changed to the **Cunard Princess**! (Cunard)*

owner of the largest passenger ship in service.

By 1975 the *Cunard Adventurer* and *Cunard Ambassador* had become the inspiration for the following two Cunard cruise ships. The *Cunard Countess* and *Cunard Conquest* (with the name changed to the *Cunard Princess* in August 1976), improved, larger and more efficient versions of the earlier pair, were constructed in Denmark and then towed to Italy for fitting out. The ships proudly flew the flag for the downmarket side of Cunard and were cheaply-built, cabins had aluminium drawer units that would catch thousands of unsuspecting passenger legs over each ship's lifetime but they would prove very popular, and remained the favourite ships of several Cunard Captains who would go on to command the *QE2* and both would have long careers with the *Cunard Countess* being scrapped in 2014 after catching fire with the Cunard Princess still in service.

The *Cunard Countess* first appeared with a white and black funnel but this had been changed to red and black by the time she entered service. Janet Armstrong, wife of former American astronaut Neil Armstrong, made Cunard history when she became the first American to name a Cunard ship and that ceremony took place in San Juan.

The *Cunard Princess* would continue to make Cunard American history as her naming in New York was the first event of its kind in that city and the first of a Cunard ship actually in America itself despite being 63 hours late in arriving at the port after enduring a pounding storm on the Atlantic. Her Serene Highness Princess Grace of Monaco broke the bottle on her first try and the contents splattered all over her hat and coat. Later that day Princess Grace joined 400 other guests on an overnight cruise on the *Cunard Princess* and when asked why she came from Monaco for the naming replied: "because I was very flattered to be asked – wouldn't you do it, if you were asked to christen a lovely ship?"

A jubilant Cunard even went as far to claim that the *Cunard Princess* would be the last new cruise ship ever built! The cost of fuel had risen to unheard of levels and the supply of cruise berths had reached saturation point.

Answering the call of Mrs Thatcher

On 19th March 1982, the Argentinean army invaded the British colony of the Falkland Islands in the South Atlantic. Within days a task force had been despatched and several commercial vessels, including P&O's the *Canberra*, had been requisitioned and converted for war service. Despite constant rumours that the *QE2* would also be 'called up' Cunard rebutted any such talk and the ship continued as scheduled with an Atlantic crossing to New York, followed by a maiden call to Philadelphia on 25th April where she officiated at the opening of the year-long tricentennial celebrations of the founding of the city in 1682.

Requisitioning of Ships Order 1982 and you are accordingly required to place her at his disposal forthwith. The Master should report for directions on the employment of the vessel to Mr R. Brooks department of Trade Sea Transport Officer Southampton who will act as the principal link between the Master and all other civil and naval/military authorities until sailing."

Captain Hutcheson said that news of the requisitioning had come as a "total surprise" and he reported that after he had broadcast the news to the passengers, cheers broke out all over the ship. All future sailings of the *QE2* were

*The **QE2** departs Southampton for the Falklands on 12th May 1982. (Cunard)*

However, there was no doubting that the *QE2*'s speed, size and facilities made her ideal for trooping and on 3rd May 1982, as the *QE2* was steaming along the south coast of England bound for Southampton, the long-expected news that she had been requisitioned by the British government for use in the Falklands campaign was confirmed.

Cunard received the following instructions from the government: "Your vessel *Queen Elizabeth 2* is requisitioned by the Secretary of State for Trade under the

cancelled as Cunard did not know for how long its flagship would be requisitioned, but it was felt that the *QE2* would be back with them within two months.

The *QE2* officially came alongside her berth at midnight on 4th May and was immediately requisitioned for war service becoming a 'STUFT' (Ship Taken Up From Trade). Over the next eight days the most amazing transformation would take place. The *QE2*'s aft decks became helicopter landing platforms after extensive alterations were undertaken including slicing away large parts of the superstructure aft. Forward, the deck was extended towards the bow right over the capstans so that a third heli-pad could be built on the foredeck. These new landing pads were capable of handling the 18,626 pounds of a Sea King helicopter plus whatever cargo it may have had to carry.

The *QE2* could not carry fuel for much more than a one-way trip so provisions had to be made for refuelling at sea. Pipes were laid from the starboard midships baggage area on Two Deck to the huge tanks below. Most of the pictures and valuable furniture were removed from the ship and stored in Pickfords warehouses ashore. Six pianos (two would remain on board for entertaining), casino equipment, plants and high-cost food items were removed and stored ashore. The *QE2*'s own china, glassware and silverware was collected, packed and stored. To reduce the natural magnetic field of the liner and help protect her from influencing magnetic mines, a degaussing cable was fitted inside the ship.

Captain Peter Jackson was advised on 6th May that he would be in command and 650 of the *QE2*'s own crew volunteered to remain with the ship throughout her war service.

On 12th May the formal embarkation of the 3,000 troops that made up 5 Infantry Brigade began. The Brigade comprised the Scots Guards, the Welsh Guards and the Ghurkha Rifles. While final preparations were being made a problem developed in the *QE2*'s engine room. One of her boilers had been shut down for maintenance and now a second boiler had developed a massive leak in its supply of distilled water which could not be traced. With the world watching it was vital that the *QE2* sail on time, so at 16.00 hours the underpowered ship headed down-river at seven knots to an anchor position three miles off the Nab where she would remain overnight. Engineers worked through the night to discover the cause of the leak which they eventually did – a valve had simply been left open. At 09.35 hours the *QE2* was underway.

The *QE2* arrived in Freetown on 18th May where she took on 1,867 tons of fuel as well as more water in an operation that was completed three hours earlier than expected and she was underway again by 23.00 hours.

The weather resulted in the *QE2* having to stay 50

miles off Ascension when she arrived on 20th May and after her departure from there strict blackout regulations were enforced on board. Black plastic sheeting was taped over the 500-plus windows and 1,350-plus portholes. A helicopter flew around the *QE2* to ensure the ship was indeed blacked-out.

Captain Jackson noted that it was "… a frightening sight, to see the ship belting along at 27 knots on a black night and without a light showing".

On 22nd May the *QE2* sailed in company with another Cunarder, the container ship *Atlantic Causeway*, with both ships still delivering and receiving stores from Ascension via helicopter. That night the *QE2* left Ascension behind and, in addition to being blacked-out, all navigation lights and radar was switched off – the *QE2* became electronically silent. She sped through the dark, through an ice field, without radar; life on the Bridge went back fifty years.

During the night of 26th and 27th May the radar was switched on every 30 minutes and at one time more than 100 icebergs could be seen on the screen. Captain Jackson would later write that "never have I known such a harrowing experience".

The next day the *QE2* met with *HMS Antrim* and the transfer of Major General Moore, Brigadier Wilson and other personnel commenced. Sea conditions were rough which made the transfer between ships extremely difficult. The *QE2* was sailing again by early afternoon and hundreds of icebergs were to be spotted as the ship sailed in and out of patchy fog.

Just after 17.00 hours South Georgia was visible on the radar and the *QE2* anchored in Cumberland Bay East two hours later. A rust-streaked the *Canberra* was waiting for the *QE2*'s arrival and, the immediate plan was to transfer survivors from *HMS Ardent* from the P&O flagship to the Cunard flagship.

The trawler *Cordella* came alongside the *QE2* at 21.20 hours and the first batch of troops were on their way to the *Canberra* a little under two hours later. Just before midnight *HMS Leeds Castle*, the *Cordella* and the tug *Typhoon* were alongside the *QE2* to transfer yet more troops for the last time until morning when the operation would start again.

From 06.00 hours on 28th May the transfer from the

QE2 would start in earnest with helicopters, the *QE2*'s own lifeboats and the trawlers the *Cordella*, *Junella*, *Northella*, *Farnella* and the *Pict* carrying troops and stores to the waiting the *Canberra* and *Norland*, the latter bringing to the *QE2* survivors from *HMS Antelope*. The *Canberra* sailed at 22.30 hours as snow fell covering the assembled ships.

The next day saw another Cunard cargo ship, the *Saxonia*, and the Royal Fleet auxiliary the *Stromness* rendezvous with the *QE2* and the auxiliary vessel brought survivors from *HMS Coventry*.

Captain Jackson was concerned about the deteriorating weather, and icebergs had drifted in and out of the entrance to Cumberland Bay during the *QE2*'s stay there. The *Junella* took the last group of troops from the *QE2* at just after 16.00 hours and as the weather continued to decline, the *QE2* left South Georgia just after 17.00 hours.

On 3rd June, after the *QE2* had faced another ice field and been refuelled at sea in a Force 7 which had to be suspended as the swell had made the pipeline chaff, Captain Jackson received orders to proceed back to Southampton. The *QE2*'s work in the campaign was done and it remained for her to now bring home 640 survivors.

The *QE2* neared Ascension once again on 4th June in order to transfer some of the most seriously wounded to *HMS Dumbarton Castle*.

On 11th June the *QE2* was home. Admiral John Fieldhouse and Cunard Chairman Lord Matthews flew out to join the ship as she made her way to Southampton. The Queen Mother wished to greet the *QE2*, and as the ship passed the Needles Lighthouse at 09.00 hours the Royal Yacht *Britannia* came abeam with The Queen Mother standing on the aft deck. The *QE2*'s crew and warship survivors gave three cheers and the liner blew her whistle in salute. As the *QE2* made her way to her berth she was escorted by a flotilla of small aircraft and thousands cheered and waved from the shore as she berthed.

The *QE2* had sailed the 6,796 mile distance from South Georgia to Southampton in 12 days, 12 hours and 18 minutes at an average speed of 23.23 knots. She had joined the ranks of Cunarders before her who had answered their country's call and served with honour.

While this book has not concerned itself with the cargo

*The Royal Yacht **Britannia**, with HM Queen Elizabeth the Queen Mother on board, welcomes the **QE2** back to Southampton on 11th June 1982. (Cunard)*

operations of ships of Cunard and its associated companies it must be noted that Cunard container ship the *Atlantic Conveyor* was hit by an Exocet missile on 25th May and sunk with the loss of 12 lives, six Cunard men, including her Captain, and six servicemen.

It would take nine weeks to restore the *QE2* and when she re-appeared in August 1982 she had been given a light grey hull which would prove extremely difficult to maintain so she reverted to the traditional black in June 1983.

In October 1982, the *Cunard Countess* was chartered for six months by the British Ministry of Defence to support troop movements between Ascension Island and the Falkland Islands while Port Stanley Airport was being reinstated. A helicopter pad was constructed at her stern and families and friends of British personnel lost in the conflict were also carried on one round voyage, to enable commemorations both at sea and ashore.

Cunard won a two-year contract from the British government in 1983 to carry workers and supplies for a new airport in the Falkland Islands. The Danish passenger-car ferry the *England* was acquired to undertake the service from Cape Town to the Falklands. In 1985, once the airport had been built the *England* was laid up while Cunard considered options for the ship which included rebuilding it into a luxury *Sagafjord/Vistafjord* style ship for Cunard use or conversion to cruise ship for selling on. None of these plans came to fruition and the *England* left Cunard in December 1986.

In 1983 Trafalgar House attempted a hostile takeover of P&O, another large passenger and cargo shipping line, which also had, like Trafalgar, various divisions and interests in similar industries. P&O objected and forced the issue to the British Monopolies and Mergers Commission. In their filing, P&O was critical of Trafalgar's management of Cunard and their failure to correct the *QE2*'s mechanical problems over the years. In 1984, the Commission ruled in favour of the merger, but Trafalgar had lost the wind in its sails and decided against proceeding. If P&O had fallen then it would have given Trafalgar several prestigious cruise lines and ships including P&O Cruises, Princess Cruises, Swan Hellenic, British India Steam Navigation and P&O Cruises in Australia. With its high profile, thanks to the 'Loveboat' television programme and the new *Royal Princess* which was under construction at the time, Princess Cruises would have given Trafalgar a second cruise line with a global image and reputation to match that of Cunard and it begs the question just what would have happened with Cunard if a deal had gone through.

While Trafalgar House insisted the various divisions of P&O Cruises would have remained the same, plans drawn up included the closing down of P&O Cruises, Swan Hellenic and British India with the two main ships, the *Canberra* and the *Oriana*, also being sold. The *Sea Princess* would have transferred to Cunard and received a traditional name (perhaps the *Caronia?*) and the *Cunard Countess* and *Cunard Princess* would have integrated into Princess Cruises with its ships concentrating on the American market while the Cunard fleet would be European based with the *QE2* being the link between.

On 12th May 1983, Trafalgar House announced that they had entered into an agreement with Norwegian American Cruises (NAC) to acquire the *Sagafjord* and *Vistafjord* together with the goodwill of that company for $73 million cash payable on delivery of the ships in October that year. Trafalgar House was quick to point out that this was further evidence of their confidence in Cunard and proved wrong those who claimed it would hinder the progress of Cunard when they took it over in 1971.

The *Sagafjord* had been built in France and had entered service in 1965 while the *Vistafjord*, which entered service in 1973 and often mistakenly said to be the last passenger ship to be built on the Tyne, came from the same yard that had produced the legends the *Mauretania* and the *Carpathia* so perhaps could claim to have some Cunard pedigree within her already! Although smaller than the *QE2* these two ships were a perfect match for the Cunard flagship and their liner / cruise ship design would mean they could deputise on Atlantic service

for the *QE2* which they would do several times when the *QE2* could not undertake her Atlantic schedule particularly during the last months of 1986 when the *Sagafjord* took over the *QE2*'s Atlantic programmes when the latter was being re-engined.

Cunard was so anxious to keep NAC's loyal German following for the Vistafjord and the *Sagafjord*'s mainly American passengers that, despite post-purchase rumours that the ships would be given traditional Cunard names and even be lengthened, Cunard changes were limited. A new brand, Cunard-NAC, was established and, after delivery to Cunard in October 1983, each ship was given Cunard funnel colours, re-flagged from Norway to Nassau (while still retaining their Norwegian officers), refurbished to a higher standard, changing some existing cabin configurations due to their increasing passenger numbers, and new balcony suites were added.

The cruising patterns of the two ships would remain more or less the same with each remaining either side of the Atlantic. The *Sagafjord* probably always offered the best Alaskan cruises in terms of duration and port content (but initially putting her in the same Alaska brochures as the *Cunard Princess* did not continue for long) while the *Vistafjord* remained in Northern Europe and the Mediterranean. The purchase of NAC allowed Cunard to establish a footing in the German market but huge efforts were made to increase the number of British passengers travelling on the *Vistafjord*.

From 1983 Cunard began chartering British Airways Concorde as part of the *QE2*'s Atlantic package for the first time and on a regular basis for the next 20 years. There were 37 charters in its first year and 137 in 1984. The *QE2* and Concorde would enjoy a close relationship - two rivals in a partnership of equals that should not have worked but it became one of the most successful travel combinations ever with Cunard buying more Concorde seats at one time than any other!

At the same time Cunard was quick to meet changing demands and lifestyles of its passengers with the introduction of the first health spa at sea on the *QE2* in 1982. The Golden Door Spa was a success and was installed on the *Sagafjord* and the *Vistafjord*. The *QE2* received the first Computer Learning Centre at sea in 1983 and one appeared shortly afterwards on the *Vistafjord*.

The Norwegian Sea Goddess Cruises was founded in the early 1980s as an ultra-deluxe cruise, all-inclusive cruise line. Its initial plan was to operate eight yacht-like ships but in the end only two, the *Sea Goddess I* in 1984 and the *Sea Goddess II* in 1985, entered service. These two ships carried 116 passengers looked after by 95 crew, quickly established themselves as the most highly-rated cruise ships afloat and were seen as the closest thing to owning your own yacht without actually owning one. The company encountered financial difficulties and, like the whole cruise industry at this time, was greatly affected by events in the Mediterranean such as the hijacking of the cruise ship the *Achille Lauro* in October 1985, and the American bombing of Libya in April 1986. The 'Goddesses' were about to be repossessed by their Finnish builders when Cunard stepped in and arranged a 12-year charter that would see them integrated into its fleet under the name Cunard - Sea Goddess Cruises. Another triumph of creativity but, while the ship names themselves were unimaginative, these ships were unlike anything else Cunard had ever owned or anything else afloat at that time, perhaps giving them traditional Cunard names would not have been appropriate while names such as the *Laconia* and the *Caronia* would have been very apt for the *Sagafjord* and the *Vistafjord*.

Cunard now had seven ships but overall the fleet was inconsistent when it came to facilities and livery. The 'Sea Goddesses' did not display Cunard funnel colours, the *QE2* had a black hull and the hull colours of the *Sagafjord* and the *Vistafjord* were different. However the additions to the fleet

flourished under Cunard with the ships vying for the highest accolades and ratings in the industry.

Throughout her career, the *QE2* had suffered several breakdowns causing embarrassing headlines around the world and, in later years, spare parts had to be specially made by hand. The *QE2*'s engines were more or less the same type as those that had powered the *Mauretania* and the *Lusitania* almost 80 years earlier and were too inefficient for a 1980s superliner. But what to do? Cunard had to decide whether to invest in a brand-new ship or stand by its flagship. In the event Cunard came to a momentous decision: she would be re-engined. It would be the biggest ship re-engining ever undertaken anywhere and was equivalent to a heart transplant for a human.

Ralph Bahna, Cunard's Chief Executive Officer, said: "The most cost-effective way of providing a superliner for tomorrow is to enhance the world's most popular existing vessel".

Up until this point, the *QE2* had already undergone a number of refurbishments and refits, keeping her passenger facilities and services up to date in comparison with newer purpose-built cruise tonnage. Yet, perhaps the emphasis was too much on passenger facilities and too little on the machinery. The economical benefits of re-placing the engine plant on the

*The **QE2** nearing the end of the biggest re-engining project ever undertaken. (Cunard)*

*With her new funnel the **QE2** assumed a more powerful and robust look after her re-engining. (Cunard)*

QE2 were even greater than originally thought, even considering the $53 million budget for the conversion, the five- to eight-month out-of-service time and the 12- to 14-month lead time for the implementation. Re-engining a ship whose hull had another 20 years and whose reputation was priceless would increase profit, life cycle cash flow, reliability, maintain a prestigious image and was cheaper than building a new ship.

On 29th July 1983 a major meeting was held in Southampton to begin to examine the feasibility of increased fuel efficiency with regard to the *QE2*'s propulsion plant. After having spent over two years evaluating all the options, including more than 15 different alternatives from various shipbuilders and seven engine makers, Cunard announced on 25th October 1985 that it had signed an £80 million contract to re-engine the *QE2* with the Lloyd Werft Shipyard in Bremerhaven, West Germany.

Atlantic and maritime history was made on 20th October 1986 when the *QE2* left New York for the last time as a steamship, and undertook her and Cunard's last crossing of the Atlantic under steam, ending a 146-year tradition. The *QE2*'s steam turbines had taken her a total of 2,622,858 miles. Five

days later she arrived at Southampton for the last time as a steamship and her arrival in Germany two days later began the race against time to complete the biggest, most complicated and most epic conversion in civil merchant shipping history.

After 179 days and 1.7 million man hours, Lloyd Werft handed back to Cunard its revitalised flagship after what still remains today the biggest merchant ship conversion ever undertaken.

During the voyage to Southampton she achieved a remarkable 33.8 knots and on 29th April 1987 Her Royal Highness The Princess of Wales and 500 underprivileged children took part in the "biggest children's party afloat!" Her first crossing and indeed her first months after the re-engining were not without problems but the investment proved itself to be a worthy one indeed and the *QE2*'s glory years were about to begin.

Cunard had wanted to sell the *Cunard Countess* and the *Cunard Princess* in 1988, because their hopes of reflagging them in the US failed, in order to become a five-star line but by 1989 operating four-star ships in emerging markets was more desirable. The *Cunard Princess* was sent to Europe in 1989 and

*The Grand Lounge on the **QE2** in April 1987. (Cunard)*

*The Queen's Room on the **QE2** in April 1987. (Cunard)*

soon became the most popular fly-cruise Mediterranean ship in the British cruise market until she left the fleet in 1995.

The importance of Cunard's 150th anniversary was not lost on Trafalgar House who saw it as a key opportunity to raise its own profile, so the Trafalgar House logo appeared on Cunard collateral produced in 1990 and even the logo was placed on the superstructure of the *QE2* and other ships in the fleet.

The importance of such a celebration was not lost on Cunard itself as the company had been unable to celebrate

several previous 4th July key milestones. The First World War was underway when Cunard reached 75 in 1915, and the *Lusitania* had recently been torpedoed and lost. The Second World War meant no celebrations in 1940 when, during its 100th anniversary, Cunard should have been celebrating the introduction of the *Queen Elizabeth*, the largest (and probably the fastest) passenger ship in the world. And even though the keel had just been laid for what would become the *QE2* in 1965, celebrating the company's 125th anniversary was

*The re-engined **QE2** passes the Needles in the English Channel in 1987. (FotoFlite)*

probably far from the minds of Sir John Brocklebank and Sir Basil Smallpeice who were then struggling to keep the Cunard ship afloat.

Sadly, on the 150th anniversary of the sailing of Cunard's first ship the *Britannia* from Liverpool to New York, 4th July 1990, the *QE2* was not on the Atlantic but returning from her six-month Japanese charter. The following weeks saw Cunard and its flagship in the media spotlight once again as 150th anniversary celebrations took place. On 17th July, the *QE2* left New York headed for Southampton. She sailed her fastest ever eastbound crossing and arrived in Southampton in four days, six hours and 57 minutes, making an average of 30.16 knots. That afternoon, 22nd July, the *QE2* left her homeport for a five-day cruise to Cobh, Liverpool, Greenock and Cherbourg; it was perhaps the most emotional cruise undertaken by the ship at that point.

The *QE2* was greeted by 60,000 people and units of the Irish Navy on her maiden arrival at Cobh, in the Irish Republic, the next day. Her arrival also coincided with the opening of the new cargo terminal at Ringaskiddy (where she berthed) and the Irish Taoiseach, Charles Haughey, was entertained to lunch to mark the event.

An estimated one million spectators greeted her maiden arrival in Liverpool on 24th July. As she made her stately progress up the River Mersey she became the first Queen liner to visit what had been Cunard's home from 1839 to 1967 and the first Cunard passenger ship to do so for over 25 years. The *QE2* anchored opposite the Cunard Building on the Pierhead and ten thousand red and blue balloons were released from the ship. Captain Woodall would have to stay on board his ship for the day as the prevailing weather meant the anchor started to drag, so Staff Captain Ron Bolton represented him at the ceremonies ashore which included the unveiling of a bust of Sir Samuel Cunard and a service at St Nicholas's Church. The *QE2* sailed that night after a magnificent firework display.

The next day saw the *QE2* make an emotional visit to the Clyde for the first time since 1968. She berthed at Greenock - the furthest up the river she could travel. She was greeted by bagpipes, a group of pensioners from John Brown's was hosted on board for lunch and she was escorted by a flotilla of hundreds of vessels of all types when she sailed.

The *QE2* made a quick call at Cherbourg on 26th July. The weather throughout the cruise had been glorious sunshine but this spell broke just before the highlight of the cruise. At this time Captain Woodall also handed over command to Captain Ron Warwick and history was made when Captain Warwick assumed command of the same ship as his father – Captain Bil

Warwick, the *QE2*'s first master. The change in command was necessary, for Captain Woodall would be required to entertain two VIPs the next day.

On 27th July 1990, the *QE2* arrived and anchored in her allocated position at Spithead. Shortly afterwards she was joined by Cunarders the *Vistafjord* and the *Atlantic Conveyor* and dozens of private yachts, motor boats and excursion vessels, all

*The Royal Yacht **Britannia**, with HM The Queen and HRH The Duke of Edinburgh on board, sails past the **QE2** on 27th July 1990 to celebrate Cunard's 150th anniversary. (Cunard)*

*HM The Queen unveiling a plaque in the Grand Lounge of the **QE2** to mark her visit on 27th July 1990. (Cunard)*

keen to take part in the planned Royal review of Cunard, and Royal Navy ships by The Queen and The Duke of Edinburgh on board the Royal Yacht *Britannia*. The Royal Yacht left Portsmouth, led by the Trinity House vessel the *Patricia* and followed by HMS *Broadsword*, at 09.25 hours and passed the portsides of the anchored Cunarders. A Concorde, a 767 and 747 then made a flypast in salute before the *Britannia* anchored and a second flypast, consisting of a Sea King, Lynx and

*The **QE2** sailing into Cobh for the first time on 23rd July 1990. (Cunard)*

Dauphin helicopters and a Harrier jump jet, took place. The Queen and Duke of Edinburgh then transferred to the *QE2* by Royal Barge and prior to lunch attended receptions in the Queens Room and Grand Lounge. The *QE2* left her anchorage at 13.45 hours and proceeded to her berth in Southampton. This was the first time The Queen had sailed on the ship she had launched 23 years earlier, and it was the first time a Reigning Monarch had sailed on another ship with commercial passengers. The *QE2* berthed ahead of the *Vistafjord* and later that evening both ships were serenaded with a firework finale.

As the 1990 recession progressed, Trafalgar House continued to invest heavily, with some £750 million having been invested in commercial property alone between 1988 and the first half of 1990. Moreover, interest was not being charged to the profit and loss account but capitalised and substantial borrowings were being carried off the balance sheet. In 1991 The Financial Reporting Review Panel threatened to apply for a court order that would require Trafalgar to charge a £142.5 million reduction in asset values through the profit and loss account rather than through reserves, which eventually led to directors restating their 1992 accounts from a £112.5 million profit to a £30 million loss!

The *Cunard Princess* would see war action when she was chartered to the United States Armed Forces Recreation Center who would use the ship as a recreational facility for troops involved in the Gulf conflict. The *Cunard Princess* arrived in Bahrain on 24th December 1990. Initially it was planned to use her on three-day cruises around the Persian Gulf but instead she remained permanently moored in Bahrain until

September 1991. Given Cunard's heroic roles in various conflicts and wars over the decades it seemed appropriate to have a ship in military service during its 150th anniversary.

The *QE2* had been scheduled to make a Bermuda cruise in early August 1992 but the cruise had to be cancelled when Cunard did not receive from the Bermudian authorities the necessary licences for the *QE2* to visit. Instead the *QE2* was rescheduled to undertake a short cruise from New York to Newfoundland, Nova Scotia and Martha's Vineyard. So on 3rd August, the *QE2* left New York with 1,824 passengers and 1,003 crew. Having spent the day of 7th August off the north east tip of the island of Martha's Vineyard, the *QE2* weighed anchor just after 20.30 hours and headed south-west.

At 21.58 hours the *QE2* had reached a point approximately 3.5 miles SSW of Cuttyhunk Island and was about to pass over the southern tip of the shoaling seabed as she prepared to skirt the main areas of the reefs, when she experienced two periods of heavy vibration in quick succession. The engines began to slow and the *QE2* began to lose speed. Captain Woodall contacted the Staff Chief Engineer in the Engine Control Room who reported that the propeller shafts were still turning at 144 rpm and that he was instructing his staff to check for possible damage. Thus mechanical breakdown was quickly ruled out and the First Officer confirmed that the *QE2* had not been involved in a collision with another vessel. The *QE2* had struck an underwater object and it was decided that the passengers would have to be disembarked.

The *QE2* then proceeded, accompanied by a Coast Guard cutter and two tugs, to Boston. It was only after the *QE2* had been placed in the dry dock that the true extent of the damage to the underwater hull became known. In all the damage covered a width of 80 feet over the keel and either side of it and extended over a length of 400 feet aft from the bulbous bow. The keel was covered in indents – some up to 240 feet in length and 14 inches deep – gouges and fractures, some of the latter being from 10 to 70 feet long and a 32 foot length and plates were buckled in place. In total 20 double-bottom tanks had sustained damaged to some extent and the port bilge keel had been severely damaged.

It soon became clear that full repairs would not be able to be carried out in as the yard did not have the staff, the resources or the correct grade of steel to complete the job. After initial repairs the *QE2* proceeded to Hamburg. The shipyard of Blohm & Voss was successful in their bid and the *QE2* left Boston on 1st September and headed for Germany. On arrival in Hamburg the liner was lifted in a floating dock and full repairs were undertaken. In all, nine Atlantic crossings and two cruises were cancelled while the *QE2* was undergoing repairs. There was intense speculation in the press that the repairs, lost revenue and compensation payments would cost Cunard up to £50 million but the company never revealed the actual cost. The *QE2*'s return to Southampton on 3rd October was a jubilant occasion with three fireboats escorting her up the Solent and the vessel returned to service the next day.

Investigations into the cause of the grounding were undertaken by both the National Transportation Safety Board (USA) and the UK Marine Accident Investigation Branch (MAIB). The actual grounding site on Sow and Pig Reef was located and surveyed. Both investigations came to similar conclusions. There could be no doubt that the cause of the grounding was that the charts for the area were wrong and there was significantly less water than charted. In fact it was discovered that the area was last surveyed on 1939 by dropping

*Above right: Welcomed by one million the **QE2** in Liverpool for the first time on 24th July 1990. (Cunard)*

*Right: The **Vistafjord** in Corfu shortly after Cunard had purchased the ship. (Mark Cornford)*

*Below: The **Sagafjord** seen from her sister the **Vistafjord** in the Caribbean in 1990. A magnificent sight as both ships passed at speed. (Mark Cornford)*

a line at regular intervals; this method, of course, can miss significant peaks! It was noted that prior to the grounding, the *QE2* had passed over an area with a 40-foot sounding without mishap or any indication of shallow water effect. The *QE2* grounded twice in quick succession; at the time of the initial grounding the depth of water was 35.0 feet while the depth of water at the second grounding was 34.2 feet. It assumed that the stationary forward and after draughts of the vessel were 32.3 feet and 31.3 feet respectively. On the assumption that no change in draught was caused by the effect of the prevailing weather conditions, it was apparent that the effect of 'squat' on the vessel caused the bow to sink by at least 2.7 feet. 'Squat' is a phenomenon where ships travelling at speed in shallow water settle lower in the water than they would normally – but the degree to which they do so is not easy to calculate. The extent of the damage suggested that, on grounding, the vessel was trimmed by the head. The Master had expected squat of 1 to 1½ feet, with change of trim by the stern. It was clear that Captain Woodall had underestimated the magnitude of 'squat' effect upon his vessel in the prevailing circumstances – a factor magnified with the increase of speed to 25 knots.

And what of the rocks? Divers found signs of contact with traces of the *QE2*'s red anti-fouling paint and shavings of steel were found on several rocks which had either been moved boldly horizontally, compressed into the seafloor or partially pulled out of the seabed by almost a foot. It was generally agreed that if a lesser vessel had sustained the damage the *QE2* had, then it would probably have been lost.

Cunard had tried to pursue several expansion projects, whether through acquisitions or newbuilds, as discussed in the next chapter, but to expand it required capital from Trafalgar House and its plans were often thwarted because it had to compete for cash with the other numerous divisions under the Trafalgar umbrella.

The *QE2* swallowed investment, time and focus which was totally necessary given the uniqueness of the ship, the role she played, her place on the world stage and her impact on the profits of the company. She perhaps did dominate too much, which probably diverted the attention of management and prevented it from being too brave. The *QE2* had to be a success. But even when plans did become reality Cunard sometimes never really helped itself. The company was self-restrained constantly with a revolving door when it came to management. Running Cunard was perhaps seen as the most sought-after job in the cruise industry, but it was, in truth, a poisoned chalice with the typical tenure of a President or Managing Director being two years – or less! Each new incumbent would come to Cunard with new ideas and rebrand this and that but were generally half-way through their grand scheme when they were replaced and then a new direction

*The **Vistafjord** seen after her refit in 1992. (FotoFlite)*

would replace the one that was either just starting to bear fruit or hadn't quite bedded-in enough to bear fruit.

In the background, Trafalgar House woes continued and massive provisions led to a £347 million loss in 1993 and Trafalgar itself became a takeover target. Its Far East associates, Jardine Matheson, through its property subsidiary Hong Kong Land, invested in Trafalgar House and took 15% of the company and later increased its share to 25%. Jardines was controlled by the Keswick family, a dynasty of Scottish origin, and Simon Keswick took the chair at Trafalgar House in 1994 and the Trafalgar stalwarts, Sir Nigel Broackes and Sir Eric Parker, who had seen themselves as the saviours of Cunard and the *QE2* when they acquired the company in 1971, were no longer responsible for it. In truth, by this time the relationship between both men was strained and Trafalgar House had many troubles to contend with.

A change in leadership and a change in direction for Cunard occurred in 1993 when John Olsen was brought in as Chairman to give the company a new focus and a new sense of direction. His tenure at Cunard saw several major investments being made, new marketing initiatives being introduced, the upgrading of the fleet, a re-focus on Cunard's heritage which is something the company had been reluctant to do, and several strategic marketing moves being made – all to establish Cunard in new and important markets. John Olsen managed to get funds from Trafalgar House but at the end of the day a lot of the deals made were perhaps not properly thought through.

A deal was struck with the German company Peter Deilmann for Cunard to market and sell its five riverboats - the *Mozart*, the *Dresden*, the *Danube Princess*, the *Prussian Princess* and the *Princesse de Provance* – in the UK and US markets under the umbrella Cunard EuropAmerica River Cruises, but after two unsuccessful years, 1994 and 1995, the deal was scrapped.

The European shipping company Effjohn International had established Crown Cruise Line in the late 1980s and constructed three ships for its new venture: the one-off *Crown Monarch* in 1990 and the two sisters, the *Crown Jewel* in 1992 and the *Crown Dynasty* in 1993, which were the real gems of Effjohn. The new cruise line with its new tonnage struggled to get itself established in the very competitive cruise market and it had limited presence and marketing ability. At this time Cunard's intention was to become the industry's largest luxury cruise line and to dispose of the *Cunard Countess* and the *Cunard Princess*. However the possible earlier involvement with the *Monterey* (covered in the next chapter) had given the company confidence in mass-market cruises so Trafalgar House had a

Cunard Crown Dynasty *seen in the Panama Canal. (Newall Dunn Collection)*

change of heart and looked to expand the lower-priced fleet, but the parent company earnings were impacted by the severe recession in Britain so was unable to provide Cunard with the capital needed to construct new ships for this market. Perhaps spotting an opportunity that would resolve the issues it had with its Crown Cruise Line, and knowing Cunard was interested in new ships, Effjohn approached. Cunard, needing to expand but without the money to do so and Effjohn, with a brand new fleet but no presence, formed the perfect match. On 27th January 1993 Cunard Crown, a 10-year joint venture premium cruise line, was announced and the merging of the two fleets began. The three Crown ships, given Cunard's funnel colours, would be joined by the refurbished *Cunard Countess* and the *Cunard Princess* – the latter two having their names printed in large script in the centre of their hulls to match the Crown ships. The crewing of each ship would remain as before and Crown Cruise Line's marketing, sales and reservations functions transferred from Florida to Cunard's New York base. Since the ownership of the Crown ships did not pass to Cunard these ships have not been included in the Fleet List at Appendix One

All three Crown ships were marketed with Cunard affixed to their names but they were never actually renamed. The *Cunard Crown Jewel* operated in the Caribbean, the *Cunard Crown Dynasty* in the Panama Canal and Alaska and, in a break for Cunard, the *Cunard Crown Monarch* was sent off to establish a presence year-round in Australia. She arrived in Sydney for the first time in November 1993 and began operating cruises to the South Pacific.

Cunard now had a fleet featuring 7,000 berths placing it in fifth position in the cruise market.

The *Crown Dynasty* was still at the shipyard when the Cunard

*The **Cunard Countess** in San Juan in November 1995 displaying her amended Cunard livery featuring the relocated Cunard name, Cunard lion rampant and 'speedstripe'. (Mark Cornford)*

Crown deal was struck so responsibility for her introduction fell to Cunard and she would be the first new ship the company had introduced since the *Cunard Princess* in 1977. The *Crown Dynasty* left her Spanish shipyard and called for promotional visits at Southampton on 2nd July 1993 before arriving in Liverpool and berthing alongside the Pier Head on 4th July – exactly 153 years since the *Britannia* left Liverpool and headed for Boston. When the *Crown Dynasty* left Liverpool that night, without any passengers, and headed for New York it marked the first time since 30th January 1968 that a Cunard ship, the *Franconia*, left Liverpool for New York, via Bermuda. Cunard had selected former First Lady Betty Ford to christen the ship in New York – just as Princess Grace of Monaco named the *Cunard Princess* in the city.

The Crown ships looked very smart in their Cunard colours but a lick of paint could not hide the flaws in the deal Cunard had struck with Effjohn. In October 1994 Cunard had the rug pulled from under its feet when the *Crown Monarch* was sold by Effjohn to new Far East owners just as she was becoming a success in a market that would become one of the most successful in the cruise industry. And then the *Crown Jewel* was sold to Star Cruises in 1995. Losing two ships within a few years of establishing Cunard Crown showed just how the deal

with Effjohn had not been thought out, as it undermined the huge amount of time, effort and money Cunard had put in to establish the brand, its ships and its foothold in the Australian market.

Just as airlines and hotels rewarded their frequent travellers and guests Cunard launched Cruise Miles in 1994 where passengers could earn cruise miles when sailing on any Cunard ship with the quantity earned depending on ship, cruise length and accommodation booked and any accumulated Cruise Miles were redeemable for cabin upgrades or future cruises. It took Cunard a long time to extricate itself from this programme when it was withdrawn in 1996.

The huge Norwegian Kloster Group was in serious financial difficulties and decided to dissolve its up-market Royal Viking Line. One ship, the *Royal Viking Queen*, was transferred to Kloster's Royal Cruise Line but Cunard finally triumphed with an acquisition when, on 30th June 1994 at 13.05 hours in London, it took the Royal Viking brand and its flagship, the *Royal Viking Sun*, in a deal with $170 million. Cunard had first approached Kloster in 1991 to purchase the ship. Royal Viking was a great addition to Cunard given its reputation, its loyal passenger base and the fact that the *Royal Viking Sun* had entered service in December 1988 and was rated as the number one ship in the world every year since. It also eliminated a major competitor and the infusion of new tonnage had the desired effect on re-vitalising Cunard but once again the company showed lack of creativity and bravery when they created the Cunard Royal Viking brand and placed its 'new' ship under that umbrella together with the ageing *Sagafjord* and the *Vistafjord* and the 'Sea Goddess' yachts. True, the highest-rated passenger ships in the world were together under one brand, but the differences in the ships themselves could not have been more obvious.

The creation of Cunard Royal Viking was just one aspect of the entire re-branding of the fleet. Several sub-brands would be formed under the so called Cunard 'Master' brand: Cunard Queen Elizabeth 2 and Cunard Crown which would operate the *Cunard Countess*, the *Cunard Princess*, the *Cunard Crown Dynasty*, and the *Cunard Crown Jewel* would join Cunard Royal Viking and Cunard EuropAmerica Cruises. "Subtle changes" were made to the Cunard logo, individual logos were created for each sub-brand and each ship received what very much looked like a 'speed-stripe' of three colours (red, gold and deep 'Britannia blue') the length of their superstructures with the lion rampant logo displayed on the side of each ship near the Cunard name. By the middle of 1995 these stripes were in position on each ship in the fleet.

How Cunard would have branded the Royal Yacht *Britannia*, when it become public the company had expressed "interest" in that ship after the UK government announced in 1994 that she was to be retired in 1997, is anyone's guess!

John Olsen ordered important physical investments in the fleet which would see every ship refurbished but it was intended to give the *QE2*, the *Sagafjord* and the *Vistafjord* the biggest internal revamps they had ever received, with the work being completed by the end of 1995.

However it was decided not to refit the *Sagafjord* and it was eventually announced that the ship would be withdrawn at the end of her Alaska season in September 1996.

Years of refitting and refurbishment had, by the 1990s, given the *QE2* an interior which was piecemeal, with styles ranging from the 1930s to the 1980s. The refits in 1990 and 1992 had gone some way to giving the ship an art deco 1930s style in several key areas but a great deal of work was necessary on her public areas. Increasing competition in the cruise industry prompted Cunard to take urgent action and 'Project Lifestyle' was developed.

The *QE2* left New York on 13th November 1994 with a team of contractors on board, arriving at Blohm & Voss on 20th November. The £45 million 'Project Lifestyle' refit would

see 32 days of re-building ahead by a workforce of 2,000 from 20 countries (and 400 of the *QE2*'s crew) working 24 hours a day in order to complete the ambitious project. In all, almost one million square feet of public area space was affected. Nearly every passenger area on board received work ranging from complete redesign to redecoration or complete replacement to just having new artwork installed. Thousands of pieces of furniture and other items had to be purchased for the refit work, including 300 tons of steel, aluminium, ceramics and wood; 2,252 new light fixtures; 74,200 square yards (62,000 square metres) of fabric for chairs and curtains; 40,000 square yards (38,000 square metres) of new carpet in 25 separate carpet designs; 12 pieces of commissioned artwork and 8,000 gallons (12,000 litres) of paint.

As well as gaining an entirely new look on board, the *QE2* was also given a new profile and image on the outside too complying with the new corporate branding introduced by John Olsen.

It soon became clear that too much work was being undertaken with not enough time being allowed to undertake it. The *QE2* returned to Southampton and on the day she was due to sail for New York, 17th December, His Royal Highness Prince Andrew visited the ship. The carefully devised tour route planned for the Royal visit had to be abandoned on the day as several of her decks still looked as if they were under construction; whole blocks of cabins had no fittings whatsoever, and the ship's corridors were carpetless and littered with pipes and wiring. Workmen were everywhere. Even the sanitised route involved the Royal Party stepping over workmen laying carpet, and the Prince wryly remarked that his experience at sea had taught him to always expect refits to overrun. He remarked to crew "I think you are very brave going to sea this week".

John Olsen's oft-repeated message to his staff was that he wanted "everyone in Britain" to know that the *QE2* had had the biggest refit ever. He certainly got his wish.

Once the Royal visit had finished, Cunard personnel had to turn their attention to the passengers in the Terminal Building who were waiting to board and who were becoming angrier by the hour. The company had managed to contact around 300 people prior to their leaving home to advise that their cabins would not be ready and advised them not to travel to Southampton. However, several hundred more had arrived at the Terminal expecting their cabins to be available, and a further 160 had to be informed at the Terminal that they could not sail with the ship. All cancelled passengers were given a full refund and a guarantee of a future free cruise as compensation, which was generous to a level previously unheard of in the travel business.

The unfinished state of the ship had resulted in the Inspector from the Marine Safety Office placing a restriction of 1,000 passengers being carried. To exacerbate the problem further this number also included the workmen who would have to sail in order to complete the unfinished areas. In all, 600 passengers would be allowed to board.

The *QE2* eventually sailed several hours late, leaving many angry passengers behind, and headed straight into a Force 8 storm which resulted in many of the workers being seasick - thus delaying the work even further.

The aft ends of Quarter and Upper Decks were mainly incomplete and workmen busied themselves to complete the unfinished areas. Staircases and corridors remained uncarpeted and blocked with furniture piled high. Some passengers had to endure constant flooding, and toilet and washing facilities that ran with rusty brown water. But most passengers were mollified by the news that the entire voyage was to be free – and that they were to receive a further free voyage as recompense for discomfort.

But the ship's progress across the Atlantic wasn't a matter of private grief as it might have been in earlier years; modern communications – including direct dial phone installed in every cabin during a previous refit – meant that before long the whole saga was unfolding on the front pages of national newspapers around the world. It was a gift for the tabloid press, especially in the quiet week leading up to Christmas, and they exploited the opportunity to the full – making use of pictures taken at the yard during the refit, but which bore no relation to the current situation on the ship. True the passengers experienced discomfort and inconvenience, but for the tribulations of the crossing to generate more coverage than the sinking of the *Lusitania*, or the Martha's Vineyard incident when the *QE2* had genuinely been in danger, was grotesque. A coterie of disgruntled passengers naturally stoked the fires, often with a view to compensation in addition to the free sailing they were already on and the further free trip promised, firstly demanding to be taken off the ship (even though she was mid Atlantic) and on arrival in New York threatening to refuse to get off! The absurd over-reaction to the incident was best exemplified by the fact that on the same day that a plane crashed in Coventry killing five people, tabloid newspapers' front pages led on a passenger complaint from the *QE2* that her toilet had "exploded"!

Matters were not helped by the perverse attitude of parent company, Trafalgar House, which was so concerned about its share price it did all it could to suppress information rather than putting its efforts into informing the press. It thus allowed speculation to fester.

When the *QE2* finally arrived in New York 12 hours late on 23rd December, the United States Coast Guard boarded the ship earlier than expected to inspect the ship and issued a certificate of 'Control Verification for a Foreign Vessel' having "…already become convinced that the ship was in a dangerous condition." They advised that a certificate to sail would only be issued if the huge pile of rubbish that had accumulated was cleared (the Marine Safety Agency in the UK had provided a certificate for the *QE2* to sail on the proviso that all the rubbish would be cleared before the ship left New York) and that the crew could prove that the fire doors on the vessel were in working order. Cunard had to also guarantee that the outstanding building work, mainly in the new Lido area , was be completed as soon as possible. In all, the USCG issued a number of requests that totalled six pages.

Matters worsened when it became clear that the USCG would actually detain the ship and prevent her from sailing until the problems had been rectified. The *QE2* became the first vessel to be detained this way in New York for many years. Detailed ships are normally served with a detention notice, but the *QE2* was not. Instead a call was made to the British Consulate in New York but the call was not logged and Cunard was only made aware of it afterwards. Admiral Card from the USCG became involved and a letter was then despatched. A series of meetings were hurriedly convened in Washington and New York to sort out the mess.

The *QE2* was eventually permitted to sail – 24 hours late – and she sailed straight into another storm which would result in the cancellation of the call at Fort Lauderdale which would disappoint even more passengers.

The problems with the *QE2* overshadowed exactly the same problems with the *Vistafjord*. Her extensive £10 million refit was nowhere near completed when she re-entered service on 30th November and left Malta for Fort Lauderdale in a worse condition than the *QE2*.

Both ships would quickly emerge better than before but December 1994 will forever be a dark period in the history of Cunard.

An agreement with Effjohn had been reached earlier in the year for the *Cunard Crown Dynasty* to fall under the full operational control of Cunard from May 1995. She would be chartered by Cunard and marketed as the *Cunard Dynasty* but would retain her original name. Changes at Cunard Crown were not over when in April 1995 it was announced that the

Cunard Princess had been sold and that she would be handed over to her new owners Mediterranean Shipping Company in May that year which, in turn, chartered her to Star Lauro in Italy.

Plans for the *Sagafjord* to be refitted along similar lines as the *Vistafjord* were initially postponed then cancelled. It is interesting to note that the younger *Vistafjord* was always the subject of more refitting and refurbishment than her older sister, and by 1995 a decision had to be made about the *Sagafjord*. A plan was devised to rename her the *Cunard Endeavour* – the name thought most appropriate for Cunard's oldest ship about to embark on a new role – and she would be the Mediterranean replacement for the *Cunard Princess* from 1996. The *Cunard Endeavour* would increase Cunard's capacity in this market as some cabins would be converted to accommodate three or four passengers. She would also replace the *Crown Monarch* in the Australian market from November to April each year. Sadly the *Cunard Endeavour* never became reality.

After being slapped across the face by one of the *QE2's* enraged passengers earlier in the year, John Olsen left Cunard in May 1995, with a rumoured £500,000 pay off, and took the blame for the disastrous refits of the *QE2* and the *Vistafjord* and the subsequent fallout. The pay off caused a stir in the press on both sides of the Atlantic with the UK's **Daily Mirror** headline being 'Cunardly Believe It'. Nigel Rich, Chief Executive of Trafalgar House, said John Olsen's departure was

only partly a consequence of the *QE2* fiasco: "He had also failed to turn around Cunard, which had suffered from years of under-investment and made a £14 million loss in the half-year to March".

On 7th September 1995, the *QE2* left Southampton under the command of Captain Ron Warwick for New York via Cherbourg. Initially it was thought that the proximity of Hurricane Luis would result in the cancellation of the call at Cherbourg but the *QE2* did call and then proceeded to cross the Atlantic. During the course of the voyage the *QE2's* officers

*Above right: The **Sea Goddess I**. (Newall Dunn Collection)*

*Right: The **Royal Viking Sun** arriving in Bermuda in October 1995 wearing the Cunard name and 'speedstripe'. (Mark Cornford)*

*Below: The **Royal Viking Sun**, in her complete Cunard livery, and **Cunard Crown Dynasty** exchanging noisy salutes as they meet in Puerto Caldera. (Mark Cornford)*

closely monitored the progress of Luis and the weather deteriorated further by the early morning of 11th September with the 'eye' of 'Luis' around 130 miles away; the wind speed had increased from 50 to 130 knots, giving the QE2 a heel of 7° to starboard. Luis was heading in a north-easterly direction and making a forward speed estimated to be between 40 and 50 knots. Then at 02.10 hours a rogue wave was sighted right ahead looming out of the darkness. Hundreds of tons of water broke over the QE2's bow sending a shudder throughout the ship. The sea cascaded all over the forward deck, including the Bridge, and it was several seconds before the water had drained away from the wheelhouse windows and vision was restored. The weight of water landing on the foredeck bent a few of the railings and dented the deck plating to such an extent that the tip of the foredeck had been buckled downwards to show the lines of the beams and longitudinal stiffening underneath.

The Captain would later add:

"It looked as if we were going straight into the White Cliffs of Dover! The fact that the QE2 handled it so well is a tribute to her. She withstood it marvellously. I think British people should take pride in such marvellous engineering".

Captain Warwick reported that the wave had been more or less level with the line of sight on the Bridge which is 95 feet above the surface of the water. His claim was later supported by data taken from Canadian weather monitors in the area which showed the wave had been from 95 to 98 feet in height and around 1,200 feet wide.

The amazing thing was that most of the passengers slept through the rogue wave and only became aware the next morning when presented with a Storm Certificate as a memento.

Despite the influence of Hong Kong Land, Trafalgar House fortunes continued to slide and on 15th December 1995 a further loss of £321 million was announced, which meant the aggregate loss over a few years was then approaching a billion pounds. Dividends were stopped and it was declared that they would not resume until sustainable profit had returned.

82 years after Samuel Cunard had established the first scheduled service across the Atlantic, Cunard was able to introduce another new concept in ocean travel when, in 1922, the American Express Company initiated the first ever continuous circumnavigation of the globe by passenger liner, when they exclusively chartered the Laconia for the purpose of a 130-day, 22-port voyage. In January 1996 Cunard was able to proudly claim another first in World Cruise history - the first time three of its ships would depart that month on World Cruises. This was to be the Sagafjord's last World Cruise for Cunard since her withdrawal from service had been announced, and joining her on the World Cruise circuit were the QE2 and the Royal Viking Sun. Three ships would depart on World Cruises but only one would complete her voyage. The Sagafjord's World Cruise ended abruptly when a fire in her Engine Room on 16th February saw her decommissioned early as repairs were not considered worthwhile.

She would return to service for a brief stint as the Gripsholm for the German Transocean cruise line before Cunard sold her to the UK-based Saga Cruises where, as Saga Rose, she would enjoy several more years cruising.

After the fire, some passengers opted to continue their World Cruise and transferred to the Royal Viking Sun. On 4th April that ship sustained hull and engine damage when she struck a coral reef off Sharm El-Sheikh in the Red Sea. Cunard had to pay $23 million in compensation for damage to the protected reef before the Egyptian authorities would release the ship. Repairs would take until the end of June before the Royal Viking Sun re-entered service sporting the Cunard funnel colours while still retaining the Royal Viking sea eagle motif on the funnel – now painted in gold. Thankfully some of the Sagafjord refugees who had flocked to the Royal Viking Sun proceeded to board the QE2 and were able to complete a World Cruise. Two decades later Cunard would sell a World Cruise package that involved sailing the world on three ships but at least this time passengers taking that option knew in advance!

The Cunard Countess was sold in November 1996 to Awani Cruises in the Far East. Despite her cheap construction the Cunard Countess had for over two decades been very popular with passengers and very successful – for many years she was the most popular Caribbean ship in the UK market.

By now Trafalgar House was as battered as the Sagafjord's engines and the Royal Viking Sun's hull, so it came as no surprise when on 18th April 1996 Norwegian shipbuilding and engineering group Kvaerner acquired Trafalgar House plc following a £904 million offer. The acquisition provided Kvaerner with a broad-based portfolio of companies, including Cunard and a staff of 34,000. For the first time in its 156-year history Cunard was out of British hands.

The Kvaerner acquisition intensified speculations that Cunard would be sold as it didn't quite fit into the Kvaerner portfolio and that the Norwegian group was keen to offload disaster-prone Cunard to help raise money to pay for Trafalgar as well as reduce the huge debt taken on by acquiring Trafalgar House.

Throughout 1996, rumours that P&O, the Vlasov Group, Virgin and Prudential all looked at acquiring Cunard from Kvaerner persisted but these groups only really wanted the Cunard name, the *QE2* and the *Royal Viking Sun*. Even though keeping Cunard was a strain and diverted focus, Kvaerner was resolute that any buyer would have to take Cunard complete with the entire fleet. For their part Kvaerner continued to support Cunard but the months of speculation made for a very unsettling time for officers and crews and for shoreside employees who would arrive at work each morning not knowing if they would have a new owner or still have a job at the end of that day. But staff remained loyal to Cunard and what was still the highest-rated fleet of ships in the world.

Kvaerner brought in Greek shipowner Paris Katsoufis as Cunard President and Chief Operating Officer and his short time in the role saw Cunard relocate from New York to Miami. As well as handling crewing and management for Cunard ships, Paris Katsoufis had the same team working on the same issues for his ageing cruise ship the *Topaz*, which dated back to 1956 when she entered service as the *Empress of Britain*, which he chartered to Thomson Cruises.

In March 1997, the *Cunard Dynasty* was chartered to Majesty Cruises Line and renamed the *Crown Majesty* but remained under Cunard management until she was sold in September that year to Norwegian Cruise Line. Cunard went for luxury again and although the now five-ship fleet was considered and rated among the finest in the world, led by a flagship that was the most famous ship in the world, nothing could diminish the fact that the fleet was mis-matched. All had a different livery and led by a flagship that marked the 30th anniversary of her launch in September that year. And it was also the turn for the *Vistafjord* to make unwelcome headlines when a suspected arsonist on board was responsible for a spate of several fires which caused the death of one of her crew.

Despite still not being happy with potential buyers wanting to take pieces from the Cunard cake and not the whole cake itself, Kvaerner, which was in financial trouble itself and had been forced to admit that the Trafalgar House acquisition had weakened it, embarked on a newbuild programme for Cunard in 1998. After many false dawns on this front, the fact that this time an actual ship-building owner was involved and was prepared to invest in new tonnage, it seemed that Cunard would finally get the first ships it had designed since the *QE2* had entered service 30 years previously.

Two 60,000-ton, 26-knot ships were to be built to undertake world cruises and offer 940 berths each in all outside cabins - with the standard size of 21 metres and 70% featuring balconies. The cabin configuration was to consist of two Owner's Suites, 12 Royal Suites, 12 regular suites, 32 demi-suites, 280 staterooms with balcony and 142 staterooms with window. The main showroom was to hold 850 while the main Dining Room would offer single-seating dining with a capacity of 960. Other public rooms would include a Computer Learning Centre, Cinema, Business Centre, Library, Card Room, Cigar Room, Nursery and an indoor swimming pool. The two ships would enter service in June 2000 and June 2001 and one ship would be targeted at the UK market while the other was aimed at the US market. Preliminary names for the ships, which were never formally decided on, were the *Britannia* and the *America* given their target markets and historical maritime resonance. When news leaked of possible new Cunarders, the UK press announced that Cunard were to call them the *Britannia* and the *Queen Mary* and then a story appeared that The Queen had declined the name the *Britannia* thinking it too close to the 1997 retirement of the Royal Yacht *Britannia* but whatever names would have been given can only be guessed at now.

There would have been an undoubted carnival atmosphere within its London, Southampton, Miami and Hamburg offices had the order been signed, but for Cunard a carnival of a different sort was on the horizon.

Chapter Ten

Trafalgar's sleeping giant?

A journalist writing in Lloyd's List International on 11th May 1993 claimed that Cunard was a company "which has done absolutely nothing in the cruise industry for the last 10 years". Perhaps the purchase of Norwegian American Cruises, the investment in the 'Sea Goddesses' and the continual investment in the *QE2* including the biggest re-engining project ever undertaken, along with introducing innovative programmes and facilities on its ships in the previous 10 years had completely passed the journalist by. But Cunard was unflatteringly labelled a 'sleeping giant' for most of those 10 years by its competitors and industry observers so perhaps that journalist was not alone in his perception of Cunard. The label was unfair and many using it failed to appreciate the constraints Cunard faced just being part of a larger group of companies under a parent company that was stretched and by now running out of time.

Cunard was trying to make waves and make waves it

Cunard's proposed ship for its new Hawaiian venture. Perhaps a return to black and white funnels for Cunard? (Cunard)

would if some of the plans it considered had come to fruition but its image was not helped by the fact that almost every other company in the industry was either ordering new ships or re-affirming their positions by eliminating rivals. P&O consumed Sitmar in 1988; Holland America took Home Lines in the same year only for it to be acquired by Carnival in 1989; Royal Caribbean got involved with Celebrity Cruises in 1997 and then there was always Carnival and its relentless growth and deals with Epirotiki, Airtours, Costa, Seabourn and so on. While industry rivals consolidated, and remember Trafalgar House had tried to eliminate P&O in 1983, Cunard remained on a steady-as-she-goes course with occasional rumours of new tonnage or possible acquisitions surfacing. But as with all things Cunard, rumours became big stories and the possibility of new liners being built captured the imagination of both the public and the press.

In fact, while Cunard was externally perceived as being

inactive the company was quite the opposite internally with various steering committees established to evaluate potential newbuilds, acquisitions, management deals and the ten-year period from the mid-1980s saw the 'sleeping giant' evaluate plans ranging from building an ocean liner capable of 40 knots, to breaking into the US market to taking on the long-defunct *United States* and operating her with the *QE2* on the Atlantic!

In 1987 Cunard entered discussions with the Finnish Shipyard Wartsila regarding their catchily titled '1300/160 Design' cruise ship which was an amended version of Royal Caribbean's the *Song of America* which had entered service in 1982. The Cunard version would see the removal of the Royal Caribbean trademarked Viking Crown Lounge from the funnel, a different engine configuration, the removal of the aft lounge and aft pool, the relocation of the Lido area and a number of changes to the cabin configuration to allow for 750 cabins and Spa area. A visit by Cunard executives to the *Song of America* in October 1987 assisted Cunard with its planning and although the executives praised the *Song of America* the plans for '1300/160' came to nothing and the project was shelved in November 1987.

For many years Cunard was obsessed with establishing a US-flag cruise line. At one point the company investigated if the *Cunard Countess* and the *Cunard Princess* could somehow be re-flagged in the United States, on the proviso that Cunard would build new ships in America, and then have the new ships replace them. The US was keen to revive its long-gone passenger shipbuilding industry so 1988 and 1989 saw Cunard deal with Tampa Shipyards Inc. on several designs for different US-flagged cruise ships with the initial 1,358-passenger capacity being increased to 1,500 and the initial '*Tampa* Ship' project becoming the 'Eagle' project.

In 1988 Cunard began negotiations on a joint venture proposal with Hyatt to establish an Hawaiian venture. At that time the growing cruise market in Hawaii was serviced by American Hawaii Cruises (with its two ships: the *Independence* and the *Constitution*) and a new entrant Aloha Pacific Cruises and its one future ship, the *Monterey*. Cunard and Hyatt considered AHC and APC to have poor reputations and limited appeal and believed that the potential for efficient sized, modern, mid-ranged cruise ships in the market was something to take advantage of. In their early discussions with Hyatt, Cunard proposed to include Hyatt with their $215 million 40,000-ton 'The *Tampa* Ship'. This version of the '*Tampa*' was based externally on the new *Seaward* (1988) from Norwegian Cruise Line, with one less deck to avoid the need for costly aluminium but with additional passenger accommodation.

Hyatt rejected this "substantially inferior *Seaward*" design so Cunard and Hyatt developed a new design ('Eagle') for two US-built, four-star, 40,000-ton, 21.5-knot ships carrying 1,542 passengers that would enter service in 1992 and 1993 for year-round operation in the Hawaiian Islands competing against American Hawaii Cruises and its two ageing ships and Aloha Pacific Cruises and its heavily rebuilt *Monterey*. Cunard would provide worldwide marketing, sales and order processing, perform passenger service functions, provide accounting services, perform purchasing functions and hire and train the staff required for the project. For its part Hyatt would provide sales support, purchasing support, provide promotional (in-hotel) support and hire and train passenger service staff. The Eagle Project had to overcome several hurdles not least the cost of building US-flag cruise ships, the use of US union labour, the possible lack of interest of Hawaii in attracting more cruise ships, limited berth facilities in the region, US Coast Guard regulations and Hawaii intra-state regulations including tough pollution regulations.

To perhaps force the hand of Cunard and Hyatt, the American yard announced in November 1989 that negotiations for two medium-sized cruise ships for the protected Hawaiian trade, in a deal worth almost $500 million, was close to being signed.

Despite designs for 'Eagle' progressing, no contract was signed and a year later Cunard and Hyatt approached American Hawaii Cruises directly in the hope of incorporating that operation direct into their proposed new Hawaiian venture with Cunard taking over management of the *Independence* and the *Constitution*. No deal could be made. In 1993 American Hawaii Cruises was close to bankruptcy and Cunard tried again to acquire the company thinking that an acquisition would bring it closer to the Asian market, enable Cunard to increase sales in Australia and Japan and give Cunard the monopoly in the Hawaii cruise trade but it was eventually deterred as getting involved in a bankruptcy could be messy for Cunard. The two American Hawaii ships needed extensive investment and Hawaii was in a major tourist recession by this time. American Hawaii was eventually purchased by Delta Queen Steamboat Co. in June 1993.

In May 1989 Aloha Pacific Cruises was experiencing financial difficulties and the *Monterey* was facing repossession by the yard Wartsila in Finland. Cunard had the opportunity to purchase the *Monterey* and use that ship with Hyatt to begin its Hawaiian venture. The *Monterey* would give the companies

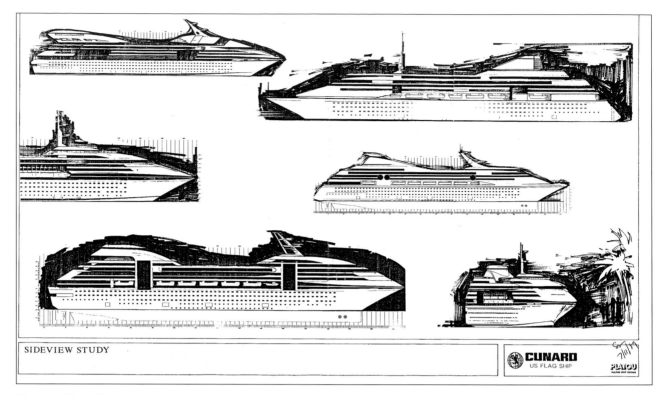

SIDEVIEW STUDY

CUNARD
US FLAG SHIP

Various profiles of Cunard's proposed 'Eagle' Hawaii ship. (Cunard)

an initial step into the market and the benefits of using the *Monterey* as a training vessel would be valuable in the start up of 'Eagle'. The problem of taking on the *Monterey* was what to do with her once the 'Eagle' ships had entered service. An inspection by a Cunard executive reported that he found her in "excellent condition" and good for another 20 years. Cunard thought her ideal for the Australian market given her suitability in terms of recognition in the market, the fact she was built for heavy seas and the capability of 25 knots.

Cunard and Hyatt were so keen to work with each other they looked into a hotel partnership together when all hopes of establishing a cruise venture sank without trace.

Cunard approached Norwegian ship owner Knut Kloster in 1989, with a view to getting involved in his massive Pheonix World City project by assuming specific operational management functions. For World City the association with Cunard would provide the project as a whole with additional tangible credibility while Cunard would benefit in several areas: it would give it a distinct and highly differentiated image in the industry, it would be an important profit maker and it would involve Cunard in floating leisure resorts which were then considered the next major innovation in the marketplace. In the end Cunard considered World City to be a somewhat unrealistic venture when the financial data they

were provided with had been scrutinised.

As well as new tonnage, Cunard was often looking at acquiring other companies that would open new markets for it or re-invigorate the company with new tonnage. It was keen to secure a 600-bed ship for the UK market that would cruise in the Caribbean in the winter and the Mediterranean in the summer, complementing the *Cunard Countess* and the *Cunard Princess* operations in those areas.

In 1988, Citibank offered Cunard the opportunity to purchase Royal Cruise Line and two of its ships, the *Crown Odyssey* (1988) and the *Golden Odyssey* (1974), for between $200 and $300 million. The third ship in the fleet, the *Royal Odyssey*, was not included in the sale but Cunard declined to explore the opportunity further unless the price was reduced to around $115 million. The company also foresaw potential issues with making the *Crown Odyssey* and the *Golden Odyssey* compatible with the *Sagafjord* and the *Vistafjord*.

Cunard had always been the undoubted jewel in the Trafalgar House crown, and the acquisitions made for it and the investment put into the *QE2* was evidence of that, but Trafalgar House was still keen to make a fleet expansion announcement before or during Cunard's 150th anniversary in 1990.

In 1989 Trafalgar's Deputy Chairman and Group Chief Executive Eric Parker announced they were considering building up to three new ships for Cunard. He claimed discussions were at the early planning stage but interestingly confirmed that two of the ships would be part of a joint-venture while the third would be fully-owned by the group. Industry speculation thought the partner would be a Japanese concern as Trafalgar House was keen to reduce the tax bill on two long charters there undertaken by the *QE2*. She had spent 89 days in Yokohama (March – June 1989) as part of the city's 130th anniversary celebrations, and then a further charter period from December 1989 to June 1990 saw the *QE2* performing similar functions she undertook in Yokohama as well as undertaking ten short cruises to Hong Kong and other nearby ports. These charters saw Cunard receive around £250,000 a day - nearly £50 million in total. As obviously lucrative as these charters were for Cunard, they were at the expense of having the *QE2* on the Atlantic where Cunard had the monopoly. Cunard would form a new cruise line, Cunard American International Cruises, with several partners who had no cruising experience but the capital Cunard needed, and offer cruises tailored to Asian tastes with offices based in Hong Kong, Tokyo, Singapore, Taipei and Bangkok. In the end the promising Far East market was not growing as fast as hoped so Cunard American International Cruises did not proceed past negotiations.

Plans to charter a ship in time to operate with the *Cunard Countess* in the Caribbean for the 1990 were thwarted as suitable tonnage could not be found, or was not available, despite housebroker H E Moss being appointed to find a vessel for Cunard that would allow them to satisfy demand for its Caribbean cruises. Royal Viking's the *Royal Viking Sky* was wanted by Cunard but no deal was made.

While the two 'Sea Goddess' ships earned Cunard awards and favourable reviews the two yacht-like ships were costing the company as much effort as the *Sagafjord* and the *Vistafjord* did when it came to marketing. Something had to be done so Cunard sought an opportunity in 1989 to combine its 'Sea Goddess' vessels with their main rival Seabourn Cruise Line and its two larger but similar vessels the *Seabourn Pride* and the *Seabourn Spirit*. Two years later Cunard would still be considering how it could work with Seabourn when Carnival Cruise Line announced their acquisition of 25% of Seabourn in November 1991. Cunard was still in favour of working with Carnival to combine the *Sea Goddess I* and the *Sea Goddess II* with the Seabourn ships with Cunard managing the combined fleets but a deal could not be arranged.

In 1991 Cunard entered negotiations with Mitsubishi Heavy Industries for two 32,000-ton cruise ships based on the Japanese NYK ship the *Asuka* which had entered service that year. The Cunard version would have refinements including reducing the number of inside cabins to around 10% of the total as opposed to 25% on the *Asuka*. A total of 1,225 persons (800 passengers and 425 crew) would be accommodated in the 20-knot ship with public rooms including an Entrance Hall, Main Dining Room, additional restaurant, Showlounge, secondary lounges, Shops, Casino, Sky Lounge, Card Room, Library and Health Spa. The first ship was to be delivered in 1994 with the second a year later and provided two ships were ordered simultaneously the price per ship was Japanese Yen 25,500,000,000. Cunard considered the public room arrangement "awkward" and the ratio of inside cabins too high and it couldn't get Trafalgar House interested in the project.

At the same time the company was working on 'Project Cyclops' the codename for its possible acquisition of Celebrity Cruises from Chandris for $480 million and thus obtain the new *Horizon* (1990), the forthcoming *Zenith* (1992) and the greatly refurbished *Meridian* as well as Celebrity's preferential trading rights in Bermuda. As well as being re-established as a major cruise company Cunard would also receive much-needed new vessels for its ageing fleet. The *Horizon* was to have been redeployed on a similar itinerary to the *Cunard Countess* while the *Zenith* and the *Meridian* would have gone into Alaska and Caribbean cruises and Mediterranean and Far East voyages respectively.

After joining forces with Cunard Crown in 1993 Cunard and Effjohn sought to establish further ties on two further completely different projects.

Effjohn and a company called Swift Line were privately proceeding with a revolutionary cruise ship project dubbed 'Swift'. By October 1993 Cunard had entered into a joint venture agreement with Swift Line to provide worldwide marketing and sales support and had given the ship the tentative name the *Mauretania*. While it's true that the 1907 four-funnelled legend was for 22 years the swiftest ship in the world, the name was entirely at odds with the futuristic design of the ship. She looked like a bullet - not what you'd expect at all from Cunard, but then neither was the *QE2* when she appeared. Cunard could certainly have re-used 'Ships have been boring long enough' for 'Swift'/the *Mauretania*. Indeed Cunard documents revealed "The *Mauretania* will be, in design and operation, truly revolutionary. From her striking exterior, which will instantly set her apart from her contemporaries – to her unique three class General Arrangement and high speed, this vessel will carve a unique niche in the cruise market". Like the name given to the ship the three-classes was an anachronism by the 1990s but the '*Q5*' was also to have as many classes and it was the US office, against the wishes of the UK office, that insisted on that number for both projected ships. Just as it was the US office that was so reluctant to have the *QE2* re-drawn as a two-class ship in the 1960s.

The *Mauretania* would offer Concierge, Premium and Family class arrangements and facilities. "Her mix of facilities will be unmatched by any vessel currently in service, and she will contain a number of unique features never seen aboard a cruise ship. These include her Concierge Apartments, totally separate and exclusive accommodations and dining facilities on the top of the ship; the Family class of cabins, served by the first full-service buffet aboard a cruise vessel; and the most comprehensive spa at sea ever designed. The *Mauretania* will be the first ship of the Fiber Optic Age, boasting a fully interactive television system, passenger business and computer center, a space observatory and a Virtual Reality entertainment facility". How times had changed! When the *Mauretania* entered service in 1907 Cunard likened her to a floating palace. The art deco splendour of the 1939 *Mauretania* was heralded by the company. And now the possible third *Mauretania* was being likened to the space age.

The *Mauretania* was to be built at a cost of $320 million at the Kvaerner Masa-Yards in Finland and be 74,000 tons with a length of 880 feet, accommodation for 2,000 passengers and 880 crew. A nude sun-bathing deck for passengers was to be included. Her initial 24 – 26 knots speed was increased by Cunard to 28.5 knots to enable her to offer seven-day Caribbean cruises to and from Fort Lauderdale in the winter and seven-day Barcelona – Barcelona cruises in the summer.

Additional statistics for the *Mauretania*:

Breadth ....95 feet
Passenger Decks..10

Cabin Breakdown

Concierge Class 400
Premium Class..1,200
Family Class..400

Family Class was modelled on the compact but comfortable cabins found on Baltic super-ferries such as the *Silja Serenade* and the *Silja Symphony* and were to be configured to carry two to four people, including children. Considerable savings in staffing and food costs would be made by Cunard as Family Class passengers would dine in a buffet restaurant rather than a full-service dining room and these savings were to be passed on to the passenger in the form of lower fares.

An order for the *Mauretania* was expected to be placed early in 1994 with her maiden voyage taking place in 1996. Twenty years on an order is still awaited – the *Mauretania* having been shelved in 1995.

In 1993 Effjohn announced: "There are plans to market the SS *United States* through Effjohn's partner, Cunard, using her as a running mate to the *Queen Elizabeth 2* on the prestigious five star Atlantic route". Cunard was about to get involved with another swift ship of sorts, the *United States*, which snatched the Blue Riband from the *Queen Mary* in 1952.

American travel entrepreneur Fred Mayer had bought the ship and had her sent to Turkey to be stripped of asbestos prior to being rebuilt. Effjohn had signed an agreement to supervise and technically support the rebuilding of the *United States* which had been laid up since 1969.

Interestingly, when Richard Hadley purchased the *United States* in the 1970s he approached Cunard then to represent his new US Cruises and its new service to Hawaii from Los Angeles.

Now Cunard investigated a similar association with Effjohn as that with Cunard Crown seeing this as the best way to avoid United States being operated as a low-cost rival /alternative to the *QE2* on the Atlantic run by a company

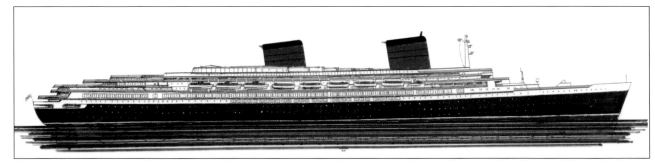

*The **United States** as a Cunarder. (Cunard)*

such as Regency Cruises, of which Fred Mayer had been involved with at one point. Cunard's plan was to operate the *United States* from 4th July 1996 on a new Le Havre to Fort Lauderdale route, thus tapping into the lucrative European market while the *QE2* would remain unchallenged from Southampton to New York. The *United States* would enable Cunard to introduce the first US-flag sea-going passenger vessel to sail in continental UK waters in 35 years ("A ship flying the American flag with an American crew will receive an enthusiastic response from the American public"). The *United States* would allow Cunard to trade on routes closed to foreign flag carries and she could sail Los Angeles – San Francisco – Honolulu without running into difficulties with the American Jones Act. It was also not lost on Cunard that taking on the *United States* would give it the two most famous ships in the world.

Cunard's technical team took over the planning of the *United States'* conversion which was expected to cost up to $295 million, with yards in Turkey, Germany and Singapore being approached.

On the technical side various re-engining proposals (diesel-mechanical propulsion, diesel-electric propulsion with two propellers or diesel-electric propulsion with four propellers) were considered but by April 1993 Cunard had decided that re-engining was not to be considered any further and that her existing aft steam plant would be upgraded. However such things such as the inclusion of stern thrusters to assist manoeuvrability and an additional outside swimming pool (to be located in between the funnels) were considered a must. Like the *QE2*, the *United States* was an exceptionally strong ship and Cunard was confident of getting another twenty years of life out of her using her existing power plant as the reduced speeds she would be sailing under their service would extend the life of the *United States*.

As for the interior nothing of the existing accommodation, public and service spaces for passengers and crew would be retained and the new *United States* would offer a four-star thoroughly American experience with accommodation divided into three types of service: Luxury (340 deluxe and First Class berths); World Class (1,300 berths) and Budget (370 berths aimed at the economy conscious and family market). Interestingly Cunard investigated building 'Court cabins' in the *United States*. 'Court cabins' were a feature of the P&O ship *Canberra* and were a simple answer to the old problem of the 'inside' cabin. Along the ship's side are many courts, or verandas, with large windows overlooking the sea

*The **United States** in lay-up for sale. (Ferry Publications Library)*

and each 'Court cabin', similarly, had a window which looked out through the veranda to the ocean.

The ship would be marketed to the American looking for a cruise experience that reminded him of home or the European passenger who wanted to start or prolong his American vacation. There would be the largest, best-equipped health club afloat and a duty-free marketplace would be similar to those offered on Baltic ferries where items such as stereos, televisions and other electronic equipment would be sold. Entertainment would be decidedly American with Broadway musicals in the Showlounge and the nightclub would be programmed by the best DJs from America's top discos, nightclubs and radio stations and movies, both in the cinema and on cabin televisions, would feature Hollywood hits past and present.

In the end, the *United States* remained in Turkey, devoid of asbestos and all of her internal fittings, until being returned to America where she is still laid up today. Cunard's interest in the project was no more after 1994.

To have labelled Cunard a 'sleeping giant' was unfair. The company had made acquisitions, had made innovations, had the most famous ship in the world with the *QE2* and, if any of the plans discussed in this chapter, had the opportunity to reaffirm its place as a giant in the cruise industry.

But then this giant would eventually join another.

Q5

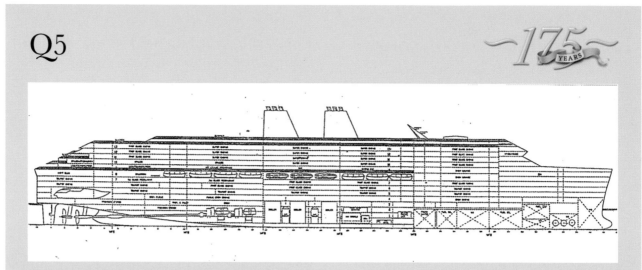

Original profile design of **Q5**. *(Cunard)*

A lot of discussions took place in the mid-1980s concerning the life span of the *QE2* and whether a new 'Queen' liner should be built. A final decision rested on the strength of the *QE2*'s hull, which was strong and was felt by ship surveyors could last another 20 years or so. Given this and the potential cost of a new 'Queen' a decision was made to re-engine the *QE2* which took place at the end of 1986. That decision would ultimately prove the correct one but Cunard and Trafalgar House knew that a new ocean liner would still be required at some point even though the *QE2*'s new engines were designed to give her a further 20-year lifespan.

Initially known as 'Century 21' it seemed fitting to begin using '*Q5*' for the project as this would become the fifth Queen liner for Cunard (or sixth if *Berengaria* was included) despite '*Q3*' never leaving the drawing board. The use of '*Q5*' rekindled memories of the British comedian Spike Milligan's 'Q...' surreal comedy TV series which ran from 1969 to 1982. It was rumoured he'd been inspired by the use of '*Q3*' and '*Q4*' by Cunard that the six seasons of 'Q...' were known as '*Q5*', '*Q6*' and so on.

While a project like '*Q5*' was usually not discussed publicly by Cunard it did become public knowledge when market research for a new ocean liner was undertaken with various groups outside Cunard. The questionnaire circulated clearly stated Atlantic crossings of 3.5 – 4 days and even one-way fares of $2,175 were printed. Despite this Cunard never formally confirmed

they were planning a new 'Queen' even when the UK press excitedly reported that Cunard was planning a new ship to be called *Princess Diana*.

Internal documents show that '*Q5*' was to have entered service in 1991 and that she would have been very revolutionary - perhaps the most revolutionary liner ever. '*Q5*' was to be a two-funnelled, 90,000-ton gas-turbine ship capable of 40 knots! Such a revolutionary ship would have offered four classes of accommodation: two Super Deluxe, a First and a Tourist Class with the latter initially having to enjoy buffet food - for which they would pay extra (this concept was way ahead of cruise lines such as Aida and Ocean Village which would appear several years later). With the *QE2* having received new engines she would have worked together with '*Q5*' but trade in Japanese, Pacific and Alaskan markets while '*Q5*' would assume the *QE2*'s Atlantic mantle.

Designing '*Q5*' was a challenge and Cunard and Trafalgar House couldn't agree on final design details and were never satisfied with their profile of the new ship. The design and development costs started to spiral. Cunard approached the noted Norwegian ship architect Njal Eide and he was drafted in to work on the design – just as James Gardner had been drafted in to work on *QE2* in the 1960s. The result was a ship streamlined to within an inch and the two funnels had been replaced with three grouped together and swept backwards toward the stern.

Cunard's *Q5* Concept Specification Document (Revision 6) dated November 1990 revealed:

Objective

- A 40-knot ship capable of crossing in four days
- 2,400 passengers
  1,400 of these in First Class
  (about 700 of these in Grills)
- Multiple Grill Restaurants
- Classic lines
- An overall experience to command superliner pricing
- Acceptable return on investment to Trafalgar House
- Panamax Hull

Marketing parameters

- Minimum deck head of 7.6 ft free space in the main portion of the cabin
- Public room deck head heights similar to *QE2*
- Accommodation range similar to *QE2* (size)
- Need a Concierge Lounge concept for Grill accommodations (in the bedroom area)
- Need to maximise the use of outside space for accommodation and inside space for public room use
- Need greater emphasis on classic ocean liner amenities like a grand staircase verses a cruise style amenity such as an atrium
- Need a good distribution of deck space in more than one area
- Need unique public spaces (eg Lincoln Center at Sea?)
- Accommodation classes cannot be mixed in one area
- No need for tendered that carry more than 250 people

Passengers   2500

Class	Number	Cabin size
Super Class (A)		600 sq ft
Super Class (B)	750 total in Super Class	400 sq ft
First Class	700	225 sq ft
Tourist Class	1050	160 – 180 sq ft

Restaurants

- Buffet facilities – comprehensive for lunch and breakfast and alternative dinner service
- Super Class – four smaller restaurants: two with a 125 passenger capacity and two with a 250 passenger capacity with one sitting each
- First Class – two restaurants each for 350 passengers with one sitting each
- Tourist Class – one restaurant for 525 passengers with two sittings

Public spaces

- Generally integrated but some special spaces for Super Class
- Generally high public space to passenger rations
- Board and Meeting Facilities (Restaurant daytime use?)

Public spaces *(cont)*

- Comprehensive Spa facility
- Maximum dual use of space (ie Buffet facility becomes disco at night etc)
- Indoor – Outdoor spaces suitable for a variety of trading areas
- Casino
- No Cinema (show movies in meeting facilities)
- Indoor and Outdoor Swimming Pools

Dimensions

- Panamax
- Draft as necessary but not to exceed 35 feet

Technical

- Speed: 37.5 knots average normal service; 41 knots maximum service speed and 44 knots trial speed
- Flat consumption curve – 100 days per year 37.5 knots; 250 days 28 knots average
- Range: 10,000 miles at 25 knots; 7,000 miles at 37.5 knots
- Water: make daily requirement in 12 hours at sea. Five days storage.
- Engines: minimize noise/vibration
  one or two fuel ship
  minimize operating costs
  cheapest fuel possible
- Sewage / garbage – advanced
- Manoeuvring – completely self sustaining without tugs under all but the most extreme conditions

Q5

- Stabilised
- Comprehensive tendering capacity

Stores / Baggage

- Very advanced systems with baggage systems towed to dedicated on shore facilities airline style and with stores loaded by container or conventionally – advance materials handling on board
- Stores space for up to 60 days depending on item

Crew

- About 1300 in good accommodation. (About 250 singles and 550 doubles). About half singles with private bathrooms. Other share one bathroom between two cabins.

Cabin detail

- Additionally small number of very large suites like Queen Elizabeth Suite on *QE2*.
- Maximise the number of outside cabins and balconies
- Maintain general separation of cabin type
- About 300 connecting cabins (within and between types)
- Bathrooms should be the best possible with marble, double sinks, hairdryers, shaving mirrors etc
- Tourist Class cabins showers, remainder baths, Super Class bath plus shower separate
- Jacuzzis in Super Class and First Class

- Highest level of between cabin soundproofing technically achievable
- All twin beds convert to doubles
- Interactive TV with radio channels
- Tape players in all cabins
- Safe in all cabins
- Refrigerator / minibar in all cabins
- Handicapped cabins in sufficient number
- Walk-in closets in First and Super Class if possible. In any case sufficient storage for World Cruises

Having invested heavily in extending the life of the *QE2*, Trafalgar House put aside for future capital investment in 'Q5' – a rights issue had raised £400 million. However, investment in Commercial Property, Scott Lithgow, as well as the Davy Corporation in 1992 (which added 30% to Trafalgar House's turnover) swallowed up too much cash flow. As a consequence, and mainly as a result of poor investment decisions in oil and gas platforms and accounting issues relating to the capitalisation of interest etc (leading to that re-statement of the 1992 accounts), any money for 'Q5' Trafalgar House had disappeared.

And so did 'Q5'.

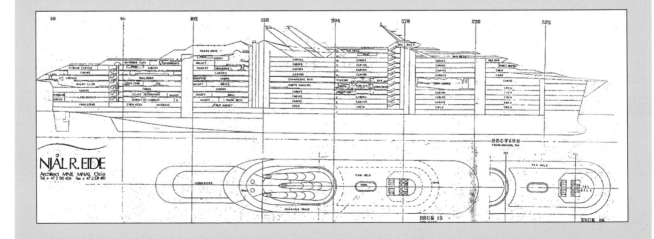

'Q5' as proposed by Njal Eide. (Cunard)

Don't stop the carnival

O n 3rd April 1998 the mighty American Carnival Corporation, comprised of 37 ships in its fully-owned Carnival Cruise Line, Holland America Line, Windstar Cruises and equity interests in Costa Cruises, Seabourn Cruise Line and Airtours plc, announced their purchase of Cunard for $500 million. Carnival Corporation, together with a group of Norwegian investors led by Christiania Markets, had thus succeeded in doing something the American JP Morgan and his giant IMMC group had failed to do 100 years earlier!

At the same time Carnival announced they had reached an agreement with Kvaerner Masa-Yards to develop a design for a new class of ships for Cunard – perhaps an indication that

*The 'new' Cunard fleet, the **QE2** and the **Caronia**, meet off Barbados on 31st December 1999. (Cunard)*

at first Carnival was happy to proceed with the two new ships, (the *Britannia* and the *America?*), Cunard and Kvaerner had been developing.

It was also announced that Seabourn Cruise Line, which was 50% owned by Carnival and 50% owned by its founder Atle Brynestad, would be merged with Cunard to make the largest company in the luxury segment of the cruise market.

Seabourn Cruise Line had been founded to compete with Sea Goddess Cruises with the next generation ships catering to that exclusive all-inclusive market. The company had three ships: the *Seabourn Pride* (1988), the *Seabourn Spirit* (1989) and the *Seabourn Legend* (1992).

The story of
CUNARD'S
~*175*~
YEARS

Micky Arison, Carnival's chairman and CEO, said: "The *QE2* is the best known cruise ship in the world and commands a vast customer following from around the world" and added that Cunard was "the strongest brand name in the in the luxury market".

Cunard's response to the media uproar in the UK that another great British brand had been lost to foreign owners was to quietly remind those making the hoo-ha that really Cunard was going back home as the company had been founded by a Canadian with American roots. For most, especially Cunard employees, Carnival was a welcome new owner – no one could doubt its success and it meant that for the first time in almost 40 years Cunard was back in the hands of actual ship owners.

Carnival completed its purchase on 28th May 1998 and owned 68.33% with Christiana Markets owning 19.26% and Atle Brynestad 12.41%. A new company, Cunard Line Limited, was created to operate Cunard and Seabourn. On 19th October 1999 Carnival Corporation exercised its option to buy the remaining 32% minority interest in a deal worth about $205 million.

The new President and Managing Director Larry Pimentel repeated mantra was that "Cunard's future would be a reflection of its past". He set about creating a new company and was joined by Chief Operating Officer Pamela Conover.

And then the announcement, that stunned Cunard employees, passengers, competitors and industry observers and had maritime historians scurrying to rewrite their lectures and the history books, came. In Oslo on 8th June 1998,

*The renaming of the **Vistafjord** as the **Caronia** in Liverpool on 10th December 1999. (Cunard)*

barely a week after taking control of Cunard, Carnival unveiled plans for 'Project Queen Mary' - the undertaking of the design and development for a new class of "stately superliner". It perhaps would have been more traditional to use 'Q6' as the project title (Spike Milligan again?) but whatever label was given to the project Cunard was at last getting a new ocean liner. For almost 30 years it had been assumed, despite leaked reports of the *Q5*, that the *QE2* would be the last Atlantic liner ever and once she had gone that would be it. It was a presumption both Cunard and Trafalgar House encouraged, and probably believed, and it was a key element in creating the almost mythical status of

The first image of 'Project Queen Mary' released in November 1999. (Cunard)

*Profile of the **Queen Mary 2**. (Cunard)*

that ship. Projects like the *Q5* always did seem to be pipe dreams but this time no-one doubted Carnival's intentions.

With extensive design work starting on the new liner project, the new management team of Cunard Line Limited had to decide exactly what to do with the nine ships of the newly-combined Cunard and Seabourn fleets. After months of evaluation and deliberation it was decided that the two 'Sea Goddess' twins would be transferred to Seabourn – an obvious choice given the type of vessels they were and they were brilliantly renamed the *Seabourn Goddess I* and the *Seabourn Goddess II*. The *Vistafjord* would be renamed the *Caronia* and join the *QE2* on the Cunard side. Both would "reflect" the Britishness expected from Cunard and both would carry the same livery – for the first time since the 1920s ships of Cunard would do this. What was surprising was the placement of the *Royal Viking Sun* into Seabourn. As the *Seabourn Sun* the new 700-passenger ship did not seem to fit with the 116 passenger Goddesses and the 212-passenger original Seabourn ships.

In November 1999 Cunard unveiled the first image of the new 'Project Queen Mary' vessel and announced that she would be the largest passenger ship in the world. Five builders were in the running to construct the ship: Fincantieri, Italy; HDW, Germany; MASA Yards, Finland; Chantiers de l'Atlantique, France and Harland & Wolff in Belfast. The latter was a surprise given its lack of passenger ship building for many years and the list was whittled down to the French and Belfast yard. Deputy Prime Minister John Prescott, who began his working life as a waiter on Cunard ships in the 1950s, should be credited for getting Harland & Wolff onto the shortlist, but no matter how it tried to compare with the French yard it couldn't, and on 10th March 2000 not only was the name the *Queen Mary 2* announced but a letter of intent for her construction was placed with Chantiers de l'Atlantique. The formal contract was signed on 6th November 2000 for the "grandest and largest passenger vessel liner ever".

What Sir Samuel Cunard would have thought about the *Queen Mary 2* is open to speculation but perhaps he would have insisted that the largest, longest, tallest, widest and most expensive liner ever (as Cunard would repeat and repeat and repeat in the years to come) would have had paddlewheels incorporated into her design!

All of the rebranding and re-positioning of the existing ships was complete by December 1999. In fact the *Royal Viking Sun* and the *Vistafjord* conversions and renaming took place at the Lloyd-Werft Shipyard in Bremerhaven at the same time the *QE2* was undergoing a £30 million investment by Carnival, which was a great show of faith in the ship.

On 10th December, the *Caronia* arrived in Liverpool and berthed alongside the Pier Head for her official renaming and re-flagging to the UK. Originally Madeleine Arison, wife of Micky Arison, was to rename the ship but she cancelled at the very last minute due to ill health, so Pamela Conover did the honours and the Deputy Prime Minister John Prescott, who was there to re-flag the ship, caused laughter and headlines when he mistakenly referred to Larry Pimentel as "Larry Pimpernel". As the English wine, chosen to reflect the new Britishness of Cunard and to remind people that Cunard ships had always been traditionally named with wine and not French champagne, smashed against the side of the *Caronia* the recently-applied black paint was stripped from the hull. There was no time for a re-touch as the *Caronia* had to quickly head mid-river for the evening rather than stay alongside as planned as she would have been impaled on a rather large rock that had been discovered at the last minute. Six hundred specially-invited guests, including many members of the UK press had been invited to sail with the *Caronia* to Southampton where she would meet up with the refitted *QE2* and the guests would transfer to her for a celebratory lunch. The journey to Southampton was simply horrendous as the *Caronia* encountered ferocious weather in the Irish Sea which made

*Above: The wheelhouse block of the **Queen Mary 2** is eased into position. (Chantiers de l' Atlantique)*

*Right: The **Queen Mary 2** and her newly-installed bulbous bow. (Chantiers de l' Atlantique)*

*Below: Gathered for the keel-laying of the **Queen Mary 2** on 4th July 2002: Captain R. Warwick (Master Designate), Pamela Conover (Cunard President and Chief Operating Officer), Patrick Boissier (Chantiers de l'Atlantique Managing Director), Mrs Boissier, Micky Arison (Carnival Corporation Chairman and Chief Executive Officer) and Mrs Arison. (Chantiers de l' Atlantique)*

Queen Mary 2

Passenger areas on the largest, longest, widest and grandest ocean liner ever built. The rooms are depicted as they were in 2004 and some have been refurbished since.

Above: Princess Grill.

Left: The Grand Lobby.

Below: G32 Nightclub.

(All photos Cunard)

Above: Commodore Club.

Right: Britannia Restaurant.

Below: One of the Duplex Suites.

(All photos Cunard)

*The **Queen Mary 2** arrives in Fort Lauderdale at the end of her maiden voyage on 26th January 2004. (Cunard)*

the annual Cunard Christmas Press Lunch one to remember for years to come and prompted some to return to the following year's lunch (on land) with 'I survived ...' T-shirts. Cunard naming ceremonies had been so rare over the decades but the *Caronia* renaming set the tone for future Cunard ceremonies that were considered distinctly Cunard in style and the most spectacular ever.

In July 2001, the *Seabourn Goddess I* and the *Seabourn Goddess II* were sold to Atle Brynestad to operate for his new Sea Dream Cruises venture and, since the *Seabourn Sun* never really did fit in at Seabourn, she was transferred to Holland America Line and became their *Prinsendam* in April 2002.

On 14th December 2001, Carnival Corporation signed a Letter of Intent with its preferred builder, Fincantieri of Italy, for an 85,000-ton cruise ship for Cunard to enter service in 2005. The new ship would be built at the yard's Marghera base near Venice and she would be the second-largest ship ever built for Cunard. Sailing under the British flag the onboard styling was to British tastes and the shipboard currency was to be pound sterling rather than the US dollar which had been on board Cunard ships for decades. The new ship would give Cunard more capacity than the company had had since the 1960s and its third 'Queen' as in March 2003 it was announced the new ship would be called the *Queen Victoria*.

At the same time a plan for either the *Noordam* or the *Nieuw Amsterdam* to be transferred from Holland America to provide a much needed infusion of new tonnage into Cunard and act as a stop-gap until planned new tonnage had been built was considered.

After P&O demerged its cruise division to create P&O Princess in 2000, the cruise line was in a vulnerable position and was positioned in third place behind Royal Caribbean International and the market leader Carnival Corporation. In May 2001 P&O Princess approached Royal Caribbean about joining forces, and when that merger was announced in November 2001 it provoked Carnival to respond and make a bid for P&O Princess itself in order to prevent its two main rivals creating the largest cruise combination in the world. Many months of intense negotiation followed but Carnival triumphed and on 17th April 2003 it was announced that P&O Princess and Carnival Corporation would form a single economic entity, Carnival Corporation & plc. The addition of P&O Princess to the Carnival family had far-reaching repercussions for Cunard and its future direction.

Pamela Conover, Cunard's President and Chief Operating Officer, pressed the button to cut the first sheet of steel for the *Queen Mary 2* on 16th January 2002 at an event attended by His Royal Highness Prince Edward whose film company Ardent had been commissioned by Cunard to film the construction. The keel laying took place on that sacred 4th

July anniversary in 2002 for Cunard and the ceremony was conducted by Master Designate Captain Ron Warwick.

Although ship construction had dramatically changed since the 1960s the differences in the speed of construction between the *Queen Mary 2* and the *QE2* were obvious, as key milestones in the construction of the *Queen Mary 2* were reached within months of each other rather than years with the *QE2*.

The *Queen Mary 2* was floated out of the massive building dock on 21st March 2003 and undertook her first sea trials in September prior to her Owners' Trials in November.

In May 2003, with the delivery of the *Queen Mary 2* now little more than six months away, and with construction begun on the *Queen Victoria*, Cunard announced that *Caronia* had been sold to UK-based Saga Group and would be delivered in November 2004 and reunited with her sister the *Sagafjord*. The *Caronia* had proved an excellent addition to Cunard over the 20 years she had been a Cunarder but by now she was ageing and not as efficient as modern ships but still very popular. While her age had something to do with her sale, Cunard's desire to have a consistent fleet was also a factor - she did not have Grill dining etc. Investigations were made to introduce at least a Queens Grill section in her main Dining Room but none of the concepts proved satisfactory.

At the same time as the *Caronia* announcement it was confirmed that 2003 would be the *QE2*'s last season on the Atlantic and that Atlantic duties would be undertaken by the *Queen Mary 2* from 2004. The *QE2* would continue her World Cruise each year from January to April and then offer cruises to and from Southampton. Removing the ship from the North Atlantic and reducing her speed for cruising would help extend the life of the ship.

In France the final stage of construction of the *Queen Mary 2* was marred by a fatal accident on 15th November 2003, when a gangway collapsed during a visit of shipyard workers and their relatives who had been invited to visit the vessel. After a 15-metre (49 feet) fall into the dry dock, a total of 32 people were injured and 16, including children, were killed.

Cunard took delivery of the *Queen Mary 2* on 22nd December 2003, and despite the terrible weather several thousand greeted her upon her first arrival in Southampton four days later. The next 18 days would see the *Queen Mary 2* undertake several shakedown cruises, host thousands of visitors and be named by Her Majesty The Queen, making the first January public engagement of her reign, prior to departing on her maiden voyage.

The naming ceremony on 8th January 2004 has been acclaimed as the most spectacular ceremony of its kind ever and featured performances by The Band of Her Majesty's Royal Marines (Portsmouth), the Royal Philharmonic Orchestra, soprano Lesley Garrett – all performing under the direction of one of Britain's most popular conductors, Anthony Inglis. One heart-stopping moment was provided when singer Heather Small was performing a specially-extended version of her anthem 'Proud' and the *Queen Mary 2* was 'unveiled' after a spectacular curtain drop.

Earlier that day, the *Queen Mary 2* was bestowed with the designation RMS (Royal Mail Ship) by the Royal Mail. She became the first Cunarder to carry the designation since 1968 as Cunard declined the honour for the *QE2*. The Cunard publicity machine was always quick to point out that the hull of its first RMS ship, the *Britannia*, could fit within the Britannia Restaurant on the *Queen Mary 2* which was now the biggest RMS vessel in history!

The *Queen Mary 2* left Southampton on her maiden voyage to Fort Lauderdale on 12th January 2004 and from then until her return to Southampton she operated a series of Caribbean cruises. On 16th April she left Southampton on her first Atlantic crossing proper and arrived in New York on 22nd April. Previous maiden arrivals had seen Cunarders surrounded by dozens of private craft but the post-911 New York restricted her arrival to fireboats and helicopters. Three days later the *QE2* arrived in New York and berthed alongside and it was then the sheer scale of the *Queen Mary 2* came into its own when passengers and crew on that ship were looking down on the *QE2*! That night, on 25th April, both ships left New York for what was the first-ever tandem crossing of the Atlantic – an event repeated by Cunard several times since. Commodore Warwick and Captain McNaught would keep their ships within a mile of each other and would changeover sides during the night to extend the photographic opportunities. Their arrival in Southampton on 1st May would be a significant day for both ships as the Boston Cup, denoting flagship status, transferred to the *Queen Mary 2* in a moving ceremony on board the *QE2*. The older ship left Southampton later that day, heading off for refit in Germany. Cunard had arranged for guests to view the sailpast from the new flagship the *Queen Mary 2*; many had tears in their eyes as the *QE2* emerged from the mist bang on cue, with her whistle blasting, as the rousing British patriotic music being played was interrupted to play Stevie Wonder's 'Isn't She Lovely' – a moment that will live in the memory of all who witnessed it.

The original 2004 schedule for the *Queen Mary 2* had to be amended in order for her to attend the Athens Olympics as

an accommodation ship. It was important to secure the presence of the ship at such events to cement her in the public psyche as well as perhaps start the transfer of such duties from the *QE2* to the new flag bearer.

While it is difficult to envisage just what would have happened if Carnival Corporation had not consumed P&O, it is safe to assume that Carnival would have used Cunard to obtain a larger market share of the UK market and aggressively compete against P&O. It was thought that several sisters to the *Queen Victoria* would have been built in order for Carnival to achieve this. But now Cunard and P&O were effectively competing for the same market in the same market, so several months after P&O had been acquired and Carnival had assessed the potential future for both Cunard and its new purchase, it was decided, with construction well advanced, that the *Queen Victoria*'s design was not quite suitable for Cunard. She did not have the number of suites and junior suites considered appropriate and lacked a second Grill restaurant for those travelling in deluxe accommodation. On 5th April 2004 it was announced she would be transferred to P&O Cruises to appear in April 2005 as their the *Arcadia*.

A new 90,000-ton *Queen Victoria*, for delivery at the end of 2007, was ordered for Cunard at the same time. This new version had her hull lengthened and strengthened with grander public spaces and extra deluxe accommodation built into its design.

In July 2004, Carnival Corp announced the relocation of Cunard from Miami to California in a move that would eliminate around 300 positions and save $20 million annually. The move was completed by the end of the year and effectively placed Cunard under the management of Princess Cruises. The association between Cunard and Seabourn was dissolved.

Over the course of her lifetime, the *QE2* made the headlines for breaking new records or surpassing records that had stood unchallenged for many years. On 4th September 2005 she became the longest-serving Cunard Atlantic liner after sailing 36 years, four months and three days and thus surpassing the record held by the *Scythia*. For many years subsequent Presidents and Managing Directors of Cunard would not want to highlight her age when it came to special anniversaries fearing it would make her pale in comparison to newer, flashier ships, but the PR Department would make a great fuss safe in the knowledge that most people knew the

Opposite page: The largest tapestry ever to go to sea in the Britannia Restaurant of the **Queen Mary 2**. *(Cunard)*

QE2 was a child of the sixties, that her age was something to be celebrated, the investment in her over the years kept her ahead of the competition in some respects and that the press would mark the anniversary anyway even if Cunard had chosen to ignore it. But each of these anniversaries or milestones would start another debate in shipping circles about just how much longer could this legend sail on for. SOLAS (Safety of Life at Sea) regulations were often cited as perhaps being the *QE2*'s Achilles heel. The round of regulations introduced in 1997 saw the likes of the *Canberra* and the *Rotterdam* withdrawn by their owners and another round, due in 2010, saw several other vintage ships retired. The *QE2*'s design meant that 2010, after minor work was undertaken, was not an issue for her.

From April 2006, future calls at New York by the *Queen Mary 2* would see Cunard ships berthing at Brooklyn at the new cruise terminal there rather than at the traditional piers, as the *Queen Mary 2's* length, and the fact that over 100 foot of her projected into the river whenever she was alongside, gave cause for concern with the American Coastguard.

Italian tradition demands that a 'Madrina' be present at the float out of ships at their yards and Cunard selected long-serving Social Hostess Maureen Ryan to officiate at the float out of the second *Queen Victoria* on 15th January 2007. Maureen had joined Cunard in 1963 at 17 and before smashing a bottle of Italian Prosecco against the side of the ship she had assisted in the welding of two coins at the base of the mast – an Italian Euro coin and a gold Queen Victoria sovereign.

The *QE2* sailed into Sydney on 20th April 2007 and met with the *Queen Mary 2*. The meeting, the first of two Cunard 'Queens' at the port since the *Queen Mary* and the *Queen Elizabeth* in the Second World War, brought traffic chaos and the city to a standstill.

As stated in Chapter 7 about the retirement of the *Queen Mary* and the *Queen Elizabeth*, the day that had to one day come, came when on 18th June 2007 Cunard surprised everyone with the announcement that the *QE2* had been sold for $100 million to Istithmar, the investment arm of Dubai World, a wholly owned company of the government of Dubai. She was to be handed over in November 2008 and after re-building would be positioned at a specially-constructed pier at The Palm Jumeirah, the world's largest man-made island, to create "a luxury floating hotel, retail and entertainment destination". No matter how the sale was dressed up the **London Evening Standard** hoardings that night proclaimed '*QE2* sold to Arabs'.

Sultan Ahmed bin Sulayem, Chairman of Dubai World, said: "*QE2* is without a doubt one of the wonders of the maritime world, and is easily the most famous serving liner in the world today".

For some the shock, outrage and upset caused by her sale meant they would never sail Cunard again but Cunard was in the shipping business and ships had to be run at a profit. While she had and was making money, the *QE2* achieving $100 million for a 40-year-old ship was unheard of and it did pass the final decision of her future to another party. Perhaps it also spared the ship from sailing past her best and the inevitable headlines that would have made.

The gamble to build the *QE2* had certainly paid off and Sir John Brocklebank and Sir Basil Smallpeice would certainly have raised a glass – and certainly should be celebrated themselves.

Before the sale announcement, Cunard made plans to celebrate the 40th anniversary of the *QE2*'s launch on 20th September 2007. Very few ships ever reached this milestone while in service so a special Round Britain cruise (15th to 23rd September 2007) was planned that would call at the Tyne, South Queensferry, Greenock and Liverpool. Initially it was thought her sale would overshadow the celebrations but that was not the case as Cunard and those on board were even more determined to celebrate a remarkable ship and a remarkable career. Her maiden arrival on the Tyne was probably one of the most exciting ever made by the ship - an arrival her Captain, Ian McNaught, had to get right as he was taking his ship home! After several aborted attempts to enter the river, the *QE2* managed it on the last attempt and on the sail up the Tyne the *QE2* was cheered by thousands. Her arrival on the Clyde exactly 40 years after her launch saw the Red Arrows perform before the *QE2*'s whistle was sounded for 40 seconds at the moment of her launch. Celebrations reached a crescendo the next day in Liverpool when all passengers attended a celebratory concert at the Anglican Cathedral in Liverpool which, as emotions ran high, told her story in word and song. Late on the last night before arriving in Southampton, the *QE2* sailed past the *Queen Mary 2* in the English Channel and both ships saluted each other.

The *Queen Victoria* had just returned to the yard after her first sea trials when, on 10th October 2007, Cunard announced the order for a 92,000-ton ship costing 500 million Euros. Her slightly higher gross tonnage made her the second largest Cunarder ever built and not surprisingly Cunard also announced she would be named the *Queen Elizabeth*. While this new ship was of a totally different type

and design to the two earlier ships named 'Elizabeth' it was an appropriate name for Cunard as there had been an Elizabeth in its fleet for longer than any other name making it perhaps the most revered in its history.

But why not the *Queen Elizabeth 3*? In Cunard history there have been three passenger ships named the *Caronia*, two named the *Carmania* and two named the *Laconia* and the second and third to use the names were never given a number in their name. The *QE2* was and will always be the exception - perhaps Cunard's most exceptional ship - and the company was reverting back to history by not adding a number. Just as the company would revert back to history when a bottle of Rothschilds 'Cunard Graves' wine was used to officially name her. The *Queen Mary 2* and the *Queen Victoria* were named using champagne which was a break with tradition as company ships had always been christened using wine from the Commonwealth which did not, thankfully, have the same result as the wine used for *Caronia* in Liverpool in 1999!

The announcement partially offset the news of the *QE2*'s sale and Cunard was able to claim the introduction of a third new ship in six years giving it, one of the oldest names in shipping the youngest fleet in the cruise industry. It was all a far cry from a decade earlier when the fleet, although highly-rated, was a rag tag collection of ships with hardly any consistency in the onboard product to the livery of the fleet. For the first time in decades the Cunard fleet would be consistent in its dining styles, cabin sizes and overall standards.

The Italian shipbuilder Fincantieri would build the *Queen Elizabeth* but she would be built at their Monfalcone yard near Trieste while the *Queen Victoria* was being built at their Marghera yard near Venice.

When the *Queen Elizabeth's* maiden voyage (a 12-day trip to the Canaries departing 12th October 2010) was announced it sold out within 29 minutes 14 seconds, which was faster than the final voyage for the *QE2* had sold.

The *Queen Victoria* and the *Queen Elizabeth* were Cunard versions of the Vista-Class design developed by Carnival Corporation and used very successfully for its Costa, Carnival, Holland America and P&O brands. The *Queen Elizabeth* was the eleventh Vista ship and this was the source of much criticism of Cunard but those quick to criticise forgot Samuel Cunard himself would approve of Carnival's choice not to take risks and build upon a proven design!

The *Queen Victoria* was handed over to Cunard on 24th November 2007. On the day before her maiden voyage she was named at a ceremony in Southampton on 10th December that year by Her Royal Highness The Duchess of

The 'first' **Queen Victoria** *which would enter service as* **Arcadia** *for P&O Cruises. (Cunard)*

Cornwall, accompanied by His Royal Highness The Prince of Wales. Sadly the bottle of champagne failed to smash after being released by The Duchess, with the press naturally raising the spectre of bad luck for the ship in the headlines the next day with further headlines being made during her Christmas cruise when an outbreak of Norovirus was linked by the press to the unbroken bottle. In fact while the actual

bottle The Duchess released did not break a stand-by bottle was broken immediately.

On 6th January 2008, both the *QE2* and the *Queen Victoria* left Southampton for New York. The Masters of each ship, Captain Ian McNaught and Captain Paul Wright kept both vessels close throughout the boisterous crossing and would swap sides each day. When they arrived in New York on 13th

An impressive view of the (second) **Queen Victoria** *heading down the English Channel. (FotoFlite)*

Queen Victoria

Cunard were keen to emphasise the ocean liner design of the **Queen Victoria**'s public spaces and they do combine a mix of the grand and the intimate.

Above: Chart Room.

Left: Cafe Carinthia.

Below: Princess Grill.

(All photos Mike Louagie)

Above: Grand Lobby. (Mike Louagie)

Below left: Britannia Restaurant. (Mike Louagie)

Below right: Royal Arcade. (Mike Louagie)

FOR YOUR LEISURE & RELAXATION

1 Connexions™ Conference Centre (Deck 3)	11 Sea View Sauna - Cunard Royal Spa (Deck 9)
2 Cunard Royal Spa & Fitness Centre (Deck 9)	12 Sports Deck (Deck 11)
3 Cunardia Museum (Deck 2)	13 Royal Court Theatre (Decks 1, 2 & 3)
4 Empire Casino (Deck 2)	14 The Grand Lobby
5 Images (Deck 3)	15 The Royal Arcade - Shops (Deck 3)
6 Library (Decks 2 & 3)	16 The Terrace (Deck 11)
7 Hydropool - Cunard Royal Spa (Deck 9)	17 The Zone and Play Zone (Deck 10)
8 Lido Pool - Aft (Deck 9)	18 Whirlpools - Lido Pool - Aft (Deck 9)
9 Pavilion Pool (Deck 9)	19 Whirlpools - Pavilion Pool (Deck 9)
10 Queens Arcade (Deck 2)	20 The Grills Upper Terrace (Deck 12)

*Unusually for a modern ship Cunard's cross-section for the **Queen Victoria** was deliberately designed to reflect those of liners past such as the one for the **Aquitania** on page 44. (Cunard)*

January they were joined by the *Queen Mary 2* for the first-ever gathering by three Cunard 'Queen' liners. Later that day the *QE2* left New York on her final World Cruise.

Her Majesty The Queen paid a farewell visit to the *QE2* in Southampton on 2nd June just as her Mother had paid a farewell to 'her' ship the *Queen Elizabeth* in 1968.

Cunard had scheduled a series of farewell cruises for the *QE2* after the sale announcement. Two existing voyages in 2008 were replaced by a British Isles voyage and two transatlantic crossings while the farewell voyage to Dubai was added to an original schedule that had nothing programmed for the *QE2* in November.

The *QE2*'s 'Farewell to the British Isles' voyage departed Southampton on 30th September and emotional calls were made at Cobh, Liverpool, Greenock, South Queensferry and the Tyne with a maiden visit to Belfast. At Greenock the weather was unusually balmy and her departure that night saw the last-ever Cunard ship to be built on the Clyde leave that river for the last time. At Cobh a new Cunard tradition began - to commemorate the loss of the *Lusitania* at the Peace

Memorial to the disaster in the middle of the town.

For the second time in two years a concert was held at the Anglican Cathedral in Liverpool to celebrate the life of the *QE2*. Carol Marlow, President and Managing Director, acknowledged the bereavement felt by many when she said:

"For the last hundred years each generation has taken particularly to its heart one ship out of all the ships of the day.

"That one ship becomes the focus of national attention, admiration, mystique and myth.

"From 1907 for almost thirty years it was the magnificent four-funnelled *Mauretania*, built on the Tyne and based here in the port of Liverpool.

"Of her, President Franklin D. Roosevelt wrote: "If ever there was a ship that possessed a soul, *Mauretania* did; she was a ship with a fighting heart".

"She was a ship thousands turned out to see in 1935, watching from the cliffs as she progressed slowly up the east coast to the breaker's yard on the Firth of Forth.

"People were sad, as they said there would never be

VICTORIA

DINING VENUES

21	Britannia Restaurant (Decks 2 & 3)

THE GRILLS

22	Princess Grill - Starboard Side (Deck 11)
23	Queens Grill - Port Side (Deck 11)
24	The Courtyard (Deck 11)
25	The Grills Lounge (Deck 11)

ALTERNATIVE DINING VENUES

26	Todd English Restaurant - Port Side (Deck 2)
27	Winter Garden - Retractable Roof (Deck 9)
28	Lido (Deck 9)

BARS & LOUNGES

29	Café Carinthia (Deck 2)
30	Chart Room (Deck 2)
31	Commodore Club (Deck 10)
32	Golden Lion (Deck 2)
33	Hemispheres (Deck 10)
34	Midships Bar and Lounge (Deck 3)
35	The Queens Room (Decks 2 & 3)
36	Churchill's Cigar Lounge (Deck 10)
37	Admiral's lounge (Deck 10)

another *Mauretania*.

"And they were right; there wasn't. But there was another icon.

"For the next year *Queen Mary* came into service – and very rapidly she outshone all the other ships of her generation.

"And when she sailed from Southampton for the final time, just 32 years after *Mauretania*'s final voyage, people were equally sad. And they said there would never be another *Queen Mary*.

"And there wasn't. But there was *QE2*!

"In the same year *Queen Mary* took up residence in Long Beach as a hotel and convention centre, *QE2* thundered down the slipway into the Clyde. Ever since she has been the world's most famous ship.

"*Queen Mary* was not forgotten, just as *Mauretania* was not forgotten, but *QE2* assumed the mantle as the 'most famous ship in the world'.

"Surprisingly so, really, as she was so modern, so far ahead of her time, so different from the ships that had gone before.

"Now *QE2* moves on – to a home in Dubai, where she will

start a new life which is likely to be as long as her current one has been.

"And people are undoubtedly sad; they say there will never be another *QE2*.

"There won't – but there is *Queen Mary 2*....

"But now for *QE2*, it's 'Time to Say Goodbye'".

She would repeat those words on board as the *QE2* sailed into Dubai on her final day of service.

On 10th October, the *QE2* left Southampton with the *Queen Mary 2* and both vessels headed for New York. The *QE2*'s call there on 16th October was her 710th at the port and that night she left America forever and, escorted by the *Queen Mary 2* she made her 812th and last crossing of the Atlantic.

Just as the *Mauretania* made a memorable farewell message to her birthplace as she sailed past the mouth of the Tyne in 1935, the *QE2*'s Captain Ian McNaught gave a farewell address to Southampton which was broadcast to the thousands who had gathered in Southampton:

"For forty years, *QE2* has been acclaimed all over the

*An emotional moment in Cunard and New York history as the **QE2** leaves the port for the last time on 16th October 2008 with the **Queen Mary 2** following. (Cunard)*

globe as a symbol of British excellence.

"And throughout her life, imprinted firmly on that symbol of excellence is one word. And the word is Southampton.

"*QE2* belongs to Southampton; this is her home, just as it will be home to *Queen Mary 2* and *Queen Victoria*.

"She has put into her home port more times than she has visited any other port in the world. And after every voyage this is always the port that she comes home to: Southampton.

"But the day has come today which had to come. And this time, her 726th time, is the last time. For when *QE2* sails tonight she will not come back home again.

"For forty years *QE2* has striven to serve Southampton and the country to her best. But now her sea days are done, and she passes on to a new life in a new home.

"On behalf of *QE2* I bid Southampton farewell and thank you for all the affection you have shown to her over all those years.

"Southampton, I salute you".

Right: HRH the Duchess of Cornwall at the naming ceremony of **Queen Victoria** *just after the bottle had refused to break. Also seen are HRH The Prince of Wales and Cunard President and Managing Director Carol Marlow. (Cunard)*

Below: The **Queen Victoria** *departs Southampton on her maiden voyage on 11th December 2007. (Cunard)*

After a visit by His Royal Highness The Duke of Edinburgh, the *QE2*'s farewell voyage left Southampton for Dubai on 11th November and called at Lisbon, Gibraltar, Civitavecchia, Naples, Malta, Alexandria and transited the Suez Canal. Her last day at sea in Cunard service, 26th November 2008, was 40 years to the day that the *QE2* had left the Clyde on her first sea trials. The next day the Cunard flag was lowered for the final time during a moving ceremony on the port bridge wing, where Cunard President and Managing Director Carol Marlow initially struggled to compose herself at the start of her speech, which saw her leave Cunard ownership.

The *QE2* was born into a world of uncertainty, built by an almost bankrupt shipyard for an almost bankrupt shipping company. Her future was predicted to be so short as to be non-existent, and many deplored her departure from the style norms of her predecessors. But she survived; more than that, she triumphed against the odds. There is not much else to be said about the *QE2* that has not been said in the many books and thousands of tributes written about her over the years. Her record speaks for itself. She had completed 1,419 voyages, carried almost 2.5 million passengers over 5,875,493.22 million nautical miles – more than any other ship ever. The "white elephant" proved them all wrong and went on to do things her own way. She is perhaps Cunard's

*The **QE2** making her final call to Liverpool on 3rd October 2008. (Cunard)*

greatest ship. She was perhaps Cunard's greatest gamble. She did overshadow whatever ship happened to be her fleetmate at the time and she was probably more famous than Cunard itself but company flagships have always been that. From 1974 to 2004 the *QE2* had the Atlantic more or less to herself and she alone ensured the continuation of Samuel's service until the baton - symbolised by the Boston Cup - could be handed to a successor that very much relied on her in terms of service, atmosphere and aspects of her design to carry the

*A scene from the Anglican Cathedral in Liverpool of the **QE2**'s 'Time to Say Goodbye' concert on 3rd October 2008. (Cunard)*

*HRH The Duke of Edinburgh presents 'Coming Home' to the City of Southampton on the **QE2**'s final day in her homeport. The painting by Robert Lloyd was specially-commissioned by Cunard to remind the City of its favourite ship for generations to come. (Cunard)*

Cunard name into the future.

Eight years later the *QE2* languishes in Dubai. For all intents and purposes it looks as if those farewell voyage passengers and crew have just left with furniture in public rooms laid exactly as it was when she was in service. Several grand schemes to have her lavishly refurbished and located in other ports around the world have come to nothing and her future is desperately in doubt.

2009 was another year of change for Cunard when it came to which city the company would be directed from when the

*The **QE2** during her last hours in Great Britain and Southampton on 11th November 2008. (Cunard)*

company was relocated from Los Angeles to Southampton to be based from the same office as P&O Cruises.

On 2nd July 2009, the keel for the *Queen Elizabeth* was laid. Her construction proceeded at an alarming rate in terms of speed. She was structurally complete when her Cunard-painted funnel was hoisted into position by Christmas 2009 and was ready to be floated for the first time on 5th January 2010. This time Cunard had chosen Florence ('Dennie') Farmer to perform the role - which she did admirably - as Madrina. Her husband, Willie, had served Cunard for 41 years after joining the company in 1938 and was Chief Engineer on the *Queen Elizabeth* and the *QE2*. For this ship Cunard had selected three coins for welding into the mast dating from 1938 (a half crown), 1967 (a gold sovereign) and 2010 (a sovereign). The years symbolised the years the *Queen Elizabeth*, the *QE2* and the *Queen Elizabeth* were launched or named.

The *Queen Mary 2*'s 2010 Atlantic programme saw the addition of seven-night crossings with that duration becoming the norm from 2011. 2014 would see several eight-night crossings added to her schedule.

On 4th October 2010 Cunard took delivery of the *Queen Elizabeth* and when The Queen named her in Southampton on 11th October 2010 she could claim the astonishing fact that she was the only person to have attended the launches of all three Cunard 'Elizabeths'. She accompanied her Mother when 12 years of age to the launch of the first *Queen Elizabeth* in 1938 and she performed the launch of the second ship to bear the name in 1967.

2011 saw the registry of the Cunard fleet change to the Bermudan flag. The *Queen Victoria* and the *Queen Elizabeth* were re-flagged in October while the *Queen Mary 2* received Hamilton on her stern on 8th December and for the first time since its founding no British-registered ships were flying under the Cunard flag. The re-registry did mean weddings could be performed on a Cunard ship and the first one took place on the *Queen Mary 2* on 29th April 2012.

When Cunard's three ships, the *Queen Mary 2*, the *QE2* and the *Queen Victoria* met in New York on 13th January 2008 it was the first time three 'Queens' had met and the first time the entire fleet had gathered together in one port. The three met again on 22nd April that year in Southampton. Both

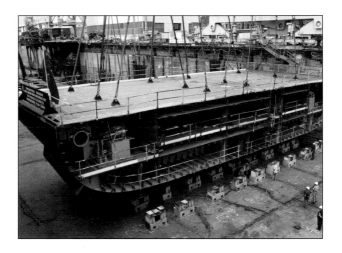

Above right: The keel laying for the **Queen Elizabeth** *on 2nd July 2009.(Brian D. Smith)*

Right: Cunard President and Managing Director seen with Fincantieri executives and Priest at the Keel Laying for the **Queen Elizabeth**. *(Brian D. Smith)*

Below: The **Queen Elizabeth** *fitting out in 2010. (Brian D. Smith)*

Queen Elizabeth

While a sister to the **Queen Victoria** *this ship would have her own style with some structural alterations made and more art deco touches.*

Above: Commodore Club.

Left: Royal Court Theatre

Below: Cunard Royal Spa.

(All photos Cunard)

Above: The Library. (Cunard)

Below left: Golden Lion Pub. (Cunard)

Below right: The Verandah. (Cunard)

*The **Queen Elizabeth** leaving the builders for Southampton. (Brian D. Smith)*

events drew large crowds, excitement and interest and underlined the fact that Cunard ships attracted crowds and made news. This is a fact not lost on Cunard and the current fleet of 'Queens' have met several times. The first meeting took place in New York on 13th January 2011, the second in

*Three ships have carried the Elizabeth name in Cunard history making it one of the most revered names for the company. **Queen Elizabeth**, 1946 (top), **Queen Elizabeth 2**, 1969 (middle) and **Queen Elizabeth**, 2010 (bottom). (Fincantieri)*

Southampton on 5th June 2012 when they marked the Diamond Jubilee of The Queen, the third meeting took place again in Southampton on 13th July 2012, followed by meetings in Lisbon on 6th May 2014, when all three were photographed together in open water and Southampton on 9th May.

Cunard was keen to mark the tenth anniversary into service of the *Queen Mary 2* and special events and photo opportunities took place throughout the first six months of 2014 with the highlight being a visit by His Royal Highness The Duke of Edinburgh to the ship in Southampton on 9th May. Her first ten years had seen the *Queen Mary 2* sail almost 1.5 million nautical miles on 419 voyages that called at 177 ports in 60 countries.

In 2014 Cunard confirmed a series of cruises and celebrations to commemorate the 175th anniversary of the departure of the *Britannia*. In what will be an event never before seen in Liverpool, the *Queen Mary 2*, the *Queen Victoria* and the *Queen Elizabeth* will be seen on the Mersey together on 25th May 2015 before the *Queen Mary 2* makes a return call to the city on 4th July and later that day will follow in the *Britannia's* wake and head for Halifax and Boston. It will be the first time a Cunard ship has taken passengers from Liverpool to America since the *Franconia* in 1968.

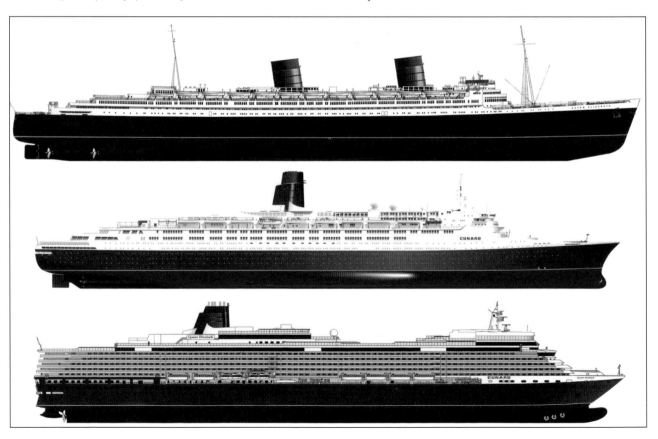

*Above: HRH The Duchess of Cornwall shares a joke with Captain Paul Wright on the **Queen Victoria**'s maiden call to Liverpool on 26th July 2010. The Duchess has made two visits to 'her' ship since naming her in 2007. (Cunard)*

*Right: HM The Queen meets artist Isobel Peachey on board the **Queen Elizabeth** before naming the ship on 11th October 2010. Cunard had commissioned the artist to paint an official portrait of The Queen to hang on board the ship. (Cunard)*

*Below: The Queen together with Captains who had commanded the **QE2** during her farewell visit to the ship on 2nd June 2008. (Cunard)*

*The **Queen Mary 2** in Liverpool on her maiden call on 20th October 2009 – the largest passenger liner ever to visit the City. (Cunard)*

*200-metres apart - the three largest Cunard ships ever built head triumphantly for Southampton on 6th MAy 2014: the **Queen Victoria** (top),*

Queen Mary 2 *(middle)and the **Queen Elizabeth** (bottom). (James Morgan)*

Celebrations will also be held in Southampton, New York, Hamburg and Sydney and the *Queen Victoria* will be in Cobh on 7th May to commemorate the loss of the *Lusitania* 100 years earlier.

As the 175th anniversary approaches, the three largest ships ever built for Cunard continue to offer an impeccable standard of service, continue to make headlines and continue to stand out thanks to the distinctive livery worn by Cunard ships since 1840. As the anniversary dawns perhaps the one black cloud is that at the time of writing the future of the *QE2* is uncertain and *Queen Mary* continues to struggle in Long Beach. But this should not detract from the triumph that is Cunard.

Cunard in 2015 - the triumph of a Great Tradition!

HRH The Duke of Edinburgh on board **Queen Mary 2** *in Southampton on 9th May 2014 to mark the ship's tenth anniversary of service. (Cunard)*

Above right: HRH The Duke of Edinburgh with Captain Christopher Wells on the Bridge. (James Morgan)

Right: The unveiling of a specially-commissioned painting by Robert Lloyd. (James Morgan)

Below: HRH The Duke of Edinburgh with the **Queen Mary 2's** *Management Team. (James Morgan)*

The Triumph of a Great Tradition'; a specially-commissioned portrait of the three Cunard Queens saluting the company's 'spiritual' home of Liverpool on 25th May 2015.

Fleet list

Cunard vessels owned and operated by the British and North American Royal Mail Steam Packet Company, the British and Foreign Steam Navigation Company, the British and North American Steam Packet Company, the Cunard Steamship Company, Cunard White Star, Cunard Line, Cunard Steamship Company, Cunard Cruise Ships, Cunard Ellerman and Carnival Corporation.

	Name	Launch	Builder	Hull	gt	Prop
1	*Unicorn*	1836	Robert Steele & Son, Greenock	W	648	P
2	*Margaret*	1839	Caird & Co, Greenock	W	700	P
3	*Britannia*	1840	Robert Duncan & Co, Greenock	W	1,156	P
4	*Acadia*	1840	John Wood & Co, Port Glasgow	W	1,154	P
5	*Caledonia*	1840	Robert Wood & Co, Greenock	W	1,156	P
6	*Columbia*	1840	Robert Steele & Son, Greenock	W	1,175	P
7	*Hibernia*	1842	Robert Steele & Son, Greenock	W	1,422	P
8	*Cambria*	1844	Robert Steele & Son, Greenock	W	1,423	P
9	*Shamrock* [1]	1847	Caird & Co, Greenock	I	714	Sgl Scr
10	*America*	1847	Robert Steele & Son, Greenock	W	1,826	P
11	*Niagara*	1847	Robert Steele & Son, Greenock	W	1,842	P
12	*Europa*	1847	John Wood & Co, Port Glasgow	W	1,834	P
13	*Canada*	1848	Robert Steele & Son, Greenock	W	1,831	P
14	*Satellite*	1848	Robert Napier & Sons, Glasgow	W	157	P
15	*British Queen* [2]	1849	Wm Denny & Bros, Dumbarton	I	772	Sgl Scr
16	*Asia*	1850	Robert Steele & Son, Greenock	W	2,226	P
17	*Africa*	1850	Robert Steele & Son, Greenock	W	2,226	P
18	*Arabia*	1852	Robert Steele & Son, Greenock	W	2,402	P
19	*Andes*	1852	Wm Denny & Bros, Dumbarton	I	1,852	Sgl Scr
20	*Alps*	1852	Wm Denny & Bros, Dumbarton	I	1,852	Sgl Scr
21	*Balbec*	1852	Wm Denny & Bros, Dumbarton	I	774	Sgl Scr
22	*Taurus*	1853	Wm Denny & Bros, Dumbarton	I	1,126	Sgl Scr
23	*Melita*	1853	Alexander Denny & Co, Dumbarton	I	1,255	Sgl Scr
24	*Teneriffe*	1853	Wm Denny & Bros, Dumbarton	I	1,126	Sgl Scr
25	*Karnak*	1853	Wm Denny & Bros, Dumbarton	I	1,116	Sgl Scr
26	*Delta*	1853	Barclay Curle & Co, Stobcross	I	645	Sgl Scr
27	*Jackal*	1853	J & G Thomson & Co, Govan	I	185	P
28	*Emeu* [3]	1853	Robert Napier & Sons, Glasgow	I	1,538	Sgl Scr
29	*Jura*	1854	J & G Thomson & Co, Govan	I	2,241	Sgl Scr
30	*Etna*	1854	Caird & Co, Greenock	I	2,115	Sgl Scr
31	*Lebanon* [4]	1854	J & G Thomson & Co, Govan	I	1,383	Sgl Scr
32	*Persia*	1855	Robert Napier & Sons, Glasgow	I	3,700	P

Footnote

[1] Owned by Charles MacIver & Co, but used on Cunard Mediterranean services.

[2] Bought by Cunard, 1853.

[3] Bought by Cunard, 1854.

[4] Bought by Cunard, 1855; formerly *Aerolith*

	Name	Launch	Builder	Hull	gt	Prop
33	**Stromboli** [5]	1856	J & G Thomson & Co, Govan	I	734	Sgl Scr
34	**Damascus** [6]	1856	Wm Denny & Bros, Dumbarton	I	1,214	Sgl Scr
35	**Calabria** [7]	1857	J & G Thomson & Co, Govan	I	2,760	Sgl Scr
36	**Palestine**	1858	Robert Steele & Son, Greenock	I	1,800	Sgl Scr
37	**Olympus**	1860	J & G Thomson & Co, Govna	I	1,794	Sgl Scr
38	**Atlas**	1860	J & G Thomson & Co, Govan	I	1,794	Sgl Scr
39	**Marathon**	1860	Robert Napier & Sons, Glasgow	I	1,784	Sgl Scr
40	**Hecla**	1860	Robert Napier & Sons, Glasgow	I	1,790	Sgl Scr
41	**Kedar**	1860	Wm Denny & Bros, Dumbarton	I	1,763	Sgl Scr
42	**Sidon**	1861	Wm Denny & Bros, Dumbarton	I	1,872	Sgl Scr
43	**Morocco**	1861	Wm Denny & Bros, Dumbarton	I	1,855	Sgl Scr
44	**Scotia**	1861	Robert Napier & Sons, Glasgow	I	3,871	P
45	**China**	1861	Robert Napier & Sons, Glasgow	I	2,638	Sgl Scr
46	**Corsica**	1863	J & G Thomson & Co, Govan	I	1,134	Sgl Scr
47	**Tripoli**	1864	J & G Thomson & Co, Govan	I	2,146	Sgl Scr
48	**Cuba**	1864	Tod & McGregor, Glasgow	I	2,832	Sgl Scr
49	**Aleppo**	1864	J & G Thomson & Co, Govan	I	2.057	Sgl Scr
50	**Tarifa**	1865	J & G Thomson & Co, Govan	I	2,058	Sgl Scr
51	**Java**	1865	J & G Thomson & Co, Govan	I	2,057	Sgl Scr
52	**Malta**	1865	J & G Thomson & Co, Govan	I	2,132	Sgl Scr
53	**Palmyra**	1865	Caird & Co, Greenock	I	2,044	Sgl Scr
54	**Russia**	1867	J & G Thomson & Co, Govan	I	2,960	Sgl Scr
55	**Siberia**	1867	J & G Thomson & Co, Govan	I	2,498	Sgl Scr
56	**Samaria**	1868	J & G Thomson & Co, Govan	I	2,500	Sgl Scr
57	**Batavia**	1870	Wm Denny & Bros, Dumbarton	I	2,593	Sgl Scr
58	**Abyssinia**	1870	J & G Thomson & Co, Govan	I	3,376	Sgl Scr
59	**Algeria**	1870	J & G Thomson & Co, Govan	I	3,428	Sgl Scr
60	**Parthia**	1870	Wm Denny & Bros, Dumbarton	I	3,167	Sgl Scr
61	**Trinidad**	1872	J & G Thomson & Co, Govan	I	1,900	Sgl Scr
62	**Demerara**	1872	J & G Thomson & Co, Govna	I	1,904	Sgl Scr
63	**Nantes**	1873	Blackwood & Gordon, Port Glasgow	I	1,473	Sgl Scr
64	**Brest**	1873	Blackwood & Gordon, Port Glasgow	I	1,472	Sgl Scr
65	**Bothnia**	1871	J & G Thomson & Co, Clydebank	I	4,535	Sgl Scr
66	**Saragossa**	1874	J & G Thomson & Co, Clydebank	I	2,263	Sgl Scr
67	**Scythia**	1874	J & G Thomson & Co, Clydeban	I	4,557	Sgl Scr
68	**Cherbourg**	1874	J & G Thomson & Co, Clydebank	I	1,614	Sgl Scr
69	**Gallia**	1878	J & G Thomson & Co, Clydebank	I	4,809	Sgl Scr
70	**Otter**	1880	Blackwood & Gordon, Port Glasgow	I	287	Sgl Scr
71	**Servia**	1881	J & G Thomson & Co, Clydebank	S	7,391	Sgl Scr
72	**Catalonia**	1881	J & G Thomson & Co, Clydebank	I	4,638	Sgl Scr
73	**Cephalonia**	1882	Laird Bros, Birkenhead	I	5,606	Sgl Scr

Footnote

[5] Bought by Cunard 1859; formerly **James Brown**

[6] Bought by Cunard during fitting out; formerly **St George**

[7] Bought by Cunard 1859; formerly **Australasian**

	Name	Launch	Builder	Hull	gt	Prop
74	*Pavonia*	1882	J & G Thomson & Co, Clydebank	I	5,588	Sgl Scr
75	*Aurania*	1882	J & G Thomson & Co, Clydebank	S	7,269	Sgl Scr
76	*Oregon* [8]	1883	John Elder & Co, Fairfield, Glasgow	I	7,017	Sgl Scr
77	*Umbria*	1884	John Elder & Co, Fairfield, Glasgow	S	8,128	Sgl Scr
78	*Skirmisher*	1884	J & G Thomson & Co, Govan	S	612	Sgl Scr
79	*Etruria*	1884	John Elder & Co, Fairfield, Glasgow	S	8,120	Sgl Scr
80	*Feltria* [9]	1891	Wm Denny & Bros, Dumbarton	S	5,254	Sgl Scr
81	*Campania*	1892	Fairfield Shipbuilding & Engineering Co, Glasgow	S	12,950	Tw Scr
82	*Lucania*	1893	Fairfield Shipbuilding & Engineering Co, Glasgow	S	12,952	Tw Scr
83	*Thracia* [10]	1895	Sir Raylton Dixon & Co, Middlesbrough	S	2,891	Sgl Scr
84	*Sylvania*	1895	London & Glasgow Shipbuilding & Engineering Co, Glasgow	S	5,598	Tw Scr
85	*Carinthia*	1895	London & Glasgow Shipbuilding & Engineering Co, Glasgow	S	5,598	Tw Scr
86	*Lycia* [11]	1896	Sir Raylton Dixon & Co, Middlesbrough	S	2,715	Sgl Scr
87	*Satellite* [12]	1896	J Scott & Co, Kinghorn	S	333	P
88	*Pavia*	1897	Workman Clark & Co, Belfast	S	2,945	Sgl Scr
89	*Tyria*	1897	Workman Clark & Co, Belfast	S	2,936	Sgl Scr
90	*Cypria*	1898	Workman Clark & Co, Belfast	S	2,936	Sgl Scr
91	*Ultonia* [13]	1898	C.S. Swan & Hunter Ltd, Wallsend	S	8,845	Tw Scr
92	*Veria*	1899	Armstrong Whitworth & Co, Walker-on-Tyne	S	3,229	Sgl Scr
93	*Ivernia*	1899	C.S. Swan & Hunter Ltd, Wallsend	S	14,067	Tw Scr
94	*Saxonia*	1899	John Brown & Co, Clydebank	S	14,281	Tw Scr
95	*Phrygia* [14]	1900	Sir Raylton Dixon & Co, Middlesbrough	S	3,352	Sgl Scr
96	*Caria* [15]	1900	Tyne Iron Shipbuilding Co, Newcastle	S	3,032	Sgl Scr
97	*Albania* [16]	1900	C.S. Swan & Hunter Ltd, Wallsend	S	7,682	Tw Scr
98	*Flavia* [17]	1901	Palmer's Shipbuilding & Iron Co Ltd, Jarrow	S	9,285	Tw Scr
99	*Carpathia*	1902	C.S. Swan & Hunter Ltd, Wallsend	S	13,603	Tw Scr
100	*Pannonia* [18]	1902	John Brown & Co, Clydebank	S	9,851	Tw Scr
101	*Brescia*	1903	J. L. Thompson & Sons, Sunderland	S	3,255	Sgl Scr
102	*Slavonia* [19]	1903	Sir James Laing & Sons, Sunderland	S	10,606	Tw Scr
103	*Caronia*	1904	John Brown & Co, Clydebank	S	19,687	Tw Scr
104	*Carmania*	1905	John Brown & Co, Clydebank	S	19,524	Trpl Scr
105	*Lusitania*	1906	John Brown & Co, Clydebank	S	31,550	Q Scr

Footnote

[8] Bought by Cunard 1884

[9] Bought by Cunard 1916; formerly *Avoca*

[10] Bought by Cunard 1909; formerly *Orona*

[11] Bought by Cunard 1916; formerly *Oceano*

[12] Bought by Cunard 1920; formerly *John Herron*

[13] Bought by Cunard on the stocks

[14] Bought by Cunard 1909; formerly *Oro*

[15] Bought by Cunard, 1911; formerly *Clematis*

[16] Bought by Cunard 1911; formerly *Consuelo*

[17] Bought by Cunard 1916; formerly *British Empire*

[18] Bought by Cunard on the stocks

[19] Bought by Cunard 1904; formerly *Yamuna*

	Name	Launch	Builder	Hull	gt	Prop
106	*Mauretania*	1906	Swan Hunter & Wigham Richardson, Wallsend	S	31,938	Q Scr
107	*Vinovia* [20]	1906	Short Brothers, Sunderland	S	7,046	Sgl Scr
108	*Adriatic* [21]	1906	Harland & Wolff, Belfast	S	24,540	Tw Scr
109	*Folia* [22]	1907	James Laing & Sons, Sunderland	S	6,704	Tw Scr
110	*Royal George* [23]	1907	Fairfield Shipbuilding & Engineering Co, Glasgow	S	11,146	Trpl Scr
111	*Ausonia* [24]	1909	Swan Hunter & Wigham Richardson, Wallsend	S	7,907	Tw Scr
112	*Franconia*	1910	Swan Hunter & Wigham Richardson, Wallsend	S	18,150	Tw Scr
113	*Olympic* [25]	1910	Harland & Wolff, Belfast	S	45,323	Trpl Scr
114	*Valacia* [26]	1910	Russell & Co, Port Glasgow	S	6,526	Sgl Scr
115	*Laconia*	1911	Swan Hunter & Wigham Richardson, Wallsend	S	18,099	Tw Scr
116	*Ascania* [27]	1911	Swan Hunter & Wigham Richardson, Wallsend	S	9,111	Tw Scr
117	*Vandalia* [28]	1912	Short Brothers, Sunderland	S	7,333	Sgl Scr
118	*Berengaria* [29]	1912	Vulcan Werke, Hamburg	S	52,226	Q Scr
119	*Andania*	1913	Scotts' Shipbuilding & Engineering Co, Greenock	S	13,405	Tw Scr
120	*Alaunia*	1913	Scotts' Shipbuilding & Engineering Co, Greenock	S	13,405	Tw Scr
121	*Valeria* [30]	1913	Russell & Co, Port Glasgow	S	5,865	Sgl Scr
122	*Volodia* [31]	1913	Russell & Co, Port Glasgow	S	5,688	Sgl Scr
123	*Aquitania*	1913	John Brown & Co, Clydebank	S	45,647	Q Scr
124	*Homeric* [32]	1913	F. Schichau, Danzig	S	34,692	Tw Scr
125	*Transylvania*	1914	Scotts' Shipbuilding & Engineering Co, Greenock	S	14,315	Tw Scr
126	*Majestic* [33]	1914	Blohm & Voss, Hamburg	S	56,621	Q Scr

Footnote

[20] Bought by Cunard, 1916; formerly *Anglo-Bolivian*. Cargo only.

[21] Acquired by Cunard White Star, 1934; sold for scrap, 1934

[22] Bought by Cunard, 1916; formerly *Principe de Piemonte*

[23] Bought by Cunard, 1916

[24] Bought by Cunard, 1911; formerly *Tortona*

[25] Acquired by Cunard White Star, 1934; sold for scrap, 1935

[26] Bought by Cunard, 1916; formerly *Luceric*

[27] Bought by Cunard 1911; formerly *Gerona*

[28] Bought by Cunard, 1915; formerly *Anglo-Californian*. Cargo only.

[29] Bought by Cunard, 1920; formerly *Imperator*

[30] Bought by Cunard, 1915; formerly *Den of Airlie*. Cargo only.

[31] Bought by Cunard, 1916; formerly *Den of Ogil*. Cargo only.

[32] Acquired by Cunard White Star, 1934; sold for scrap, 1936

[33] Acquired by Cunard White Star, 1934; sold for scrap, 1936

	Name	Launch	Builder	Hull	gt	Prop
127	*Aurania*	1916	Swan Hunter & Wigham Richardson, Wallsend	S	13,936	Tw Scr
128	*Vardulia* [34]	1917	Russell & Co, Port Glasgow	S	5,691	Sgl Scr
129	*Calgaric* [35]	1917	Harland & Wolff, Belfast	S	15,119	Trpl Scr
130	*Verbania* [36]	1917	R. Duncan & Co, Port Glasgow	S	5,021	Sgl Scr
131	*Verentia* [37]	1918	Harland & Wolff, Belfast	S	5,185	Sgl Scr
132	*Vellavia* [38]	1918	Armstrong Whitworth & Co, Walker-on-Tyne	S	5,272	Sgl Scr
133	*Venusia* [39]	1918	Harland & Wolff, Belfast	S	5,222	Sgl Scr
134	*Vasconia* [40]	1918	Russell & Co, Port Glasgow	S	5,680	Sgl Scr
135	*Vitellia* [41]	1918	Earles Shipbuilding & Engineering Co, Hull	S	5,272	Sgl Scr
136	*Virgilia* [42]	1918	Russell & Co, Port Glasgow	S	5,697	Sgl Scr
137	*Vennonia* [43]	1918	Caledon Shipbuilding & Engineering Co, Dundee	S	5,225	Sgl Scr
138	*Vindelia* [44]	1918	William Gray & Co, West Hartlepool	S	4,430	Sgl Scr
139	*Scythia*	1920	Vickers Ltd, Barrow-in-Furness	S	19,730	Tw Scr
140	*Albertic* [45]	1920	A.G.Weser, Bremen, Germany	S	18,940	Tw Scr
141	*Albania*	1920	Scotts' Shipbuilding & Engineering Co, Greenock	S	12,767	Tw Scr
142	*Samaria*	1920	Cammell Laird & Co, Birkenhead	S	19,597	Tw Scr
143	*Lancastria* [46]	1920	Wm Beardmore & Co, Dalmuir	S	16,243	Tw Scr
144	*Antonia*	1921	Vickers Ltd, Barrow-in-Furness	S	13,867	Tw Scr
145	*Laconia*	1921	Swan Hunter & Wigham Richardson, Wallsend	S	19,695	Tw Scr
146	*Ausonia*	1921	Armstrong Whitworth & Co, Walker-on-Tyne	S	13,912	Tw Sc
147	*Andania*	1921	Hawthorn Leslie & Co, Hebburn	S	13,950	Tw Scr
148	*Doric* [47]	1922	Harland & Wolff, Belfast	S	16,484	Tw Scr

Footnote

[34] Bought by Cunard 1919; formerly *Verdun*; cargo only

[35] Acquired by Cunard White Star, 1934; sold for scrap, 1934

[36] Bought by Cunard, 1919; formerly *Trafalgar*; cargo only

[37] Bought by Cunard, 1918; formerly *War Lemur*; cargo only

[38] Bought by Cunard, 1918; formerly *War Setter*; cargo only

[39] Bought by Cunard, 1918; formerly *War Snake*; cargo only

[40] Bought by Cunard, 1919; formerly *Valverda*; cargo only

[41] Bought by Cunard, 1919; formerly *War Pintail;* cargo only

[42] Bought by Cunard 1919; cargo only

[43] Bought by Cunard, 1918; formerly *War Carp;* cargo only

[44] Bought by Cunard 1919; formerly *War Wagtail*; cargo only

[45] Acquired by Cunard White Star, 1934; sold for scrap, 1934.

[46] Launched as *Tyrrhenia*; renamed 1924

[47] Acquired by Cunard White Star, 1934; sold for scrap 1935

[48] Acquired by Cunard White Star, 1934

[49] Acquired by Cunard White Star, 1934

	Name	Launch	Builder	Hull	gt	Prop
149	*Franconia*	1922	John Brown & Co, Clydebank	S	20,175	Tw Scr
150	*Ascania*	1923	Armstrong Whitworth & Co, Walker-on-Tyne	S	14,013	Tw Scr
151	*Lotharingia*	1923	Wm Hamilton & Co, Port Glasgow	S	1,256	Tw Scr
152	*Alsatia*	1923	Coaster Construction Co, Montrose	S	1,310	Tw Scr
153	*Aurania*	1924	Swan Hunter & Wigham Richardson, Wallsend	S	13,984	Tw Scr
154	*Alaunia*	1925	John Brown & Co, Clydebank	S	14,030	Tw Scr
155	*Carinthia*	1925	Vickers Ltd, Barrow-in-Furness	S	20,277	Tw Scr
156	*Laurentic* [48]	1927	Harland & Wolff, Belfast	S	18,724	Trpl Scr
157	*Bosnia*	1928	J. L. Thompson & Sons, Sunderland	S	2,402	Sgl Scr
158	*Bactria*	1928	J. L. Thompson & Sons, Sunderland	S	2,407	Sgl Sc
159	*Bantria*	1928	J. L. Thompson & Sons, Sunderland	S	2,402	Sgl Scr
160	*Bothnia*	1928	J. L. Thompson & Sons, Sunderland	S	2,402	Sgl Scr
161	*Britannic*	(49)	1929 Harland & Wolff, Belfast	S	26,943	Tw Scr
162	*Georgic* [50]	1931	Harland & Wolff, Belfast	S	27,759	Tw Scr
163	*Queen Mary*	1934	John Brown & Co, Clydebank	S	81,235	Q Scr
164	*Mauretania*	1938	Cammell Laird & Co, Birkenhead	S	35,739	Tw Scr
165	*Queen Elizabeth*	1938	John Brown & Co, Clydebank	S	83,675	Q Scr
166	*Valacia* [51]	1913	Short Brothers, Sunderland	S	7,052	Sgl Scr
167	*Vasconia* [52]	1944	Short Brothers, Sunderland	S	7,058	Sgl Scr
168	*Vardulia* [53]	1944	J. A. Jones Construction Co, Brunswick, Georgia, USA	S	7,276	Sgl Scr
169	*Vandalia* [54]	1945	California Shipbuilding Corp, Los Angeles, USA	S	7,276	Sgl Scr
170	*Brescia* [55]	1945	Consolidated Steel Corp, Wilmington, USA	S	3,834	Sgl Scr
171	*Asia*	1946	Sir James Laing & Sons, Sunderland	S	8,723	Sgl Scr
172	*Media*	1946	John Brown & Co, Clydebank	S	13,345	Tw Scr
173	*Parthia*	1947	Harland & Wolff, Belfast	S	13,362	Tw Scr
174	*Andria* [56]	1947	J. L. Thompson & Sons, Sunderland	S	7,226	Sgl Scr
175	*Arabia*	1947	Sir James Laing & Sons, Sunderland	S	8,632	Sgl Scr
176	*Caronia*	1947	John Brown & Co, Clydebank	S	34,274	Tw Scr
177	*Alsatia* [57]	1947	J. L. Thompson & Sons, Sunderland	S	7,226	Sgl Scr
178	*Assyria*	1950	Swan Hunter & Wigham Richardson, Wallsend	S	8,530	Sgl Scr

Footnote

[50] Acquired by Cunard White Star, 1934

[51] Bought by Cunard, 1946; formerly *Empire Camp*; cargo only

[52] Bought by Cunard, 1946; formerly *Empire Pendennis*; cargo only

[53] Bought by Cunard, 1947; formerly *Samfoyle*; cargo only

[54] Bought by Cunard, 1947; formerly *Granville Stewart*; cargo only

[55] Bought by Cunard, 1947; formerly *Hickory Isle*; cargo only

[56] Bought by Cunard 1951; formerly *Silverbriar*; cargo only

[57] Bought by Cunard 1951; formerly *Silverplane*; cargo only

	Name	Launch	Builder	Hull	gt	Prop
179	*Pavia* [58]	1953	Wm Hamilton & Co, Port Glasgow	S	3,411	Sgl Scr
180	*Lycia* [59]	1954	Wm Hamilton & Co, Port Glasgow	S	3,543	Sgl Scr
181	*Saxonia* [60]	1954	John Brown & Co, Clydebank	S	22,592	Tw Scr
182	*Ivernia* [61]	1954	John Brown & Co, Clydebank	S	22,637	Tw Scr
183	*Phrygia* [62]	1954	Wm Hamilton & Co, Port Glasgow	S	3,534	Sgl Scr
184	*Carinthia*	1955	John Brown & Co, Clydebank	S	21,947	Tw Scr
185	*Sylvania*	1956	John Brown & Co, Clydebank	S	22,017	Tw Scr
186	*Lucellum* [63]	1958	Cammell Laird & Co, Birkenhead	S	12,202	Sgl Scr
187	*Andania* [64]	1959	Wm Hamilton & Co, Port Glasgow	S	7,004	Sgl Scr
188	*Luxor* [65]	1959	J. L. Thompson & Sons, Sunderland	S	12,700	Sgl Scr
189	*Alaunia* [66]	1960	Wm Hamilton & Co, Port Glasgow	S	7,004	Sgl Scr
190	*Lucigen* [67]	1962	Smith's Dock Co Ltd, Middlesbrough	S	12,800	Sgl Scr
191	*Media* [68]	1963	John Readhead & Sons, South Shields	S	5,586	Sgl Scr
192	*Parthia* [69]	1963	Caledon Shipbuilding & Engineering Co, Dundee	S	5,586	Sgl Scr
193	*Saxonia* [70]	1963	John Readhead & Sons, South Shields	S	5,586	Sgl Scr
194	*Ivernia* [71]	1964	Caledon Shipbuilding & Engineering Co, Dundee	S	5,586	Sgl Scr
195	*Sagafjord* [72]	1964	Societe des Forges de la Mediterranee, Le Segne	S	24,002	Tw Scr
196	*England* [73]	1964	Helsinger Skibsvaerfr, Elsinore	S	8,116	Tw Scr
197	*Scythia* [74]	1964	Cammell Laird & Co, Birkenhead	S	5,837	Sgl Scr
198	*Samaria* [75]	1964	Cammell Laird & Co, Birkenhead	S	5,837	Sgl Scr
199	*Scotia* [76]	1966	Cammell Laird & Co, Birkenhead	S	5,825	Sgl Scr
200	*Atlantic Star* [77]	1967	Ateliers et Chantiers de Dunkerque et Bordeaux	S	11,839	Sgl Scr
201	*Queen Elizabeth 2*	1967	John Brown & Co, Clydebank (later Upper Clyde Ship Builders)	S	65,863	Tw Scr
202	*Lustrous* [78]	1968	Eriksberg m/v, Gothenberg	S	14,923	Tw Scr
203	*Luminous* [79]	1968	Eriksberg m/v, Gothenberg	S	14,923	Tw Scr
204	*Atlantic Causeway* [80]	1969	Swan Hunter Shipbuilders Ltd, Wallsend	S	14,946	Tw Scr

Footnote

[58] Cargo only

[59] Cargo only

[60] Renamed *Carmania*, 1963

[61] Renamed *Franconia*, 1963

[62] Cargo only

[63] Bought by Cunard 1964. Cargo only

[64] Cargo only

[65] Bought by Cunard 1964. Cargo only

[66] Cargo only

[67] Bought by Cunard 1964. Cargo only

[68] Cargo only 69 Cargo only

[70] Cargo only

[71] Cargo only

[72] Bought by Cunard, 1983

[73] Bought by Cunard, 1982

[74] Bought by Cunard 1969; cargo only

[75] Bought by Cunard 1969; cargo only

[76] Cargo only

[77] Bought by Cunard, 1983. Cargo only.

[78] Cargo only

[79] Cargo only

[80] Cargo only

	Name	Launch	Builder	Hull	gt	Prop
205	*Atlantic Conveyor* [81]	1969	Swan Hunter Shipbuilders Ltd, Wallsend	S	14,946	Tw Scr
206	*Lumen* [82]	1971	Eriksberg m/v, Gothenberg	S	14,923	Tw Scr
207	*Cunard Adventurer*	1971	Rotterdamsche Drangdok, Rotterdam	S	14,151	Tw Scr
208	*Saxonia* [83]	1971	Aalberg Vaerft, Aalborg	S	12,059	Sgl Scr
209	*Servia* [84]	1971	Aalberg Vaerft, Aalborg	S	12,059	Sgl Scr
210	*Cunard Campaigner* [85]	1971	Astilleras Espanoles, SA, Seville, Spain	S	15,598	Sgl Scr
211	*Cunard Caravel* [86]	1971	Astilleras Espanoles, SA, Seville, Spain	S	15,498	Sgl Scr
212	*Luminetta* [87]	1971	Eriksberg m/v, Gothenberg	S	14,923	Tw Scr
213	*Lumiere* [88]	1971	Eriksberg m/v, Gothenberg	S	14,925	Tw Scr
214	*Cunard Ambassador*	1972	P. Smit, Rotterdam	S	14,157	Tw Scr
215	*Alsatia* [89]	1972	Smith's Dock Co, Middlesbrough	S	7,722	Sgl Scr
216	*Carmania* [90]	1972	Nylands Verksted, Oslo	S	7,323	Sgl Scr
217	*Cunard Carronade* [91]	1972	Astilleras Espanoles, SA, Seville, Spain	S	5,498	Sgl Scr
218	*Cunard Calamanda* [92]	1972	Astilleras Espanoles, SA, Seville, Spain	S	15,498	Sgl Scr
219	*Scythia* [93]	1972	Aalberg Vaerft, AS, Aalborg	S	12.059	Sgl Scr
220	*Andania* [94]	1972	Smith's Dock Co, Middlesbrough	S	7,742	Sgl Scr
221	*Vistafjord* [95]	1972	Swan Hunter Shipbuilders Ltd, Wallsend	S	24,292	Tw Scr
222	*Samaria* [96]	1972	Aalberg Vaerft, Aalborg	S	12.059	Sgl Scr
223	*Andria* [97]	1972	Smith's Dock Co Ltd, Middlesbrough	S	7,689	Sgl Scr
224	*Carinthia* [98]	1973	Nylands Verksted, Oslo	S	7,330	Sgl Scr
225	*Alaunia* [99]	1973	Smith's Dock Co, Middlesbrough	S	4,938	Sgl Scr
226	*Cunard Cavalier* [100]	1973	Astilleras Espanoles, SA, Seville, Spain	S	15,498	Sgl Scr
227	*Cunard Carrier* [101]	1973	Astilleras Espanoles, SA, Seville, Spain	S	15,498	Sgl Scr
228	*Cunard Champion* [102]	1973	Astilleras Espanoles, SA, Bilbao, Spain	S	15,448	Sgl Scr

Footnote

[81] Cargo only

[82] Cargo only

[83] Bought by Cunard, 1976; formerly *Gladiola*; cargo only

[84] Bought by Cunard, 1976; formerly *Orchidea*; cargo only

[85] Cargo only

[86] Cargo only

[87] Cargo only

[88] Cargo only

[89] Bought by Cunard, 1976; formerly *Edinburgh Clipper*; cargo only

[90] Bought by Cunard, 1976; formerly *Orange*; cargo only

[91] Cargo only

[92] Cargo only

[93] Bought by Cunard, 1976; formerly *Iris Queen*

[94] Bought by Cunard, 1976; formerly *Glasgow Clipper*; cargo only

[95] Bought by Cunard, 1983; renamed *Caronia*, 1999

[96] Bought by Cunard, 1976; formerly *Chrysantema*

[97] Bought by Cunard, 1976; formerly *Teeside Clipper*; cargo only

[98] Bought by Cunard, 1976; formerly *Cantaloupe*; cargo only

[99] Bought by Cunard, 1976; formerly *Cardiff Clipper*; cargo only

[100] Cargo only

[101] Cargo only

[102] Cargo only

	Name	Launch	Builder	Hull	gt	Prop
229	*Cunard Chieftain* [103]	1973	Astilleras Espanoles, SA, Bilbao, Spain	S	15,448	Sgl Scr
230	*Cunard Countess*	1974	Burmeister & Wain, Copenhagen, Denmark	S	17,495	Tw Scr
231	*Lucellum* [104]	1974	Davie Shipbuilding Ltd, Lauzon, Canada	S	12,202	Sgl Scr
232	*Cunard Princess* [105]	1974	Burmeister & Wain, Copenhagen, Denmark	S	17,495	Tw Scr
233	*Lucerna* [106]	1975	Davie Shipbuilding Ltd, Lauzon, Canada	S	23,736	Sgl Scr
234	*City of Plymouth* [107]	1978	Appledore Shipbuilders Ltd, Appledore	S	1,599	Sgl Scr
235	*City of Lisbon* [108]	1978	Appledore Shipbuilders Ltd, Appledore	S	1,599	Sgl Scr
236	*City of Manchester* [109]	1978	Appledore Shipbuilders Ltd, Appledore	S	1,599	Sgl Scr
237	*Liverpool Star* [110]	1979	Appledore Shipbuilders Ltd, Appledore	S	1,599	Sgl Scr
238	*Oxford* [111]	1981	Appledore Shipbuilders Ltd, Appledore	S	1,599	Sgl Scr
239	*Sea Goddess I* [112]	1983	Wartsila, Helsinki, Finland	S	4,253	Tw Scr
240	*Atlantic Conveyor* [113]	1984	Swan Hunter Shipbuilders Ltd, Wallsend	S	25,301	Tw Scr
241	*Sea Goddess II* [114]	1984	Wartsila, Helsinki, Finland	S	4,253	Tw Scr
242	*Royal Viking Sun* [115]	1988	Wartsila Marine Industries, Helsinki, Finland	S	37,845	Tw Scr
243	*Seabourn Pride* [116]	1988	Schichau Seebeckwerft AG, Bremerhaven	S	9,975	Tw Scr
244	*Seabourn Spirit* [117]	1989	Schichau Seebeckwerft AG, Bremerhaven	S	9,975	Tw Scr
245	*Seabourn Legend* [118]	1991	Schichau Seebeckwerft AG, Bremerhaven	S	9,975	Tw Scr
246	*Queen Mary 2*	2003	Chantiers de l'Atlantique, St Nazaire, France	S	148,528	QP
247	*Queen Victoria*	2007	Fincantieri Cantieri Navali Italiani, Venice	S	90,049	Tw P
248	*Queen Elizabeth*	2010	Fincantieri Cantieri Navali Italiani, Monfalcone	S	90,901	Tw P

Footnote

[103] Cargo only

[104] Cargo only

[105] Launched as *Cunard Conquest*. Renamed 1977

[106] Cargo only

[107] Bought by Cunard (Trafalgar House) 1987 Cargo only

[108] Bought by Cunard (Trafalgar House) 1987 Cargo only

[109] Bought by Cunard (Trafalgar House) 1987 Cargo only

[110] Bought by Cunard (Trafalgar House) 1987. Cargo only

[111] Bought by Cunard (Trafalgar House) 1987. Cargo only

[112] Bought by Cunard 1998

[113] Cargo only

[114] Bought by Cunard 1998

[115] Bought by Cunard, 1994. Renamed *Seabourn Sun* 1999

[116] Bought by Cunard, (Carnival Corporation) 1998

[117] Bought by Cunard, (Carnival Corporation), 1998

[118] Bought by Cunard, (Carnival Corporation), 1998.

Key

W Wood **I** Iron **S** Steel **P** Paddle wheel **Sgl Scr** Single screw **Tw Scr** Twin screw **Trpl Scr** Triple screw

QS Quadruple screw **QP** Quadruple pods **Tw P** Twin pods **gt** Gross tonnage

Cunard goes to war

They shall grow not old, as we that are left grow old:

Age shall not weary them, nor the years condemn.

At the going down of the sun and in the morning,

We will remember them

Extract from *'Ode of Remembrance'* taken from Laurence Binyon's poem, *'For the Fallen'*, 1914.

1853 Crimean War

14 ships served as troops transports, hospital ships, and store ships - carried over 100,000 personnel, 7,500 horses, large quantities of stores and war materials.

1861 'Trent' Incident

Two ships served conveying troops and stores to Canada.

1867 Fenian Troubles

Two ships served as Depot ships at Liverpool for accommodation of troops.

1879 Zulu War

Four ships served as troop transports.

1891 First Boer War

Two ships served as troop transports

1882 Egyptian Campaign

Four ships served as troop transports

1885 Russian War Scare

Two ships served as Armed Merchant cruisers - a third was retained though not actually used.

1899/1902 Second Boer War

Eight ships served as transports. Steamed 404,713 miles and carried 75,000 troops, refugees, prisoners and mules.

The Georgic *pictured after bombing. (University of Liverpool Cunard archive)*

1914 - 1918 First World War

Company's fleet at outbreak of war:

25 ships (315,988 gross tons)

Lost through enemy action:

7th May	1915	*Lusitania*
6th November	1915	*Caria*
17th December	1915	*Veria*
4th October	1916	*Franconia*
19th October	1916	*Alaunia*
1st January	1917	*Ivernia*
11th February	1917	*Lycia*
25th February	1917	*Laconia*
11th March	1917	*Folia*
17th March	1917	*Thracia*
5th May	1917	*Feltria*
27th June	1917	*Ultonia*
21st August	1917	*Volodia*
19th December	1917	*Vinovia*
27th January	1918	*Andania*
4th February	1918	*Aurania*
30th May	1918	*Ausonia*
9th June	1918	*Vandalia*
17th July	1918	*Carpathia*
24th August	1918	*Flavia*

Of fleet at outbreak of war:

13 ships lost (151,751 gross tons)

Of those acquired during war:

seven ships lost (53,709 gross tons)

Three ships served as Armed Merchant cruisers, others as hospital ships, troop transports and aircraft carrier.

900,000 American officers and men were carried, plus a large repatriation movement after the Armistice. In all 3.5 million miles were sailed and nine million tons of general cargo carried.

1939 - 1945 Second World War

In September 1939 the fleet was quickly requisitioned for war service. Led by the **Queen Elizabeth**, which entered service in 1940, and the **Queen Mary**, the ships performed valuable work throughout the war.

Over 2,473,000 passengers were carried, a total distance of 5,360,000 miles was steamed from September 1939 until the end of 1945.

In addition to these achievements the Company managed on account of the Ministry of War Transport, 39 other ships (347,456 gross tons) and handled nine million tons of cargo.

Lost through enemy action:

5th September	1939	**Bosnia**
6th June	1940	**Carinthia**
16th June	1940	**Andania**
16th June	1940	**Lancastria**
3rd November	1940	**Laurentic**
14th July	1941	**Georgic**
12th September	1942	**Laconia**

1982 Falklands Conflict

Four ships served as troop and cargo transports of which one was lost. Two ships chartered for Falklands service after the Conflict.

Lost through enemy action:

25th May	1982	**Atlantic Conveyor**

1990 – 1991 First Gulf War

One ship served as rest and recuperation vessel.

Churchill Wartime Crossings

May	1943	**Queen Mary**
August	1943	**Queen Mary**
September	1944 (round trip)	**Queen Mary**

People lost

It is difficult to establish the exact number of Cunard personel who died while serving their country. 74 officers and Cunard Building (Liverpool) personnel died in the First World War while the number for the same positions in the Second World War was 61. When the **Lusitania** sank 401 crew perished alone.

In 1914 at the outbreak of war a "very large proportion" of the Company's navigating officers and an estimated 1,500 sailors, firemen and stewards joined up and 88 of those were killed or drowned. When a brigade of business men was formed in Liverpool in 1914 120 Cunard staff from the Liverpool office enlisted on the first day while the total number of office staff in British offices joining up was 387 and 65 from the Canadian and American offices - a total of 452. Of these 53 lost their lives and many received serious wounds with several permanently disabled.

Many Cunard people received the D.S.O., D.S.C., M.C., M.M. Etc and one was awarded the Victoria Cross.

*The **Mauretania** dazzle painted, being manoeuvred into her berth at New York. (University of Liverpool Cunard archive)*

Cunard and the British Royal Family

Date		Ship	Event
August	1861	*Arabia*	HRH Prince Alfred sailed from Halifax to Liverpool, arriving 17th August
21st September	1861	*Niagara*	HRH Prince Alfred sailed from Liverpool to Halifax
11th July	1913	*Mauretania*	HM King George V and HM Queen Mary visited in Liverpool
June	1924	*Aquitania*	HRH The Prince of Wales (later King Edward VIII) visited in Southampton
29th August	1924	*Berengaria*	HRH The Prince of Wales sailed from Southampton to New York
	1924	*Aquitania*	HRH The Prince of Wales sailed from New York to Southampton
19th July	1927	*Mauretania*	HM King George V and HM Queen Mary visited in Liverpool
17th December	1928	*Berengaria*	HRH Prince George sailed from New York to Southampton
29th March	1933	*Queen Mary*	HRH The Prince of Wales visited in Clydebank
	1933	*Berengaria*	HRH The Prince of Wales visited in Southampton
26th July	1933	*Berengaria*	HM King George V and HM Queen Mary visited in Southampton
5th March	1934	*Queen Mary*	HRH The Prince of Wales visited in Clydebank
26th September	1934	*Queen Mary*	HM King George V, HM Queen Mary & The Prince of Wales visited in Clydebank for the launch
	1935	*Laconia*	TRH Prince & Princess Arthur of Connaught took a one-week Mediterranean cruise
26th May	1936	*Queen Mary*	HM King Edward VIII, HM Queen Mary, TRH The Duke & Duchess of York, TRH Princess Elizabeth & Princess Margaret, the Duke & Duchess of Kent, and the Duchess of Gloucester visited in Southampton
27th September	1938	*Queen Elizabeth*	HM Queen Elizabeth & TRH Princess Elizabeth & Princess Margaret visited in Clydebank for the launch
8th October	1946	*Queen Elizabeth*	HM Queen Elizabeth & TRH Princess Elizabeth & Princess Margaret travelled on sea trials on the Clyde
6th November	1946	*Queen Elizabeth*	HRH The Duke of Windsor sailed from Southampton to New York arriving 11th November
27th December	1946	*Queen Elizabeth*	HRH The Duke and the Duchess of Windsor sailed from Southampton to New York arriving 1st January 1947
10th May	1947	*Queen Elizabeth*	HRH The Duke and the Duchess of Windsor sailed from New York to Southampton arriving 15th May
20th October	1947	*Caronia*	TRH Princess Elizabeth & Prince Philip visited in Clydebank for the launch
24th July	1948	*Queen Elizabeth*	HM King George VI, HM Queen Elizabeth and HRH Princess Margaret visited in Southampton
18th December	1948	*Caronia*	HRH Prince Philip sailed from Gourock to Southampton arriving 20th December
21st December	1949	*Queen Elizabeth*	HRH The Duke and the Duchess of Windsor sailed from Southampton to New York arriving 26th December
16th November	1950	*Queen Elizabeth*	HRH The Duke and the Duchess of Windsor sailed from Southampton to New York arriving 21st November
30th November	1950	*Queen Elizabeth*	HRH The Duke of Windsor sailed from Southampton to New York arriving 6th December

Date		Ship	Event
24th May	1951	*Queen Elizabeth*	HRH The Duke of Windsor sailed from New York to Southampton arriving 29th May
29th August	1951	*Queen Elizabeth*	HRH The Duke and the Duchess of Windsor sailed from New York to Southampton arriving 4th September
5th December	1951	*Queen Elizabeth*	HRH The Duke and Duchess of Windsor sailed from Southampton to New York arriving 10th December
28th February	1952	*Queen Elizabeth*	HRH The Duke of Windsor sailed from Southampton to New York arriving 4th March
21st May	1952	*Queen Elizabeth*	HRH The Duke and the Duchess of Windsor sailed from New York to Southampton arriving 27th May
7th March	1953	*Queen Elizabeth*	HRH The Duke of Windsor and HRH The Princess Royal sailed from New York to Southampton arriving 12th March
1st April	1953	*Queen Elizabeth*	HRH The Duke of Windsor sailed from Southampton to New York arriving 6th April
21st October	1954	*Queen Elizabeth*	HM Queen Elizabeth The Queen Mother sailed from Southampton to New York, arriving 26th October
18th November	1954	*Queen Mary*	HM Queen Elizabeth The Queen Mother sailed from New York to Southampton arriving 23rd November
14th December	1955	*Carinthia*	HRH Princess Margaret visited in Clydebank for the launch
27th October	1964	*Mauretania*	HM Queen Elizabeth The Queen Mother visited in Milford Haven
14th July	1967	*Queen Elizabeth 2*	HRH Prince Philip visited in Clydebank
20th September	1967	*Queen Elizabeth 2*	HM The Queen, HRH Prince Philip & HRH Princess Margaret visited in Clydebank for the launch
6th November	1968	*Queen Elizabeth*	HM Queen Elizabeth The Queen Mother visited in Southampton
19th November	1968	*Queen Elizabeth 2*	HRH Prince Charles sailed from Clydebank to Greenock
1st May	1969	*Queen Elizabeth 2*	HM The Queen & HRH Prince Philip visited in Southampton
29th May	1969	*Queen Elizabeth 2*	HRH Prince Philip visited in Southampton
5th March	1970	*Queen Elizabeth 2*	HRH Princess Margaret & The Earl of Snowdon visited in Barbados.
11th June	1982	*Queen Elizabeth 2*	HM Queen Elizabeth The Queen Mother welcomed back to Southampton after the Falklands War

Three Cunarders meet in Bremerhaven in November 1999. **QE2, Royal Viking Sun** *(being transformed into* **Seabourn Sun***) and* **Vistafjord** *(about to*

Date		Ship	Event
2nd December	1982	*Queen Elizabeth 2*	HM Queen Elizabeth The Queen Mother visited in Southampton.
3rd May	1986	*Queen Elizabeth 2*	HM Queen Elizabeth The Queen Mother visited in Southampton.
29th April	1987	*Queen Elizabeth 2*	HRH The Princess of Wales joined off Cowes and sailed to Southampton
14th December	1988	*Queen Elizabeth 2*	HM Queen Elizabeth The Queen Mother visited in Southampton.
27th July	1990	*Queen Elizabeth 2*	HM The Queen & HRH Prince Philip sailed from Spithead to Southampton
3rd April	1991	*Queen Elizabeth 2*	HRH Prince Edward visited in Southampton
15th June	1991	*Queen Elizabeth 2*	HRH Prince Philip & HRH Prince Edward visited in Southampton
12th June	1993	*Queen Elizabeth 2*	HRH Prince Edward visited in Southampton; left by helicopter off the South Coast
17th December	1994	*Queen Elizabeth 2*	HRH Prince Andrew visited in Southampton
17th July	1995	*Queen Elizabeth 2*	HRH The Princess Royal visited in Edinburgh
28th September	1996	*Queen Elizabeth 2*	HRH Prince Edward visited in Southampton
16th January	2002	*Queen Mary 2*	HRH Prince Edward attended the steel cutting in St. Nazaire
8th January	2004	*Queen Mary 2*	HM The Queen & HRH Prince Philip visited in Southampton for the launch
9th January	2004	*Queen Mary 2*	HRH Prince Edward visited in Southampton
21st September	2007	*Queen Elizabeth 2*	HRH The Duke of Kent visited in Liverpool
10th December	2007	*Queen Victoria*	TRH The Prince of Wales & The Duchess of Cornwall visited in Southampton for the launch
2nd June	2008	*Queen Elizabeth 2*	HM The Queen visited in Southampton
11th November	2008	*Queen Elizabeth 2*	HRH Prince Philip visited in Southampton
25th June	2010	*Queen Mary 2*	HRH The Princess Royal visited in Southampton
26th July	2010	*Queen Victoria*	HRH The Duchess of Cornwall visited in Liverpool.
11th October	2010	*Queen Elizabeth*	HM The Queen visited in Southampton for the launch
23rd May	2012	*Queen Mary 2*	HRH The Princess Royal visited in Southampton
13th December	2012	*Queen Victoria*	HRH The Duchess of Cornwall visited in Southampton
9th May	2014	*Queen Mary 2*	HRH Prince Philip visited in Southampton

*come **Caronia**) (Cunard)*

The knighted commodores

According to Mark Twain, who – unlike Charles Dickens – was very impressed by Cunard, "The Cunard people would not take Noah as first mate till they had worked him up through all the lower grades". And he was right.

Officers slowly worked their way up usually starting on a humble vessel and as they climbed they transferred to one of the Atlantic express liners; and then, when they were eventually awarded a captaincy it would be back down again from the grand ocean greyhounds to being master of a lesser vessel. And then, rather like snakes and ladders, they would work upwards again in the hope of becoming master of one of the famous express liners. And those who were particularly blessed, just before retirement might achieve the rank of Fleet Commodore.

Alone among shipping companies, Cunard has had seven of its Commodores knighted by the monarch.

Commodore Sir James Charles, KBE CBE RD RNR (1865 - 1928)

James Charles began his sea-going career as an apprentice in sailing ships, and joined Cunard in 1895.

He achieved prominence in command of the **Mauretania** in the First World War when he safely carried thousands of American soldiers to Europe. As a consequence, he received a knighthood.

His final command was the **Aquitania**, where he proved to be not just a generous host but a superb sailor who docked the ship in both Southampton and New York without the aid of tugs - something which supposedly could not be done.

In July 1928 he completed his 728th transatlantic crossing – his last before retirement. He went to his quarters to sign for the last time the official papers required of captains, but shortly afterwards when his steward entered the cabin he found Sir James sitting strangely still. The steward called to him, but there was no answer. His job was done.

Commodore Sir Arthur Rostron, KB CBE RD RNR (1869 - 1940)

Commodore Sir Arthur Rostron, by accident of history the most celebrated Cunard captain of them all, joined the company from Waverley Line's iron clipper the **Cedric the Saxon** in 1895. In 1896, the **Cedric the Saxon** disappeared without trace.

His first Cunard command was the **Brescia** in 1907, and in 1912 he made his appointment with history by taking command of the **Carpathia**. His calm efficiency and thoughtful common sense resulted in the rescue of all the survivors of the sinking of the **Titanic** – and international celebrity for Rostron.

For ten years he was master of the **Mauretania**, his favourite ship, a position he held in 1926 when he was knighted. In 1928 he became Commodore of the fleet and took command of the flagship, the **Berengaria**.

Commodore Sir Edgar Britten, KB RD RNR (1874 - 1936)

Born in Bradford, about as far from the sea as you can get, Edgar Britten defied parental opposition and ran away to sea at the age of 15. As a cabin boy earning a mere 5 shillings (25p) a month rather than an apprentice, Britten had to educate himself. He did, and obtained a master's certificate in both sail and steam.

He joined Cunard in 1901, and in 1913 assumed his first command - the small and unglamorous the *Phrygia*.

Over the years he commanded most of the fleet, rising in 1931 to captain of the *Berengaria*. It was while still in that position that he was knighted by King George V in 1934, and the following year became Commodore of the newly created White Star Line.

Also in 1935 he was appointed first master of the *Queen Mary*, and was in command both on her maiden voyage and when she took the Blue Riband.

In a strange echo of Sir James Charles, Sir Edgar collapsed in his quarters in the *Queen Mary* as he was preparing to put to sea in October 1936. He died the same day.

Commodore Sir Robert Irving, KB OBE RD RNR (1877 - 1954)

While other Commodores tended to be of lowly origin, Robert Irving was certainly not. Coming from a wealthy and well-connected Scottish Border family, he was chieftain of his clan. His family seat, Bonshaw Tower, had been built in 900AD and was home to the Irvings for hundreds of years. He joined Cunard in 1904, but served in the Royal Navy during the First World War when he was mentioned in dispatches for his part in the Battle of Jutland.

After the war he served in many Cunard ships, eventually rising to command of the *Aquitania* in 1931. The following year he was appointed ADC RNR to King George V and in 1937 took command of the *Queen Mary*. He became Fleet Commodore in 1938 and was knighted in 1943.

He retired to his family seat in 1944.

Commodore Sir James Bisset, KB CBE RD RNR LLD (1883 - 1966)

Like most seafarers of his generation, James Bisset began his seagoing life as an apprentice under sail. He joined Cunard in 1907 as a fourth officer and stayed for 40 years. He was second officer on board the *Carpathia* when, in 1912, the little ship rushed through ice in the dark to rescue all the survivors of the *Titanic*.

His first command came in 1931, and he became master of the *Queen Mary* in 1942 – just in time to begin the famous transatlantic trooping duties when GIs were brought to Europe 15,000 at a time on the unescorted ship. He took Churchill across the Atlantic three times in the war, and the two became friends.

In 1945 he was appointed Commodore of Cunard White Star, and in July of the same year was knighted by King George VI.

In 1946 he took the *Queen Elizabeth* on her first commercial voyage, and retired shortly thereafter.

Commodore Sir Cyril Illingworth, KB RD RNR (1883 - 1958)

Cyril Illingworth began life at sea under sail, and after gaining his master's certificate in 1908 he joined Cunard in 1910 - or, as he put it, 'leaving the sea to go into steam'.

He rose through the ranks, serving in most of the ships of the fleet, finally becoming master of the **Queen Mary** in 1942. His first year was traumatic as it was then that the **Queen Mary**, carrying 11,000 GIs, sliced through the escort cruiser the **Curacoa**, resulting in 39 deaths. Illingworth was forbidden to stop or the safety of both the GIs and the ship, a vital part of the war effort, would have been at risk.

In August 1947 he was appointed Commodore, and retired in October 1948; he was awarded a knighthood by King George V1 in the Birthday Honours of 1949.

Commodore Sir Ivan Thompson, KB (1894 - 1970)

Liverpudlian Ivan Thompson spent all his seafaring life in steam. He joined Cunard in 1916. He was at sea throughout both wars and had the remarkable good fortune never to have been mined or torpedoed.

His first command was the **Georgic** in 1945, but after a number of different commands became master of the **Queen Elizabeth** in 1951 and of the **Queen Mary** a year later.

He became Commodore of the Fleet in 1954, and in the same year he was in command when HM Queen Elizabeth The Queen Mother sailed to America on the **Queen Elizabeth** and back on the **Queen Mary**. He was knighted by The Queen in 1955.

*Commodore Donald MacLean on the bridge wing of the **Queen Elizabeth**. (University of Liverpool Cunard archive)*

Bibliography

Author	Publication	Publisher & date
Anonymous	The Official Guide to the Cunard Steamship Company	Sutton Sharpe & Co 1877
Arnott, Captain Robert	Captain of the Queen	Quadrant Books 1984
Aylmer, Gerald	*Mauretania*: the ship and her record	Tempus Publishing 2000
Bisset, Commodore Sir James	Commodore	Angus & Robertson 1961
Blake, George	RMS Queen Mary	B.T. Batsford 1936
Bonsor, Nicholas	North Atlantic Seaway	Brookside Publications 1975
Brinnin, John	The Sway of the Grand Saloon	Delacorte Press 1971
Britten, Commodore Sir Edgar	A Million Ocean Miles	Hutchinson & Co 1936
Butler, Daniel Allen	Warrior Queens	Pen & Sword 2002
Butler, Daniel Allen	The Age of Cunard	Lighthouse Press 2003
Butler, Daniel Allen	The Other Side of the Night	Caseuate 2009
Cracknell Long, Vera	From Britain with Love	Danecroft Publishing 1988
Ellery, David	*Queen Mary*: 101 Questions and Answers	Conway 2006
Fenby, Jonathan	The Sinking of the *Lancastria*	Simon & Schuster 2005
Fox, Stephen	Transatlantic	Harper Collins 2003
Grant, Kay	Samuel Cunard	Abelard Schuman 1967
Grossmith, Frederick	The Sinking of *Laconia*	Paul Watkins 1994
Harvey, Clive	*RMS Queen Elizabeth*	Carmania Press 2007
Haws, Duncan	Triumph of a Great Tradition	Cunard 1990
Haws, Duncan	Merchant Fleets: Cunard Line	TCL Publications 1987
HMSO	British Vessels lost at Sea 1914/18, 1939/45	Patrick Stephen 1988
Hill Dickinson & Co.	The Cunard Company & the Government	Hill Dickinson & Co. 1905
Hughes, Tom	The Blue Riband of the Atlantic	Charles Scribner's Sons 1971
Hurd, Archibald	A Merchant Fleet at War	Cassell & Co. 1920
Hutchings, David	*QE2* – a ship for all seasons	Waterfront 2002
Hyde, Professor Francis	Cunard on the Atlantic, 1840-1973	Macmillan Press 1975
Johnson, Howard	The Cunard Story	Whittet Books 1987
Jordan, Humfrey	*Mauretania*: landfalls and departures	Hodder & Stoughton 1936
Konings, Chris	*Queen Elizabeth* at War	Patrick Stephens 1985
Lacey, Robert	The Queens of the Atlantic	Sidgwick & Jackson 1973
Langley, Robert	Steam Lion	Nimbus 2006
Lord, Walter	A Night to Remember	Bantam 1956
MacLean, Commodore Donald	Queens' Company	Hutchinson & Co 1965
Maxtone Graham, John	The Only Way to Cross	Patrick Stephens 1972
McCart, Neil Atlantic	Liners of the Cunard Line	Patrick Stephens 1990
McCutcheon, Jeannette	RMS Queen Mary: transatlantic masterpiece	Tempus Publishing 2000
McKenzie Kennedy, C.	The Atlantic Blue Riband	William Sessions Ltd 1993
Miller, William & Hutchings, David	Transatlantic Liners at War	David & Charles 1985
Newall, Peter	Cunard Line: a Fleet History	Ships in Focus Publications 2012
Open Agency	Cunard Queens	The Open Agency 2011
Open Agency	The Fleet	The Open Agency 2004
O'Sullivan, Patrick	The *Lusitania* Mysteries	The Collins Press 1998
Potter, Neil & Frost, Jack	The *Queen Mary*	George Harrap & Co. 1971
Potter, Neil & Frost, Jack	The *Queen Elizabeth 2* – the authorised story	George Harrap & Co 1969
Preston, Diana	Wilful Murder	Doubleday 2002
Satchell, Alister	Running the Gauntlet	Chatham Publishing 2001
Sauder, Eric	*RMS Lusitania*: the ship and her records	Tempus Publishing 2005

BIBLIOGRAPHY

Author	Publication	Publisher & date
Simpson, Colin	*Lusitania*	Longman 1972
Slader, John	The Red Duster at War	William Kimber 1988
Smallpeice, Basil	Of Comets and Queens	Airlife 1981
Smith, Ken	*Mauretania*: the Pride of the Tyne	Newcastle Libraries 1997
Steele, Tom	*Queen Mary*	Chaidon Press 1995
Thatcher, Carol	*QE2*: 'Forty Years Famous'	Simon and Schuster 2007
Thatcher, Carol	A Voyage of Discovery	Lancaster Publishing 1999
Treasure Jones, Captain John	Tramp to Queen	The History Press 2008
Walker, Alastair	Four Thousand Lives Lost: the Enquiries of Lord Mersey	The History Press 2010
Warwick, Commodore Ronald	*QE2*	W.W. Norton & Co. 1999
Warwick, Sam and Roussel, Mike	Shipwrecks of the Cunard Line	The History Press 2012
Winfield, Pamela	Sentimental Journey	Constable 1984

Magazines

The Modern World of Conquest,	1937	The Irish Skipper,	June 2005
Antiques,	July 1982	Sports Diver,	January 2006
Trafalgar House Magazine,	1983	The Deal,	2006
The Mariners' Mirror, February	1996	Ships Monthly,	August 2006
Work Boat World, July	1998	Then and Now,	September 2006
Granta,	1998	Stamp Magazine,	September 2007
Antiques Magazine,	May 1999	Ships Monthly,	November 2007
Apollo, October	1999	Lloyds Loading List,	November 2007
Nautical Research Journal,	Winter 2005		

Newspapers

Liverpool Mercury,	5th April 1888		
Liverpool Daily Post,	5th July 1890	New York Sun	27th December 1949
Liverpool Echo,	13th December 1936	New York Herald Tribune	25th May 1951
Glasgow Herald,	30th December 1954	New York Herald Tribune	12th November 1951
Liverpool Echo,	July 1990	New York Times	11th March 1953
Yorkshire Evening Post,	26th October 1997	New York Times	7th April 1953
Daily Express,	14th May 2005	New York Herald Tribune	7th April 1953
The Sunday Times,	26th October 2010	New York Herald Tribune	21st October 1954
Daily Telegraph,	1st May 2014	New York Daily Post	26th October 1954
Daily Telegraph,	28th June 2014	New York World Telegraph & Sun	26th October 1954
New York Herald Tribune	12th October 1946	New York Times	26th October 1954
New York Times	9th November 1946	New York World Telegraph & Sun	27th October 1954
New York Daily Post	11th November 1946	New York World Telegraph & Sun	28th October 1954
New York Times	10th May 1947	New York Times,	16th July 1974
New York Times	28th July 1948	The Times,	21st May 1990

Other

The Cunard Archive, Liverpool University

Unreleased files of Dan Wallace, John Whitworth, Tom Kameen, Sir Basil Smallpeice, Sir Percy Bates and Lord Mancroft.

Unpublished correspondence of Duncan Haws, Lord Essendon, Sir Percy Bates, Alfred Bates, Commodore Sir Percy Illingworth, Lord Royden, Sir Ashley Sparks, Lord Mancroft, Colin Simpson, Tom Kameen, Lord Aberconway and John Rannie.

Official Reports

MAIB report,	July 1993	MAIB Report,	March 2003
US Coastguard Report,	May 1993	MAIB Report,	July 2003

Television Documentary proposals

'The Queens at War'. Sir David Nicholas CBE
'Big, Bigger, Biggest', Windfall Films

Index

*The **QE2** at sea in April 2005 (Cunard)*